Raising
Biracial Children

Raising Biracial Children

KERRY ANN ROCKQUEMORE
AND TRACEY LASZLOFFY

AltaMira
PRESS

A Division of
ROWMAN & LITTLEFIELD PUBLISHERS, INC.
Lanham • New York • Toronto • Oxford

AltaMira Press
A division of Rowman & Littlefield Publishers, Inc.
A wholly owned subsidary of The Rowman & Littlefield Publishing Group, Inc.
4501 Forbes Boulevard, Suite 200
Lanham, MD 20706
www.altamirapress.com

PO Box 317, Oxford, OX2 9RU, UK

British Library Cataloguing in Publication Information Available

Library of Congress Cataloguing-in-Publication Data
Rockquemore, Kerry.
Raising biracial children / Kerry Ann Rockquemore and Tracey Laszloffy.
    p. cm.
Includes bibliographical references and index.
ISBN 0-7591-0900-1 (cloth : alk. paper) — ISBN 0-7591-0901-X (pbk. : alk. paper)
1. Racially mixed children—United States. 2. Race awareness—United States. 3. Socialization—United States. 4. Child rearing—United States. I. Laszloffy, Tracey A. II. Title.
HQ777.9.R63 2005
305.23—dc22

2005008437

Printed in the United States of America

∞™ The paper used in this publication meets the minimum requirements of American National Standard for Information Sciences—Permanence of Paper for Printed Library Materials, ANSI/NISO Z39.48-1992.

This book is dedicated to William, June, Jerome, Billy, and the families who shared their stories with us and taught us so much about race, relationships, struggle, and hope.

Contents

Illustrations

Preface

Raising Biracial Children arose from our observation that while the multiracial population in the United States is increasing, we are missing a systematic understanding of the racial identity development process among mixed-race children. In addition, we observed a chasm between the world of academic researchers (for whom studying biracial identity has become a "hot area") and the everyday world of parents and practitioners who are raising mixed-race children. In short, there was a pressing need for an extensive *synthesis* of existing research, a *model* for better understanding the unique process of racial identity development for mixed-race children, and an *application* of the most salient findings addressed directly to those who care for them. Our aim is to provide parents, educators, therapists, social workers, and others with an accessible framework for understanding healthy mixed-race identity development and to translate those findings into practical care-giving strategies.

At the core of our work is the presentation of a model of racial identity development that reflects the diverse reality of the mixed-race experience. Having spent the last ten years immersed in a national study of mixed-race people and meeting with countless other interracial families and multiracial clients in therapy, we have heard them describe many different ways of being mixed-race in post–Civil Rights America. Both the existing literature and our training in clinical models that assume a "one size fits all" approach to racial identity development conflicted with the experiences mixed-race people shared with us. This conflict suggests that traditional models do not accurately reflect the life experiences of mixed-race people today. In fact, we believe that racial identity models that assume there is a singular, correct way for mixed-race people to identify are often harmful because they attempt to squeeze everyone into a narrow box and pathologize all of those who do not fit.

Eventually, our research, clinical experience, and everyday dialogues with mixed-race people led us to formulate a new model that reflects the empirical reality that mixed-race people choose many different racial identities and do so for various reasons. Our model places special emphasis on the interaction between structural, psychological, and relational factors that influence identity development. By embracing the multiple ways that mixed-race people racially self-identify and affirming that no one identity is any better or more inherently valuable than another, we are able to turn our focus to an examination of the *pathways* children travel that lead them to adopt a particular racial identity. In other words, the central argument of this book is that whichever racial label an individual uses to describe his racial identity is less important than the pathways he traveled to get there.

We believe this new identity model will allow both parents and professionals to move beyond attempts to "fit" mixed-race children into a singular "correct" racial identity, and instead recognize that there exists a range of acceptable identifications. More importantly, it is necessary to attend to the pathways that influence how children come to understand themselves racially and shape why they eventually develop particular self-understandings.

Several excellent books recently have been published to help parents and practitioners understand the multiracial experience, including Donna Jackson Nakazawa's *Does Anybody Else Look Like Me?*, Maria Root and Matt Kelley's edited volume *Multiracial Child Resource Book,* and Marguerite Wright's *I'm Chocolate, You're Vanilla.* These books differ from *Raising Biracial Children* because they approach multiracial identity from a developmental perspective. Their authors view racial identity development as occurring in a set of age-appropriate stages through which children move in a sequential, linear fashion toward the endpoint of a biracial identity. In contrast, we emphasize that children are embedded in broader contexts (such as family, school, neighborhoods) and individual identity development is best understood by considering the structural components of a child's environment as well as the quality of relationships that make up their social world. Because we each learn to understand ourselves through the relationships we have with others, we place these relationships at the core of our analysis. The result is a multidimensional, fluid, relational, and contextual model of identity development.

OUR TERMINOLOGY AND FOCUS

A clear and meaningful discussion of racial issues is often confounded by limited terminology and questions over the reality of race and racism. We, like most social scientists, are fully aware that race is a social, as opposed to a biological, construct. We currently exist at a historical moment of deep tension between our knowledge of the social construction of race and the persistence of racism in our society. Race is simultaneously real and unreal, both a figment of our collective imagination and a real constraint on opportunities and daily interactions.

As difficult as it is to effectively discuss race in America, it is all the more difficult when we consider those who fall between taken-for-granted racial categories. Because we have long assumed that racial groups exist and that individuals can be placed in one (and only one) category, we have developed elaborate rules to govern those who straddle categorization. But as the biological basis of race crumbles, so too has our confidence in categorization rules and regulations. And yet the *language* that we use to describe race remains caught in this quagmire.

For the purposes of our discussion, we use the term "mixed race" to describe the population of children who have one black and one white parent, irrespective of their self-identification. We use the term "multiracial" to describe the broader population of people who have multiple ancestry. Our use of the term "mixed race" should not suggest to the reader an endorsement of a biological view of race. In other words, because we understand race to be socially constructed, a child is not a literal mixture of two races, but instead, she is the offspring of parents who are socially categorized as different races. As a corollary, in our discussion of appearances and racial identity, when we say a child "looks black" or "looks white," we are referring to those physical traits that are typically associated with blacks and those that are typically associated with whites. While the use of this terminology may, in some ways, reify the existing categorization system, our discussion of the social reality of mixed-race children necessitates their usage.

Some readers may wonder why we are focusing on black/white mixed-race children and not multiracial children of various combinations. Our decision to focus exclusively on black/white mixed-race people is based on several factors. First and foremost, for the purpose of discussing how individuals reconcile different racial identities, it is instructive to focus on the two racial groups that are the furthest away from each other in terms of social distance. Blacks and whites continue to be the two groups in society with the most problematic history of aggression, the most clearly articulated animosity, and the most restrictive and ideologically loaded rule of group membership (the one-drop rule). We can think of no more difficult status in the United States than to reconcile having a black parent and a white parent; therefore, we keep black/white mixed-race people at the center of our analysis.

We also recognize that there are important qualitative differences between having one black and one white parent, versus one Asian and one white parent, versus one Native American and one black parent. These differences include the societal valuation of each group, how ethnicity interacts with race, language differentials, the nature of stereotypes (positive or negative) applied to different groups, and the vastly different rules of inclusion and exclusion. While the model we propose is best illustrated by focusing on black/white mixed-race people, it also can be applied to any multiracial child. This is because all multiracial children must make choices about their racial identification, navigate validation or invalidation around their choice, and resolve their in-between status while traveling pathways shaped by acceptance and/or denial. Therefore, while this book is most directly applicable to those raising black/white mixed-race children, the model we present here can be helpful for caregivers of all multiracial children.

MULTIPLE AUDIENCES

We have written this book with a multiple audience in mind. At a practical level, we are speaking to parents raising mixed-race children as well as teachers, therapists, social workers, and other social service professionals who work with them. At a theoretical level, we are speaking to researchers and theorists studying the multiracial population. Depending on the reader's personal history, educational experience, occupation, and specific interests, some parts of the book may be more relevant than others. For readers interested in our theory of mixed-race identity development, chapters 1 and 2 will be of particular interest. Those interested in finding practical, hands-on strategies to use with mixed-race children may benefit more from skimming chapter 1 and 2 and moving directly into the subsequent chapters that conclude with strategy sections.

In chapter 1, we present the Continuum of Biracial Identity (COBI) model to describe the range of racial identifications that mixed-race children develop. We argue that each place along the continuum is an equally valid blending of blackness and whiteness and caution readers against privileging certain identifications over others. This chapter culminates in a discussion of the critical role that validation and/or rejection play in racial identity development.

Chapter 2 suggests a shift of focus among clinicians and researchers away from the racial identity label that mixed-race people use and toward the process in which that identity emerged. The COBI model is predicated on the notion that a healthy identity is not a matter of the actual label a child adopts, but rather of how she developed that identity. Specifically, we encourage readers to evaluate health by examining the degree to which acceptance and/or denial of one's mixed-race parentage shapes the pathway an individual has traveled to arrive at a particular racial self-understanding. To illustrate the shift from label to pathway, we provide case studies to demonstrate how individuals can use the same racial identifier, yet vary considerably with regard to how they arrived at this identity.

After fully developing the COBI model, we begin to examine the contextual and relational factors that influence racial identity development. In chapter 3 we discuss the historical roots of racism, how it persists in contemporary America, and how it affects the way mixed-race people are categorized, understood, and treated by others. It is only by understanding how race and racism manifest in the broader social context that we can fully grasp the difficulty that children face in resolving their mixed-race status.

The central question addressed in chapter 4 is how families influence the racial identity development of mixed-race children. We identify specific relational factors within families that influence how children learn to understand themselves racially and shape their acceptance and/or denial of their mixed-race status. The chapter concludes with specific strategies for parents, extended family members, and caregivers.

Chapter 5 focuses on community institutions that exert a socializing influence on mixed-race children, paying special attention to schools. Within our discussion, we consider the messages that teachers, peers, and friends send about race and the powerful impact each has to accept and/or reject the racial identities that mixed-race children have developed. We also suggest strategies for parents and professionals to respond to situations in which community members challenge and contest the racial socialization that children receive at home.

Physical appearance is critical to our understanding of race, categorization, and group membership. Because of this, we devote chapter 6 to this important but delicate topic. In doing so, we challenge readers to question the direct relationship that is assumed between appearance and identity, and instead consider that children's racial identities are sometimes inconsistent with their skin color and other physical traits. We also discuss how appearances can become a bone of contention during adolescence and offer strategies to mitigate the often painful effects of appearance on racial identity development.

The final factor we consider in our racial identity development framework is gender, which we discuss in chapter 7. Here we explain how gender invisibly yet profoundly shapes identity development for girls. We examine how race and gender oppression interact to create unique challenges for mixed-race girls, and how beauty issues can underpin painful events that shape acceptance and/or denial of mixed-race status. We also explore the tensions that routinely develop between black and mixed-race girls and how they influence identity development. We suggest several strategies that adults can use to help counteract negative societal messages around blackness and beauty and to promote self-love and sisterhood between girls.

We conclude in chapter 8 with a discussion of the evolving nature of race relations in the United States. We summarize how the use of the COBI model assists in that transition, explain why the blending of a structural and psychological components are necessary for new theories of racial identity development, and explore our hopes for future research on interracial families and the multiracial population.

ACKNOWLEDGMENTS

Last but not least, we would like to warmly thank all of those who have walked with us as we wrote this book. We each have colleagues who have generously read and reviewed chapters and full drafts of the manuscript. We want to especially thank David Brunsma, Rainier Spencer, and Erica Childs for their

comments and conversation on various drafts of this manuscript, the anony-
mous reviewers who provided us with critical and constructive feedback, and
our editor Grace Ebron who gave us great freedom in revising the manuscript.
Jennifer Caputo and Marissa Berk-Smith both generously contributed untold
hours of their time to conduct library research and supplementary interviewing. We are deeply grateful to Gloria Lee, Michael Dailey, and Julia Novesky
for their diligence in creating and refining the appendixes.

In addition to our gratitude to all of those who directly supported our writing activity, we wish to thank those who supported us intellectually and personally throughout the process. Kerry Ann has been professionally blessed by
the support of the African American Studies Department at the University of
Illinois at Chicago. Rare is the academic department where applied work is
valued, interdisciplinary scholarship nurtured, and intellectual community so
vibrant. Beth Richie is to be commended for her leadership in creating such
an academic community. Special thanks goes to Kerry Ann's writing group
members David Stovall, Badia Ahad, Michelle Boyd, Cynthia Blair, Amanda
Lewis, Kennette Crockette, Anita Charlot, and Keith McCoy who have held her
feet to the fire once a week for the past two years. In hindsight, we are also
both thankful for the misery we experienced at the University of Connecticut.
Had we not spent many hours huddled in our offices crying, commiserating,
and creating an escape plan, this project would never have been born. Thank
you Charlie Super for bringing us together. We both were also emotionally
and spiritually supported by families, friends, and partners who in many un-
recognized ways took care of the details of life so that we could have the luxury of time to complete our writing. Kerry Ann especially thanks her
husband, William, whose daily cooking, cleaning, and caretaking enabled her
to write, and whose unconditional love is the inspiration for her work. Tracey
would like to acknowledge her parents June and Jerome for their uncompro-
mising support, wisdom, and love. Their faith and encouragement are the
foundation of all her accomplishments. She also acknowledges Billy, who was
there for her from the first day of this project and supported her throughout.
We thank each of them for their constant encouragement, which has given us
the confidence to pursue our passions and voice our ideas, even when doing
so has been unpopular and unwelcome.

Raising Biracial Children was most profoundly shaped by the mixed-race
people, parents, and practitioners who shared their lives with us. During

interviews, in therapy, at conferences, in their homes, and at chance meetings, we have never had to look far for interracial family members willing to assist us. Some read our work, others listened to our ideas, and many urged us to make our writing more accessible. Their feedback clarified our message and their stories breathed life into this manuscript. For this we will always be grateful.

1

Moving beyond Tragedy: A Multidimensional Model of Mixed-Race Identity

In April 1997, twenty-two-year-old Tiger Woods won the Masters Golf Tournament and became an instant celebrity. The media raved about his athletic talent and, as an "African American," they paralleled his accomplishments with Jackie Robinson's in baseball. Confusion followed shortly thereafter when Woods appeared on the *Oprah Winfrey Show* and was asked if it bothered him, the only child of a black American father and a Thai mother, to be labeled "African American." He replied, "Yeah it does. Growing up, I came up with this name: I'm a 'Cablinasian.'" He went on to explain that "Cablinasian" was an acronym, created to reflect the fact that he is actually one-eighth Caucasian, one-fourth black, one-eighth American Indian, and one-half Asian.

Tiger Wood's refusal to accept the media's characterization of him as black and his public attempt to identify himself as multiracial was a watershed event. It raised the profile of the Multiracial movement and provided a celebrity face for the federal legislation aimed at adding a "multiracial" category to the 2000 Census. However, the most salient outcome of Wood's assertion of himself as multiracial was that he redefined the "tragedy" that has been attributed to multiracial identity throughout history. Prior to his public self-identification, multiracial people were depicted as suffering from tragic confusion about their racial identity. After just one appearance on *Oprah*, the *idea* of multiracial identity as a valid choice for mixed-race people burst into the spotlight and caused an intense public debate over the "correct" way for mixed-race people to define themselves racially.[1]

Tiger Woods's self-definition as Cablinasian garnered so much media attention because it challenged the dominant norm that those with any "black blood" are simply black. In his self-definition, he articulated the idea that mixed-race people could claim and acknowledge all their racial ancestries. He is, however, only one of at least 6.8 million self-identifying multiracial people in the United States.[2] More importantly, his self-identification as multiracial represents but one of many racial identity choices made by mixed-race people in American society today. The debate over his racial identity mirrored the debate among social scientists over racial identity development for mixed-race people. Despite the demographic and social changes that have taken place since the Civil Rights movement, many social scientists—as well as journalists, politicians, social workers, therapists, educators, researchers, and parents—remain wedded to models that define what is the "correct" racial identity for children of interracial unions.

Over the years, social scientists have shifted their position on what is considered *the* "healthy" ideal for mixed-race people, all the while clinging to the assumption that there is *one* ideal racial identity for members of this population. The clearest example of the shifting paradigms in racial identity research is in the case of individuals with one black and one white parent, where researchers have shifted between two different ideal identities: black and biracial. Before the mid-1980s, researchers assumed that the only healthy way for members of this group to identify racially was as exclusively black. This conceptualization was grounded in the historical and cultural norm of the "one-drop rule," which mandated that individuals with any black ancestry were designated as members of the "black race."[3] Because the one-drop rule operated as an unquestioned assumption held by researchers, racial identity was not understood as a negotiable reality, nor was it an area where individuals had options. Because anyone with black ancestry was assumed to be black, black identity models were used to assess the racial identity development of mixed-race people. In this context, mixed-race people who resisted categorization as exclusively black were often seen as "confused" and were pathologized by researchers.[4]

Beginning in the late 1980s, the study of racial identity among mixed-race people shifted as the one-drop rule was challenged and reconceptualized. A new generation of researchers, many of whom were themselves multiracial, advanced a new way of defining healthy identity for mixed-race people. While the prevailing view suggested that an exclusively black identity was the ideal and only correct choice, this new generation of researchers suggested that biracial was the only healthy choice.[5] With this new assumption, researchers now assert that those who define themselves as black suffer from "denial." They are now pathologized in the same way that the previous generation of researchers stigmatized those who claimed any identity other than black. As an example of the shift in assumptions, Jewelle Taylor Gibbs, a prominent developmental psychologist, proposes that a healthy self-concept requires integration of all an individual's racial identities.[6] Therefore, she refers to clients who identify exclusively as black as being "overidentified with their black parents."[7] Similarly, Carlos Poston's Biracial Identity Development model contends that an "integrated" identity (i.e., one that comprises all aspects of an individual's racial backgrounds) is the healthy ideal and is the self-realized end point of his stage model.[8] Although many counseling researchers have relied on Gibbs and Poston's models, they represent only two of a growing number of multiracial identity frameworks.[9] The new theories illustrate an emergent trend in contemporary research where *black* identity has been replaced by *biracial* identity as the psychological ideal.[10]

The upside of the emergence of new biracial identity models is that there is growing support for the idea of "multiracial" as a legitimate category of racial identification. The downside is that this shift in models has had the unintended consequence of marginalizing singular racial identities (especially black identity) in order to establish the legitimacy of biracial and multiracial identity. Identity models that privilege either a singular black identity or a biracial identity are each problematic for the same reasons. Both assume a "one size fits all" model by focusing on *either* "black" *or* "biracial" as the only healthy option.

The purpose of this book is to challenge the very assumption that there is *one* appropriate way for mixed-race people to understand their racial identity. We argue that mixed-race people may develop one of many different racial identities, none of which are any more or less valid, no more or less correct, than the others. Certainly, mixed-race people face unique challenges. However, the greatest challenges arise when individuals develop a racial identity that is routinely rejected by others in their environment. It is this rejection, more than the actual identity one chooses, that poses the greatest risk to over-all psychological health and functioning for those who are mixed-race.

Toward that end, we present here a new way of thinking about racial identity among mixed-race people that we refer to as the Continuum of Biracial Identity (COBI) model. Our COBI model has emerged from the work we have been immersed in over the last five years interviewing multiracial people across the United States, and meeting with countless interracial families and multiracial clients in therapy. During our research and clinical interviews, we have heard mixed-race people describe their racial self-understanding in many different ways. Listening to them has led us to conclude that "one size fits all" models of mixed-race identity fail to reflect the diverse ways that mixed-race people understand themselves racially. More importantly, we believe that these models are potentially harmful to those who get labeled as "unhealthy" because they do not see themselves the way existing identity models say they "should." The COBI model reflects our belief that there are multiple ways that mixed-race people identify themselves racially, and no one way is any better, more correct, or more valuable than another. It resists attempts to "fit" mixed-race people into a singular correct identity, and instead recognizes that multiple and equally valid racial identifications exist among the growing multiracial population.

WHAT IS IDENTITY?

"Identity" is a term that is used in many different settings, yet its meaning is often unclear. The term "identity" becomes confusing when combined with the biologically unreal, yet socially real, construct of race.[11] Because identity is at the very heart of this project, we wish to be clear in our definition and use of the term. Simply put, we conceptualize identity as the way we understand ourselves in relation to others and our social environment. Our identities are constructed through a *reflexive process* involving interaction between our self and others in our environment (e.g., families, schools, neighborhoods, and houses of worship).

Children learn about race (and racial categorization) through their interactions with others. Within the context of these interactions, they come to understand who they are in the world. Their sense of identity is also shaped by existing social categories that to some extent limit the perception of options that are available for racial definition. For example, a mixed-race child who is raised solely by her black parent and grows up in a predominately black community may perceive that the only legitimate way she can identify herself racially is as black. While other possibilities exist, her immediate environment and her interactions with others in that environment may limit her perception of other possibilities, which influence how she will self-identify.

It is important to emphasize that identity is a *social process* and not a static, fixed end product that has any type of permanence attached to it. Our self-understanding is in a continual state of evolution. Moreover, the process of identity development does not occur through a single interaction, but instead progresses over an ongoing series of highly complex and coded interactions. Therefore, when we discuss racial identity, we neither believe there is only one correct way for mixed-race people to define themselves, nor do we believe that identity exists as a fixed state. It is not something that individuals "achieve" and then maintain unaltered for the remainder of their life. Instead, racial identity is an ongoing process of understanding one's self racially in relation to others and amidst societal definitions of racial group membership. Identity, therefore, is constantly in a state of development, modification, adjustment, negotiation, and evolution.

THE COBI MODEL

The COBI model we present in this book suggests that mixed-race people can locate themselves at any place along a blending continuum (see model 1.1). Each pole of the continuum represents the singular racial identification of a child's parents (one end represents black and the other white). The middle of the continuum represents an equal blend of the two, not in biological terms, but in terms of identification. Mixed-race people can locate themselves

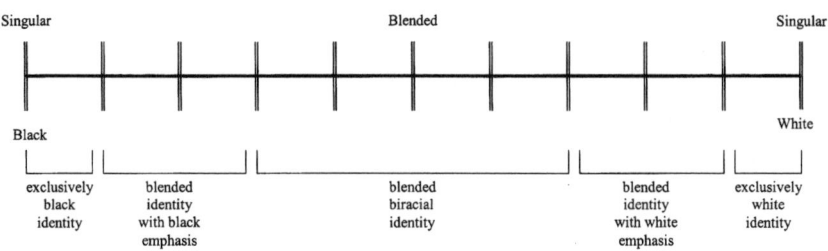

MODEL 1.1
Continuum of Biracial Identity

anywhere along this continuum and that location can change over their life-time. In other words, among those who have one black and one white parent, we find people who identify as black, white, biracial, all of the above, and none of the above. In the following section, we elaborate on each of the different ways that mixed-race people identify themselves along this continuum.

Singular Identities

Mixed-race individuals may racially self-identify with only one of their birth parents. For example, if an individual has one black and one white par-ent, she may understand her racial identity as either exclusively black *or* ex-clusively white. While multiracial activists and some researchers have pathologized the singular identity option, it is important to recognize that it is possible for a singular identity to be a valid and rational choice and can re-sult in a well-adjusted individual with high self-esteem. By way of example, a respondent in Lise Funderberg's descriptive study of multiracial identity had a white mother and a black, white, and Cherokee father. While acknowledging the reality of her multiracial background, she developed a singular black iden-tity and described that process in this way: "What I did was place things in my own mind a certain way a long time ago and then just leave them there and go forward. That placement was not only just an acceptance, but a celebration of being a person of color and going from there. . . . I am black. There's nothing else involved in it; there's no other discussion."[12]

Historically, choosing a singular identity meant developing a nonwhite racial identity because of a long-standing classification norm known as hy-podescent. This norm relegates multiracial people to the racial group of the lower-status parent. Because of the unique history of slavery in the United States, classification in accordance to this norm has been the strictest for in-dividuals with any known black ancestry. According to the one-drop rule, no matter how far an individual may be removed generationally from a black ancestor, he can never be classified as white. Therefore, individuals who have one black parent have long been forced to adopt a singular black identity and this was considered the only identity "option" for black/white mixed-race persons throughout most of American history. So deeply embedded was this cultural norm that it was not even conceptualized as an "option," nor would individuals have considered any other racial identity. In fact, Maria Root refers to the singular black identity as an "acceptance of the identity society assigns."[13]

Despite the persistence of the one-drop rule, researchers such as Dorcas Bowles and Maria Root have discussed a singular white identity as a viable, albeit rare, identification.[14] In a study of 225 black/white mixed-race people in Detroit, researchers found that 13 percent of their respondents identified exclusively as black and 4 percent identified exclusively as white.[15] Aside from these few studies, however, research documenting the existence of the singular white identity is scarce and often a topic of great discomfort for multiracial researchers, activists, and counselors dealing with multiracial people.[16] This discomfort stems from the idea that some consider the singular white identity equivalent to "passing." We disagree with equating white identification with passing. Historically, passing implies that an individual has a nonwhite identity, yet pretends to be white for various social and economic reasons. Individuals with a singular white identity are not passing because they truly understand their racial identity as white (despite the fact that one of their parents is black).[17]

Blended Identities

Gloria Anzaldúa introduced the term "border identity" to describe a hybrid social identity that spans across the boundaries of existing categories.[18] As a self-described mestiza straddling the geographic boundaries of Mexico and the United States, as well as the cultural differences between Mexican and Anglo culture, she describes her sense of border existence as follows:

> Living on borders and in margins, keeping intact one's shifting and multiple identity and integrity, is like trying to swim in a new element, an "alien" element. There is an exhilaration in being a participant in the further evolution of humankind, in being "worked" on. I have the sense that certain "faculties," not just in me, but in every border resident, colored or noncolored and dormant areas of consciousness are being activated, awakened. Strange, huh? And yes, the "alien" element has become familiar—never comfortable, not with society's clamor to uphold the old, to rejoin the flock, to go with the herd. No, not comfortable but home.[19]

As we suggest visually in model 1.1, blending occurs along a continuum and does not imply that it will be perfectly even or equal. Among those who use labels such as "biracial," "mixed," "mulatto," "mestizo," or "hapa" to describe their racial identity, we find a variety of self-understandings and degrees of blending with some leaning far more in one direction than another.

In other words, it is important to make a distinction between those who have a blended identity that appears to balance both black and white in equal ways versus those who define themselves as blended but who clearly emphasize either their blackness or their whiteness to a greater degree. In fact, most mixed-race people tend to fall somewhere in the middle range of the continuum, understanding themselves as biracial, but leaning more in one direction versus the other.

Maria Root characterizes biracial identity as the "ability to hold, merge, and respect multiple perspectives simultaneously."[20] Similarly, G. Reginald Daniel describes the blended identity as one that "resists both the dichotomization and hierarchical valuation of African American and European American cultural and racial differences."[21] The blended identity as a separate racial identity option positions "biracial" as an entirely new racial category, breaking with the norm of hypodescent as setting the parameters for racial identity among multiracial people. "Biracial" identity is the choice that Multiracial movement activists and a number of multiracial identity researchers have argued is the only healthy option for mixed-race people.[22] Yet we find those situated in the middle of the continuum vary greatly in their understanding of what it means to them to have a biracial identity. Reducing the issue of psychological health to whether or not an individual utilizes the label "biracial" mistakes the complexity of self-understanding for what box an individual checks off.

Transcendent Identities

Some mixed-race people describe themselves as having no racial identity, and therefore as having "transcended" racial categorization altogether.[23] This approach is reminiscent of Robert Park's "marginal man" theory where, by virtue of being located in between accepted social positions, individuals discount racial categorizations completely.[24] Failing to fit within the rigidly defined groupings of the existing classification system, they disregard race altogether, and instead consider the hierarchical system of race an abstraction, and others' attempts to place them in it an annoyance.

The transcendent identity is a rare but emerging identification strategy for mixed-race people. The literature has been remarkably silent on this identity option, yet various researchers have documented its existence. G. Reginald Daniel discusses how being mixed-race produces a transcendent understanding of oneself and suggests that this option is more likely to be found among those who are comfortable in the communities of both their backgrounds in roughly equal amounts.[25]

Because they are mixed-race, transcendents believe they have an objective outsider's perspective on the subjective, socially constructed phenomena of race.[26] John, who was a respondent in Rockquemore and Brunsma's study, acknowledged having one black and one white parent, but he resisted efforts to get him to clarify how he defined himself racially. Instead, he continually asserted that race was socially constructed. His parents had encouraged him to understand himself as "human" and to rebuff others' attempts to categorize him racially. Eventually, he responded to questions about his racial identity by saying: "I'm just John, you know. I never thought this was such a big deal to be identified, I just figured I'm a good guy, just like me for that, you know. But, when I came [to college] it was like I was almost forced to look at people as being white, black, Asian, or Hispanic. And so now, I'm still trying to go 'I'm just John,' but uh, you gotta be something."[27] The transcendent identity as described here is especially noteworthy because individuals claim to opt out of the categorization game altogether, instead nurturing self-understandings that are not grounded in race.

THE ROLE OF VALIDATION AND REJECTION

Because identity refers to how we understand ourselves relative to others, and because our identities are constantly evolving, interactions with others are crucial to the racial identity development process. In short, others affect how we see and understand ourselves racially. At the heart of these interactions reside experiences with validation and rejection. Whether our racial identity is validated or rejected by others is communicated through various verbal and nonverbal messages. These messages reveal how others perceive us as well as how they feel about what they perceive and, therefore, play a significant role in how we develop our racial self-understanding. (See model 1.2.)

Mutual Identification

When we assert some aspect of our identity to others, there are two levels at which validation or rejection may occur. The first involves whether the other person sees us in the same way we see ourselves. We refer to this visual agreement as "mutual identification." If others do not perceive us the way we

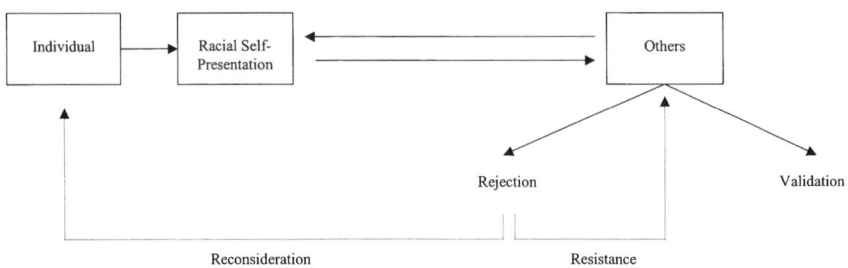

MODEL 1.2
The Relationship between Validation, Rejection, and Racial Identity

perceive ourselves, an immediate rejection occurs. For example, a person who defines himself as biracial yet is consistently assumed by others to be black experiences rejection around his preferred racial identity because of a failure of mutual identification. If however, there is agreement between how others see us and how we see ourselves, validation occurs, and we have achieved some level of mutual identification.

Racial Response

Above and beyond basic mutual identification, the second level at which validation or rejection occurs is related to how others feel about a particular racial identity. For example, Tara is a mixed-race woman who identifies herself as black.[28] Because Tara looks black and presents herself as black to others, she is validated at the level of mutual identification. However, like most black people in America, Tara has experienced rejection from whites. She has routinely encountered racial discrimination and prejudice. As she stated, "My problem is not that people don't accept me as black. My problem is that people, basically white people, reject me because they see me as black and they don't respect black people. I feel disrespected as a black person by most white people." While Tara's racial identity is validated at the basic level of identification (others see her the way she sees herself), she experiences rejection at the second level from people who have a negative response to her blackness.

Experiences with validation or rejection play a critical role in mediating the process of identity development in general, and racial identity development more specifically. In fact, validation or rejection of one's chosen racial identity contributes greatly to the overall wellness of mixed-race people.[29] Irrespective of the identity mixed-race people construct, the degree of validation or rejec-

tion they experience from others, especially those who are emotionally significant to them, can either reinforce their self-understanding and support a
sense of identity cohesion, or can undermine their sense of self and create psychic distress. Research indicates that children and adolescents that develop
blended biracial identities are most likely to encounter experiences with rejection, suggesting that such persons may be at a greater risk of psychic distress than those developing other racial identities.[30]

A CASE OF VALIDATION/REJECTION

The importance of validation and rejection in terms of mixed-race identity
may seem abstract when considered theoretically. To illustrate this in a more
tangible way, we present a case study discussing how validation and rejection
operate in the racial identity development process.

Kathy is a mixed-race young adult whose mother is African American and
father is white.[31] She appears white because of her fair skin, freckles, green eyes
and long, curly, light brown hair. Kathy had experiences of validation and rejection of her racial identity from her early to late adolescence, and each of
these experiences had critical affects on her racial identity development.

Kathy attended a public high school where the student population was ap-
proximately 50 percent African American and 50 percent white. During this
time, Kathy, who self-identified as biracial, socialized almost exclusively with
white students. According to Kathy, while both white and black students accepted her self-identification as biracial, she felt that white students responded
to this identity in a validating way, while black students rejected it.

When she was in tenth grade, Kathy transferred to a Catholic school where
all but ten of the students were white. Of these ten, six were black and four
were biracial. Kathy described her experiences at her new school in the following way:

> When I got to my new school I was really taken in by these people [students of
> color] and it was just a total different world. It was like [in public school] I was
> really never accepted by black females because, . . . they were jealous because you
> have "good" hair and "light" eyes. I remember thinking what were they jealous
> of? I didn't choose to be like this, I don't mind it, you know what I mean, so it
> was really their problem, I think. Then I went to Catholic school . . . I didn't re-
> ally know anybody, and I was just like hopefully, it will be better. Of course it
> was better because there were less black people for me to contend with. . . .

Maybe because it was a Catholic prep school that was four thousand dollars a year that made people really appreciate education and different cultures and you know, and these people really took me in and it was nice. So we [the black and biracial students], it was a close knit group, it was kind of like family within that high school.

At the Catholic school, like in her former high school, the students accepted her self-identification as biracial, but in this new context, all her peers (black, white, and biracial) validated her identity choice as legitimate and valuable. The fundamental distinction between her experiences at the two schools was that at the first one, the black students rejected her for choosing to identify as biracial because they saw it as an antiblack sentiment. They interpreted her biracial identity as a rejection of them as black people, and so they rejected her in turn. In her second school, the black students not only accepted that she identified as biracial, but also accepted this as a valid identity option.

When Kathy went to college she attended a predominately white university. Because she had checked "black" on her admission form, she was invited to attend a six-week program for black students the summer before her first year. During the program, she made many close friends among the group of thirty participants and felt part of a black community for the first time in her life. She said, "it was great, finally it was like oh, they don't care that I'm so light, or light-skinned or whatever, so that was nice. Especially freshman year, I totally identified with the black population here. And I was telling my parents, this is so opposite of what I've been kind of running away from all my life because finally these people are like, you're just a person, you know what I mean."

In this environment, the black students Kathy met accepted that she identified herself as biracial. In addition to validating her identification as a legitimate choice, they also conveyed a strong sense of pride as black people and actively encouraged Kathy to connect more directly with her blackness. Interestingly, this is precisely what Kathy did. By her final year of college, she shifted how she defined herself from biracial with an emphasis on whiteness to biracial with an emphasis on blackness. After graduation, Kathy remained at the institution working in the admissions office to increase the number of black students enrolled at the university.

Kathy felt that her college peers accepted her as biracial. At the same time they included her in the community of black students and were proud of being black. They helped her feel comfortable enough to explore and eventually connect with her blackness, which until then had been the source of confusion and alienation.

Kathy is an example of a person with three distinct experiences with validation and rejection at the second level (racial response) that affected her evolving racial identity. In each of the three educational settings described in this example, none of her peers, irrespective of race, challenged that she was biracial by parentage. She was validated as biracial at the first level of mutual identification. At the second level, however, she had dramatically different experiences with validation and rejection in each school setting. In some settings, "biracial" was viewed as worthy and positive, and was therefore validated. In other settings, it was rejected as an illegitimate, self-hating, and hostile identification.

In her first high school, the white students regarded biracial as a valid identity choice, but the black students rejected it. In her second high school, white, black, and other mixed-race students accepted biracial as a valid identity choice. It wasn't until college that Kathy had the opportunity to interact with black people who not only validated her biracial identity as legitimate, but at the same time were able to present her with ways to understand and relate to blackness that were affirming and rewarding to her. This freed her to consider her blackness in a deeper way for the first time in her life, and upon this greater engagement in a validating environment, her racial identity shifted from biracial with a white emphasis to biracial with a black emphasis.

Stories like Kathy's help us to see the complexity that exists in the lives of mixed-race people. When we listen to mixed-race people explain their reality, three major issues become clear: 1) there is no *one* way in which all mixed-race people understand their racial identity, 2) models that privilege one racial identity as the ideal fail to comprehend the multidimensionality and variation within the mixed-race population, and 3) racial identity development is a dynamic social process where the degree of validation and rejection mixed-race individuals experience plays a key role in influencing the racial identity choices they make throughout their lives.

Our COBI model asserts that there is a full range of possibilities regarding how mixed-race people may define themselves racially. The choices individuals make are shaped by the experiences they have with others and the ways that they are validated or rejected for making particular identity choices. In the next chapter, we explore how experiences with others, particularly those that involve validation and rejection, influence identity choices and ultimately shape the extent to which mixed-race people accept or deny the reality of their mixed-race parentage. We also explain how issues of acceptance and denial are at the heart of what defines healthy identity.

NOTES

1. Woods's name became so synonymous with multiracialism that Representative Tom Petri's bill (H.R. 830) mandating that a freestanding multiracial category be added to the 2000 Census became known the "Tiger Woods Bill." The bill was never passed.

2. For an analysis of multiple-race responses on the 2000 census, see Nicholas Jones and Amy Symens Smith, *The Two or More Races Population: 2000* (Washington, D.C.: U.S. Census Bureau, 2001).

3. F. James Davis, *Who Is Black? One Nation's Definition* (University Park: Pennsylvania State University Press, 1991); Allison Davis, Burleigh Gardner, Mary Gardner, and W. Lloyd Warner, *Deep South: A Social Anthropological Study of Caste and Class* (Chicago: University of Chicago Press, 1941).

4. Fernando Henriques, *Children of Conflict: A Study of Interracial Sex and Marriage* (New York: Dutton, 1975); Joyce A. Ladner, *Mixed Families: Adopting across Racial Boundaries* (Garden City, N.Y.: Anchor Press/Doubleday, 1977).

5. Dorcas Bowles, "Bi-Racial Identity: Children Born to African American and White Couples," *Clinical Social Work Journal* 21.4 (1993); Philip Brown, "Biracial Identity and Social Marginality," *Child & Adolescent Social Work Journal* 7.4 (1990); G. Reginald Daniel, "Black and White Identity in the New Millennium: Unsevering the Ties That Bind," *The Multiracial Experience: Racial Borders as the New Frontier*, ed. Maria P. P. Root (Thousand Oaks, Calif.: Sage Publications, 1996); Roger Herring, "Developing Biracial Ethnic Identity: A Review of the Increasing Dilemma," *Journal of Multicultural Counseling & Development* 23.1 (1995); W. Carlos Poston, "The Biracial Identity Development Model: A Needed Addition," *Journal of Counseling & Development* 69.2 (1990); and Jewelle Taylor Gibbs, "Biracial Adolescents," *Children of Color: Psychological Interventions with Culturally Diverse Youth*, ed. Jewelle Taylor Gibbs and Larke Nahme Huang (San Francisco: Jossey-Bass, 1998).

6. Gibbs, "Biracial Adolescents."

7. Gibbs, "Biracial Adolescents."

8. Poston, "The Biracial Identity Development Model: A Needed Addition."

9. For examples of studies using Gibbs and Poston's models, see Herring, "Developing Biracial Ethnic Identity: A Review of the Increasing Dilemma"; S. Kato, "Coats of Many Colors: Serving the Multiracial Child and Adolescent," *Journal of Family and Consumer Sciences* 92 (2000); and Carmen Braun Williams, "Claiming a Biracial Identity: Resisting Social Construction of Race and Culture," *Journal of Counseling Development* 77.1 (1999). New models of biracial identity include James H. Jacobs, "Identity Development in Biracial Children," *Racially Mixed People in America,* ed. Maria P. P. Root (Thousand Oaks, Calif.: Sage Publications, 1992); George Kitahara Kich, "The Developmental Process of Asserting a Biracial, Bicultural Identity," *Racially Mixed People in America,* ed. Maria P. P. Root (Thousand Oaks, Calif.: Sage Publications, 1992); Teresa LaFromboise, Hardin Coleman, and Jennifer Gerton, "Psychological Impact of Biculturalism: Evidence and Theory," *The Culture and Psychology Reader,* eds. Nancy Rule Goldberger and Jody Bennet Veroff (New York: New York University Press, 1995); and Christine Kerwin, Joseph G. Ponterotto, Barbara L. Jackson, and Abigail Harris, "Racial Identity in Biracial Children: A Qualitative Investigation," *Journal of Counseling Psychology* 40.2 (1993).

10. Several researchers have raised the possibility that biracial people understand their social identities in multifaceted ways: Daniel, "Black and White Identity in the New Millennium: Unsevering the Ties That Bind"; Robin Miller, "The Human Ecology of Multiracial Identity," *Racially Mixed People in America,* ed. Maria P. P. Root (Thousand Oaks, Calif.: Sage Publications, 1992); Kristen Renn, *Mixed Race Students in College: The Ecology of Race, Identity, and Community on Campus* (Albany: State University of New York Press, 2004); Kerry Ann Rockquemore, "Between Black and White: Exploring the 'Biracial' Experience," *Race & Society* 1.2 (1998); Kerry Ann Rockquemore and David Brunsma, *Beyond Black: Biracial Identity in America* (Thousand Oaks, Calif.: Sage Publications, 2002); Maria P. P. Root, "The Multiracial Experience: Racial Borders as Significant Frontier in Race Relations," *The Multiracial Experience: Racial Borders as the New Frontier,* ed. Maria P. P. Root (Thousand Oaks, Calif.: Sage Publications, 1996); and Kendra Wallace, *Relative/Outsider: The Art and Politics of Identity Among Mixed-Heritage Students* (Westport, Conn.: Ablex, 2001). However, this work has been less central to the therapeutic community than research that has privileged biracial identity as the ideal.

11. See Michael Omi and Howard Winant, *Racial Formation in the United States: From the 1960s to the 1990s,* 2nd ed. (New York: Routledge, 1994).

12. Respondent quoted from Lise Funderburg, *Black, White, Other: Biracial Americans Talk About Race and Identity,* 1st ed. (New York: W. Morrow and Co., 1994).

13. Maria P. P. Root, "Resolving 'Other' Status: Identity Development of Biracial Individuals," *Women & Therapy* 9.1–2 (1990).

14. Bowles, "Bi-Racial Identity: Children Born to African American and White Couples;" Root, "Resolving 'Other' Status: Identity Development of Biracial Individuals"; and Root, "The Multiracial Experience: Racial Borders as Significant Frontier in Race Relations." It should be noted that Root, while allowing the singular white identity as an option, narrows the geographic and cultural parameters for this possibility (i.e., she considers a white identity to be unavailable in the South).

15. Rockquemore and Brunsma, *Beyond Black: Biracial Identity in America.*

16. Bowles, "Bi-Racial Identity: Children Born to African American and White Couples"; Root, "Resolving 'Other' Status: Identity Development of Biracial Individuals"; and Root, "The Multiracial Experience: Racial Borders as Significant Frontier in Race Relations."

17. Kerry Ann Rockquemore and Patricia Arend, "Opting for White: Choice, Fluidity, and Black Identity Construction in Post–Civil Rights America," *Race & Society* 5 (2003); France Winddance Twine, "Brown Skinned White Girls: Class, Culture, and the Construction of White Identity in Suburban Communities," *Gender, Place, and Culture* 3.2 (1996).

18. Gloria Anzaldúa, *Borderlands/La Frontera: The New Mestiza,* 1st ed. (San Francisco: Spinsters/Aunt Lute, 1987).

19. Anzaldúa, *Borderlands/La Frontera: The New Mestiza.*

20. Root, "The Multiracial Experience: Racial Borders as Significant Frontier in Race Relations," xxi.

21. Daniel, "Black and White Identity in the New Millennium: Unsevering the Ties That Bind," 133.

22. Multiracial activists privileging biracial identity in their work include Nancy Brown and Ramona Douglass, "Making the Invisible Visible: The Growth of Community Network Organizations," *The Multiracial Experience: Racial Borders as the New Frontier,* ed. Maria P. P. Root (Thousand Oaks, Calif.: Sage Publications, 1996); Carlos Fernandez, "Government Classification of Multiracial/Multiethnic People," *The Multiracial Experience: Racial Borders as the New Frontier,* ed. Maria P. P.

Root (Thousand Oaks, Calif.: Sage Publications, 1996); and Susan Graham, "The Real World," *The Multiracial Experience: Racial Borders as the New Frontier,* ed. Maria P. P. Root (Thousand Oaks, Calif.: Sage Publications, 1996). Multiracial researchers who focus on an integrated biracial identity as the ideal include Brown, "Biracial Identity and Social Marginality"; Lynda D. Field, "Piecing Together the Puzzle: Self-Concept and Group Identity in Biracial Black/White Youth," *The Multiracial Experience: Racial Borders as the New Frontier,* ed. Maria P. P. Root (Thousand Oaks, Calif.: Sage Publications, 1996); Roger Herring, "Biracial Children: An Increasing Concern for Elementary and Middle School Counselors," *Elementary School Guidance & Counseling* 27.2 (1992); Poston, "The Biracial Identity Development Model: A Needed Addition"; Root, "Resolving 'Other' Status: Identity Development of Biracial Individuals"; and Gibbs, "Biracial Adolescents."

23. Rockquemore, "Between Black and White: Exploring the 'Biracial' Experience."

24. Robert Ezra Park, *Race and Culture* (New York: Free Press, 1928).

25. G. Reginald Daniel, *More Than Black?: Multiracial Identity and the New Racial Order* (Philadelphia, Pa.: Temple University Press, 2002).

26. Daniel, "Black and White Identity in the New Millennium: Unsevering the Ties That Bind"; Renn, *Mixed Race Students in College.*

27. Respondent quoted from Rockquemore and Brunsma, *Beyond Black: Biracial Identity in America,* 82. All names used are pseudonyms, with the exceptions of celebrities and cases drawn from published autobiographical material.

28. Tara was Laszloffy's student.

29. Kerry Ann Rockquemore and Tracey A. Laszloffy, "Exploring Multiple Realities: Using Narrative Approaches in Therapy with Black/White Biracials," *Family Relations: Interdisciplinary Journal of Applied Family Studies* 52.2 (2003).

30. Rockquemore and Brunsma, *Beyond Black: Biracial Identity in America.*

31. This case is drawn from Rockquemore, "Between Black and White: Exploring the "Biracial" Experience.

2

Acceptance and Denial: Shifting Our Gaze from Labels to Pathways

The COBI model is a multidimensional framework for understanding racial identity development among mixed-race people. It challenges the assumption that any particular identity is "right" or "wrong" or more or less psychologically healthy than others. It also disputes the notion that a "biracial" identity is the only psychologically healthy possibility, a perspective that has gained popularity through the political success of the Multiracial movement and academic support of new scholarship on mixed-race people. In contrast, our COBI model emphasizes the fact that variation exists among mixed-race people and their identities emerge from a variety of environmental factors. It asserts that healthy racial identity for mixed-race people is less about which *racial label* a person chooses and more about *the pathway* individuals travel toward their identity. By understanding this, parents and clinicians can better recognize the range of racial identities that they may encounter among mixed-race children. They also will be better able to create environments and experiences that support healthy pathways for racial identity development.

We believe that racial identity emerges through a social process that is shaped by a variety of conditions, including particular ideas about race (some of which are unique to specific contexts while others are reflective of society at large), the constraints that physical appearances impose, and the interactions that occur between mixed-race people and others. These interactions involve negotiation whereby mixed-race people present themselves racially in a particular way and others may validate and/or reject them, further impacting how mixed-race people understand themselves racially. In many ways, identity is the product of numerous split second unconscious agreements between individuals and others about how they are perceived and therefore how they will be defined. Throughout this process, validation and rejection are powerful mediating factors.

The focus of this chapter is how individuals can develop a racial identity in both *healthy* and *unhealthy* ways. In other words, there are many possible pathways leading to the same racial identification. Some pathways are healthy in that they involve acceptance of the reality of having one black and one white parent, and others are unhealthy because they are rooted in denial of this fact. Acceptance of mixed-race parentage may lead to any of the identity choices previously discussed, just as denial also may lead to any of these same choices. It is our contention that health is *not* defined by the racial label a person adopts, but rather it is a matter of the pathway one travels to arrive at that label. More specifically, health is determined by the degree of acceptance associated with the pathway one travels to a particular racial self-understanding.

When we use the term "acceptance" we are referring to a state of being that involves cognitive as well as emotional dimensions. One may appear to accept the reality of having one black and one white parent because she can intellectually acknowledge this fact, but this is not the same as truly accepting it emotionally and psychologically. Genuine acceptance occurs when a person has integrated the fact of mixed ancestry into her sense of self and has a peaceful relationship with it, rather than a reactive and unresolved relationship. Denial, in its most extreme form, involves disavowal of mixed-raced parentage. In less extreme cases, individuals may intellectually "accept" their multiple ancestry but are unable to emotionally and psychologically "accept" and integrate it, resulting in reactivity and a lack of resolve. Within the COBI model, any racial identification can be healthy or unhealthy depending on the pathway that led to it. Pathways that reflect acceptance or an evolving state of acceptance are healthy, while those that are steeped in denial are unhealthy.

We turn now to a discussion of how mixed-race individuals may arrive at the same racial identity by very different pathways. To illustrate how acceptance or denial can drive both conscious and unconscious processing, we present a number of case studies. We pull these cases from a variety of sources, including existing research, autobiographies, published case studies, popular media, and clinical cases. This eclectic mix of data reveals the variety of stories that mixed-race people develop about their racial identities. It also provides opportunities for the reader to recognize elements that may reflect his or her own life and the lives of people they know as well as exposing the complicated emotions that surround racial identity development.

SINGULAR IDENTITIES: PATHWAYS OF ACCEPTANCE AND DENIAL
Black/white mixed-race people who understand their racial identity in alliance with only one of their birth parents more often identify as exclusively black than exclusively white.[1] The singular black identity is far more prevalent than the singular white identity because of the historical legacy of the one-drop rule and the myth of white racial purity.[2] The one-drop rule demands that anyone who has even "one drop" of black ancestry is black. Because this norm remains so entrenched in our society, many mixed-race people (irrespective of how they may understand themselves) are considered black by others.

Numerous celebrities who have one black and one nonblack parent identify themselves as black, including Halle Berry, Lenny Kravitz, Rain Pryor, Giancarlo Esposito, and Jasmine Guy. In addition, the popular press has recently been flooded with autobiographical accounts of mixed-race people with one black and one white parent who identify exclusively as black. Such accounts include: Lisa Jones's *Bulletproof Diva*, James McBride's *The Color of Water*, Judy Scales-Trent's *Notes of a White Black Woman*, Barak Obama's *Dreams from My Father*, and Gregory Williams's *Life on the Color Line*.[3]

Pathways of Acceptance
At first glance, one might assume a singular identity involves denial of one half of a person's racial parentage, but this is not necessarily the case. Some are able to acknowledge and accept the reality of having one black and one white parent while simultaneously defining themselves as either black or white. Singer Lenny Kravitz, who defines himself as black, explained his racial identity in the following way:

> Luckily, I was not one of those children [with insecurities about my racial identity]. I knew lots of them who were mixed: "Am I black? Am I white? What am I?" I used to see kids at school who were fair like me or even more fair. They wanted to be white; they didn't want to be black because it's too hard being

black. And then the white kids are like, "You're black, so get away from us," and the black kids are like, "You're white." I never had that. My mother had taught me: "Your father's white, I'm black. You are just as much one as the other, but you are black. In society, in life, you are black." She taught me that from day one . . . you don't have to deny the white side of you if you're mixed, accept the blessing of having the advantage of two cultures, but understand that you are black. In this world, if you have a spot of black, you are black. So get over it.[4]

Lenny Kravitz's nuanced statement about his racial identity makes clear that he accepts having one white and one black parent. However, he also considers himself black. There is no evidence of denial or lack of resolution about this reality. We believe this illustrates a healthy pathway precisely because he has accepted his mixed parentage, consciously considered his personal circumstances and the broader social environment in which he is embedded, and come to the conclusion that he is a black man who has a white father.

While it is far more common for individuals with one black and one white parent to identify as black, some do develop a singular white identity.[5] This identity is only possible for those who physically look white. We raise this uncommon identity because a white identity is not, in and of itself, problematic for mixed-race people. Again, the issue is what pathway led to this particular choice. Adopting a singular identity grounded in acceptance of mixed-race parentage is reflective of health as compared to those who come to this identification through a pathway of denial.

Michelle is a nineteen-year-old student beginning her second year at a private Catholic university in the Northeast who described her racial identity as white on a survey.[6] After moving several times before she was of school age, Michelle's parents settled in an affluent suburb of Boston, where they are now both practicing physicians. She grew up in an all white neighborhood and attended private elementary and then public high schools that were both primarily white. Though she did have a close relationship with one black girl and her current best friend is Asian, Michelle's friendship network has been largely white, as have all of her boyfriends.

Michelle describes her physical appearance as white, having olive skin and "good" curly hair. She said that people are often surprised to find out she is "part African American." For Michelle, being African American is a *symbolic identity* akin to how third and fourth generation whites relate to being German

American or Italian American.[7] Describing her racial identity development, she said:

> Well, I think that because I've been raised mostly around white people, in a white neighborhood in white schools, I wouldn't say that I'm black. Maybe if I had been raised in an all black community, and I think . . . sometimes I see myself as just kind of white, like my culture and my ethnicity, I guess. But I would put in the part that I'm part African American because, I don't know, I kind of, I think it's interesting and unique, and I like people to know, I guess. Sometimes I'm also curious, I never really know if people can tell, and sometimes people will ask, what's your ethnic background?

It is clear from this statement that "African American" is an aspect of her identity that she can choose to expose or hide, and that she understands this as a feature of her *ethnic* background. She offers that she is "part African American" as something to distinguish her from bland whiteness. Michelle's physical appearance affords her the privileges of whiteness, and this is supported by her socialization. She acknowledges the fact that her father is black and her mother is white and she does not display any discomfort, awkwardness, or unrest about this fact. In short, Michelle looks white, describes herself culturally as white, and is assumed white by others. She does not hide her mixed-race parentage, but is fully conscious of the fact that she experiences the social world as a white person. Michelle is an example of someone who has a singular white identity while accepting the fact of being mixed-race. Multiracialism has little direct meaning in her daily life, but she does not manifest any denial, discomfort, or lack of resolve about it.

Pathways of Denial

Individuals can also arrive at a singular identity from a pathway of denial. This leads to identification with one racial group, but it is a decision that is grounded in painful experiences, internalized self-hatred, and/or an oppositional stance. While highlighting cases where racial identity choice is driven by acceptance is important, it is critical here that we focus equal attention on the unhealthy pathways. We do so to illustrate what a singular identity grounded in denial may look like. When encountered, caregivers and clinicians can focus on teasing out the underlying relationships that may move an individual onto a healthier pathway.

In the case of the singular racial identity, mixed-race people choose one (and only one) of their parents' races as their own exclusive identification. But when denial is a factor, they may not admit to others that they have a parent of a different race, or only do so when directly questioned. They may make overtly hostile remarks toward the race of the parent they reject. A mixed-race person who has adopted an extreme position of black separatism and indiscriminately refers to whites as "devils" or "crackers" is an example of denial. This type of identification strategy is most common when: 1) an individual fits phenotypic expectations of one group and not the other, and/or 2) when a child has a painful relationship with one parent and racializes her or his negative feelings.

While extreme, the case of Leo Felton is highly illustrative of an individual choosing a singular identity as white that is firmly grounded in denial. Leo came into the media spotlight in 2002 when he was convicted of plotting to blow up black and Jewish landmarks in Boston. As the story gained momentum, it was discovered that Leo, an avowed white supremacist (complete with swastika tattoos) was, in fact, the offspring of a black architect and a white former nun. Leo's case is interesting because it demonstrates how an individual can fully deny, first to himself and then to others, the fact of his black parentage.

Leo's appearance is ambiguous. He has olive skin and angular features and could easily be taken for Italian. The marriage between his parents was short lived so he was raised primarily by his white mother and her white female partner in a predominately white community. Leo had various emotional problems as a child, but he was institutionalized after flying into a rage that resulted from being called "half-breed" by a black child. When Leo later went to prison, he quickly bonded with white inmates and his antiblack attitudes were transformed by contact with white supremacist ideas. He not only read and accepted white supremacist ideology, but became an active leader, teacher, and resource person within the prison system. This led to the plotting of illegal acts after his release that landed him back in prison.

It is difficult to imagine the level of denial involved in a mixed-race person maintaining a white identity and a commitment to white supremacy. Yet Leo lived in this state of denial for many years, describing himself to others as one-quarter English and three-quarters Italian. When the media "outed" him as black, he was forced into a highly public identity crisis. Revealing his black ancestry forced his denial to the surface and contradicted his white supremacist identity. Given the magnitude of this denial, Leo provides an excellent illustration of an unhealthy pathway to white identity.

While Lenny Kravitz, Michelle, and Leo Felton all adopted singular identities, they differed dramatically in the degree of their acknowledgment, acceptance, and internal resolution. Lenny and Michelle demonstrate an acceptance of having one black and one white parent and the resolution of that fact with their phenotype, cultural background, and environment. In contrast, Leo is in denial of the fact of his black/white mixed parentage and his commitment to white supremacy precludes any possible healthy resolution. While both Leo and Michelle have singular identities as white, Michelle's capacity to accept her mixed-race parentage indicates healthier processing than Leo, who is in complete denial.

BLENDED IDENTITIES: PATHWAYS OF ACCEPTANCE AND DENIAL

In contrast to singular racial identification, those who develop an identity that is more blended conceptualize their racial identity as "biracial" or "mixed." By this, they are asserting a new and separate category, one that is neither one race nor another, but a blending of all their racial ancestries.[8] Because such an identity challenges the idea of mutually exclusive racial categories, those who adopt a blended identity often encounter rejection from others. We should also point out that the term "blended" includes a wide range of possibilities. Hence, one can be blended with an emphasis on whiteness, blended with an emphasis on blackness, or completely blended such that one draws on one's black and white heritage equally. Next we explore how individuals develop blended identities from pathways of acceptance *and* denial.

Numerous celebrities have asserted a blended identity in the past few years including: Mariah Carey, Paula Abdul, and Derek Jeter. Derek Jeter responds to questions about his racial identity by stating "I'm biracial. . . . People ask if I'm black or white. I'm both. I'm not one race . . . no matter how you look at it. I can't pick one or the other group because I'm part of both."[9] Derek is unable and unwilling to disentangle the mixture of culture, race, and the social influences of both his parents and articulates his sense that something unique and separate emerges from the blending of black and white. Because blended identities are, in many ways, a newly emergent phenomenon, celebrities who claim this particular identity label tend to receive a great deal of press coverage for refusing to accept a singular identity. For this reason, more attention tends to be directed toward this racial identity choice than singular identification.

Pathways of Acceptance

Blended identities, like singular identities, can be motivated by either acceptance or denial. Jayne is an example of someone with a blended identity built on a foundation of acceptance.[10] Physically, she looks very much like a light-skinned black person, and this is what most people (white and black) assume she is when they meet her. This requires Jayne to regularly correct people so that they understand her self-identification. While she now feels comfortable challenging others, this position took her many years to achieve.

Growing up, Jayne's parents actively encouraged her to identify as black and she had many black people in her social network (extended family, friends, in her neighborhood, and at school). Throughout her childhood, Jayne perceived herself as black and identified strongly with black people. She was adamant that she would never identify as biracial because "I didn't see anything good about whiteness. I saw white people as privileged and racist, even when they didn't know they were, so why would I want anything to do with being white? Plus, the people I saw who said they were biracial just seemed to be trying not to be black, and that wasn't me. I was proud to be black."

In high school, Jayne encountered rejection for the first time from some black female peers who were resentful of her light complexion. After seeing that Jayne's mother was white, their rejection intensified causing Jayne to experience a crisis for the first time around her sense of blackness. What had once been a solid source of identity and pride now became a question mark tinged with negativity. She started to question whether or not she actually was black. She also began to feel hostility toward the black girls who were treating her badly, which affected her thinking about blackness more broadly. During this time, she also met and started to date a white man, Kevin, something she never imagined she would do. This relationship transformed her because she began to develop a more complex view of whiteness. Kevin was the first white person she had a close relationship with who was clearly white in his orientation. Through her relationship with Kevin, Jayne expanded her view of being white. She was able to see whiteness in more positive terms, much the same way the black girls who rejected her helped her begin to see some negative dimensions associated with blackness.

When Jayne entered college, she was confused about her racial identity. People assumed she was black based on her appearance, and she went along with that, but internally she was no longer at peace. Her parents had encouraged her to embrace blackness and reject whiteness, but her personal life experiences had challenged her to evaluate whiteness and blackness in more multidimensional ways. As a result, she struggled with how to define herself racially. To help deal with her confusion, she started to see a therapist who specialized in working with racial issues. The therapist encouraged Jayne to consider whiteness and blackness in more nuanced ways than she had while growing up. At her therapist's urging, Jayne joined a student group called "Students for a Multiracial World," where students of all races came together to discuss how race informed their personal life experiences, their relationships with each other, and the world at large. They used the group as a forum for exploring race-related tensions on campus and promoting racial acceptance.

The group was a life-altering experience for Jayne. She told her therapist that she was finally able to see that while she was growing up, she felt she had to be either entirely black or white. Because her parents actively encouraged her to choose black, she understood herself as black. Upon reflection, she realized that she did not want to choose one over the other because this assumed one was entirely bad and the other entirely good. She came to understand that there were positive and negative aspects of whiteness and blackness, and she was beginning to derive a sense of empowerment from acknowledging what she liked and disliked about each. Through this process, Jayne decided to identify as biracial because this allowed her to embrace her whole self—black and white, and all the complexity that their combination represented.

Pathways of Denial

While many psychologists consider a blended identity the only healthy racial identification for mixed-race people, a blended identity does not, in and of itself, indicate a healthy resolution of mixed-race status. As we have argued, it is not the racial label that should be the central focus in evaluating psychological health, but the underlying process that led to that identity. In the case of individuals who adopt a blended identity, there are numerous pathways that can lead to this identification that are rooted in denial of one's mixed-race status.

Among those who adopt a blended identity through a process rooted more in denial than acceptance, we find individuals who deeply desire to be only one race. This desire is often fueled by negative feeling toward their other race. Given positive associations with one race and negative associations with the other, they find it difficult to fundamentally accept that they are the product of both racial groups. For various reasons, these individuals are not able to successfully assert and maintain a singular identity, and therefore they adopt a blended identity *as a default*.

Most often, individuals adopt "biracial" as a default category when they truly desire to have a singular identity but their physical appearance disallows single-race self-identification. For example, a person may want to adopt a singular identity as white but cannot because of her physical traits and the one-drop rule. Therefore, she may "settle" on "biracial." In this case, "biracial" is not an affirmation of multiple ancestries, but rather an identity of concession because she really wants to be white, but knows she won't be accepted by others as such because of her physical appearance. In other words, for mixed-race people who want to distance themselves from blackness but cannot, biracial is the "next best option." It signifies being "not black."

Another related manifestation occurs when individuals adopt a biracial identity as a reflection of some underlying fragmentation. While the idea of biracial implies a balanced *integration* of black and white, for some, this identity label reflects a reality in which they are sometimes black, sometimes white, and sometimes biracial depending on where they are and who they are with. Here there is an underlying confusion and lack of resolution of their mixed-race parentage. We provide two cases here to illustrate each of these unhealthy pathways leading to a blended identity. We hope this presentation will challenge the assumption that biracial identification automatically constitutes healthy racial identity development. Just because an individual responds to questions about his or her racial identity by saying "I'm biracial" doesn't mean all is well. We intend our cases to challenge the taken-for-granted assumption of psychological health surrounding biracial identity and extend the discourse to focus on processes, as opposed to labels.

When You Want to Be White, But Can't

Samantha is a twenty-four-year-old mixed-race woman who is in her third year of graduate school.[11] She was born and raised in a Midwest college town.

Samantha is very light skinned, but has dark eyes and hair texture that signify African descent. The daughter of a black male professor and white female homemaker, she grew up living primarily in university-owned housing surrounded by the children of other faculty and graduate students. Though the community was ethnically and racially diverse due to the large population of international graduate students and their children, Samantha had little contact with African Americans, and no experience living in a black community. Her mother was the primary caregiver, so while she described being close to both of her parents, she developed an especially intimate relationship with her mother.

Samantha described feeling "uncomfortable" and "different" in black social contexts, like family gatherings with her black relatives. While she had friendly relationships with the black children that were in her school and neighborhood, she also described feeling "different" from them. A recurring theme in her biography was that she did not live up to black people's expectations of blackness. Because of this, she was told that she "acted white" or "thought she was white" and this was intended as an insult. She described this phenomenon in the following way: "There's this perception [among black people] that I try to be white. Well, I don't try; if I'm white that's just cause that's how I am. Like, if you perceive me to be different in a white way, like, well, that's how I grew up, it's not, like a choice that I made."

While having no serious negative incidents with black children, she recalls some blacks accusing her of having an easier life because she was light skinned and/or had a white mother. Samantha's close friends were primarily white children, but also nonblack children of color, a trend that continues in her current social networks. While she says she dates men of "all races," every boyfriend she could recall specifically when interviewed was white.

Despite writing on a survey that she had "no racial identity," Samantha described herself as "biracial" in a straightforward and consistent manner throughout a face-to-face interview. Yet as the conversation progressed, it became increasingly apparent that except for her physical appearance, everything about Samantha reflected a white identity. Most revealingly, she claimed that *culturally* she is white: "If mainstream culture . . . can be said to be white, then culturally I am white."

While Samantha says that she is biracial, the pathway that led to this assertion is not grounded in acceptance. On a strictly cognitive level, she accepts the fact of having a black parent. However, this acceptance is superficial and is not reflected on a deeper psychological level. She has no relationship whatsoever with blackness or black people, and no understanding of what it means to be black in America. Basically, she has a positive relationship with whiteness but a strained one with blackness. She has no memory of any negative experiences with whites, does not relate to feelings of racial oppression, and views blacks as having misconceptions about and an "overly pessimistic" view of white people. She also remembers negative experiences in adolescence and young adulthood with black people which contribute to her overall sense of alienation from blacks and identification with whites.

Samantha marked that she had "no racial identity" on a survey, said that she was "biracial" in an interview, and later clarified that culturally she was "white." She can best be described as a white person who happens to look black. In her mind, the distinction between race and culture allows her to emphasize her whiteness and distance herself from blackness. The fact that she is of African descent does not mean that she knows anything about African American culture or that she experiences life as an African American person. When she says she is "biracial" it does not reflect genuine acceptance of her whiteness and blackness. Aside from the most superficial and cursory acknowledgment of her black parentage, she largely disavows this aspect of herself.

For Samantha and those like her, "biracial" is what you become when you do not want to be black, but know that you will not be validated by anyone as white because of your physical appearance. Despite being culturally white, her skin color and hair texture mark her as black and would so easily discredit a claim to white identity that it is unlikely that she would be accepted as white by others. Because of her denial, Samantha's assertion of biracial is reflective of a lack of health. She has only resolved the issue of racial identification at the level of labeling, yet remains deeply conflicted about the disjuncture between how she understands herself and how she appears to others.

Shifting Identities and the Fragmented Self

A blended identity may also emerge among those who suffer from an underlying sense of identity confusion. While the term "biracial" implies a blending and balancing of two races, in some instances individuals adopt this label as a reaction to an underlying lack of resolution about who they are and how to integrate their multiple ancestries. This lack of clarity about an individual's *identity* is distinct from the issue of shifting *behaviors*. It is possible for a person to have a clear, resolved identity and yet to engage in behavioral adaptations in different situations to match the demands of different environments.[12] This is clearly illustrated in the movie *Multi-Facial*, in which Vin Diesel plays an actor who spends a day auditioning for various roles. He moves from Italian, to Hispanic, to black by changing his clothing, language, and demeanor. In each scene, however, what changes is his presentation of self, not his fundamental self-understanding. He is code-switching from one context to another because in order to literally play different roles, he must shift his self-presentation enough to fit others' expectations.

Our concern is with those whose internal self-understanding is fragmented, leaving them unable to resolve and integrate their dual racial heritage in a balanced way. Often such individuals describe themselves as biracial but they also say that they have racial *identities* (in contrast to *behaviors*) that shift according to their context at any given time. To be clear, they are not simply adopting different behaviors in different contexts to elicit particular responses from others. Instead, what shifts is how they understand themselves internally. Embedded in this shifting is a lack of certainty about their racial identity and an overreliance on pleasing others by adapting to their expectations.

Individuals are more likely to adopt a biracial label that is reflective of an underlying lack of integration about their mixed-race ancestry during adolescence and early adulthood because this stage of life is naturally fraught with confusion over the question of "who am I"? Racial identity is likely to be one of a broad array of identity issues that individuals struggle to understand, define, and resolve. We hear about this confusion most frequently among college students who have moved from home environments where their biracial identity was accepted to a racially polarized campus environment where they feel forced to choose. In the short term, individuals can find themselves operating in multiple social circles that create competing allegiances.

Jayson is a mixed-race college student who grew up in an entirely white social context, was assumed to be white by strangers, and had little contact with African Americans.[13] During the first few years of college, he actively tried to learn about black history and culture at his predominately white university. He later transferred to a large state university with a tense and polarized racial environment where students of different races rarely interacted outside of the classroom. Here, he was simultaneously a member of the golf team and the radical black student organization. The golf team was predominately white, while the radical student group was entirely African American and overtly hostile toward whites. Jayson spent his first year at the new university moving in and between these two circles, assumed white by one group, black by the other, and accepted by both as a group member. Jayson was able to manage his bifurcated reality for a short time, but it was an unsustainable situation. When members of the black student group spotted him socializing with a white woman, they insisted that dating whites was incompatible with the group's separatist ideology.

Because of the dual lives that Jayson was leading, he felt internally conflicted. He experienced the world as a white person and understood himself as white. However, he felt guilty about that self-understanding because, ideologically, he also wanted to have a sense of himself as black and wanted to be accepted by blacks. As a result, he told people that he was "biracial." But nothing about his self-understanding or the reality of how he was living his life reflected any blending or integration. Apart from his acceptance as black by the student group (which only required his stating that his father was black), he lived in the world as a white person. Biracial was only a label—one that in no way reflected an underlying sense of clarity about the meaning of being both white and black.

Jayson was suffering from a lack of integration and his shifting identity was a transitional point along the path to accepting the fact of his blackness, which he felt he had "missed out on" during his childhood. His lack of connection to blackness, combined with his white appearance, made integrating the two difficult. As a positive step, Jayson took black studies classes and proactively cultivated relationships with black peers. In this way, he was not only trying to learn *intellectually* about black history and culture, but he was also trying to learn about *being* black. From these peers, he tried to learn blackness as a secondary cultural framework because he had not learned it as the primary framework in his childhood.[14] His problem occurred because in his efforts to learn about blackness, he encountered a highly restricted form of blackness in the separatist group. Their expectations literally disallowed him to integrate the various aspects of his social life, and his self. Consequently, "biracial" was not an honest descriptor of how Jayson understood himself racially but a label that masked an underlying struggle to resolve his fragmented racial identity.

Transcendent Identities: Pathways of Acceptance and Denial

One final way that mixed-race people understand their racial identity is by refusing to have any racial identity whatsoever. Even though someone may claim to have "transcended" racial categorization altogether, he or she can arrive at this self-understanding through pathways marked by either acceptance or denial, and therefore this identity can be indicative of either healthy or unhealthy identity development.[15]

Pathways of Acceptance

Some individuals resolve their identification in such a way that a transcendent identity is an endpoint of a thoughtful process of acceptance. Here, the individual intellectually challenges narrow racial identity categories that reinforce a racial hierarchy by asserting no racial identity. They acknowledge the racial identity imposed by society, but they do not accept any racial categorization as a place of personal self-definition.

John was a mixed-race college student who appeared white and claimed to have no racial identity.[16] He was raised in a two-parent household that was intellectually stimulating because his parents encouraged him to read, write, and discuss political and social matters openly. He attended racially diverse public schools and had an equally diverse set of friends. In talking about race, he would recite the sociological explanation of race as a socially constructed and scientifically flawed categorization system. While he acknowledged that he existed in a society where racism was undeniable, he did not consider himself a member of any racial group.

John wanted to be understood by others as the unique individual that he was, to be appreciated for his particular gifts and talents, and not to be "pigeonholed" into a preformulated category that carried with it a multitude of assumptions about the content of his character. He did not understand himself as black, white, or biracial. He described himself as a musician, a thinker, a kindhearted individual, a good friend, a Catholic, and a hard-working student with dreams and ambitions. For him, race had interfered with others seeing his authentic self, and he knew it would continue to "color" how others viewed him, his work, and his personal talents. John was willing to use the racial label "black" when needed (on applications and to serve as a mentor), but he refused to accept racial categorization as a means of self-definition. As a result, he used various strategies to challenge and reshape the way others in his immediate sphere of influence thought about race and his identity.

John's case represents someone who adopts a transcendent identity that is healthy because it does not involve denial of the reality of having one black or one white parent, nor does he deny the reality of racism in America or the inequalities it breeds. He readily acknowledges the social reality of race and racism, but he also is vocal about his opposition to the use of race as a basis for categorizing people. While he accepts the fact of his black and white parentage and the nature of the social reality he lives within, he opts to define himself racially in a way that expresses his objection to the use of race as a category for defining people.

Pathways of Denial

In contrast to a transcendent identity that recognizes the social reality of race and racism in the United States, others come to a transcendent self-understanding through a pathway of denial. They believe that racism and racial discrimination have disappeared in post–Civil Rights America. They argue that references to racial categorization reify societal misconceptions about the existence of race, and that the discussion of racial inequalities, in and of itself, perpetuates the fiction of racial groups and encourages "victimized" identities.

We believe this path to racial self-understanding is problematic, not because of its politics, but because it represents a denial of the fact that mixed-race individuals are embedded in a society that uses racial group membership as an organizing construct, and that racial group membership has empirically demonstrable consequences. For example, Peter is a mixed-race man who physically appears white.[17] He does not acknowledge the existence of racism and the innumerable challenges racism creates for people of color, including his brother, who looks black. Similarly, he denies that white people (or those who look white) are socially privileged. Peter asserts that he does not have any racial identity. He believes that "race is a draconian concept and a progressive society necessitates that people dispel of the idea of race altogether." He is passionate in his stance of refusing to define himself racially: "My mother defines herself as white and my father as black . . . as for me I don't have a racial identity. I refuse to give any power to the idea of race. I refuse to let it limit my life. It's the idea that 'I think, therefore I am.' In this case, I think I am simply human and therefore I am simply human and that's all there is to it."

While Peter's position is reasonable on intellectual grounds, it contains subtle forms of denial. While race may be a social creation, the fact that the social world he inhabits believes it exists does make it "real" in terms of everyday experience. Because he looks white and is assumed to be white by others, he has the privilege of not having to think about race at all times. His white appearance affords him the benefit of being able to act "as if" race can simply be ignored, a privilege his brother does not possess and that Peter refuses to acknowledge. In this way, Peter embodies a degree of denial of how race operates in the social world, and this suggests some lack of healthfulness regarding his racial identity development. Often, people like Peter exist in a state of denial until the moment they experience an undeniable act of racism. This moment may be long delayed because of their physical appearance. But when the inevitable occurs, it can spin them into crisis because they have invested an enormous amount of energy denying that racism exists and, as a result, have no psychological tools to cope with it. It is in these moments that their whole worldview and identity are called into question, requiring a reappraisal of the social world and their place in it.

THE COBI MODEL AND RACIAL IDENTITY DEVELOPMENT AMONG MIXED-RACE PEOPLE

Our COBI model assumes that mixed-race people can define themselves racially in a variety of ways, and we make no claim that one particular identity is better or worse than another. Accordingly, our focus in this chapter is not on which label individuals choose, but rather what pathway has lead to their identification. We believe that healthy racial identity for mixed-race people is shaped by cognitive and emotional acceptance of the fact of having one white and one black parent. Hence, two mixed-race people might define themselves in the exact same way, yet their self-definition may have different implications depending on the extent to which this label reflects an underlying acceptance of their mixed-race parentage.

Our racial identities represent how we understand and define our self based on hundreds of thousands of interactions we have with others over our lifetime. In every interaction, we present ourselves to others, who react to these self-presentations in various ways. They may validate or reject us, which in turn influences how we perceive and further present ourselves. This reflexive process occurs constantly and our identities are forged somewhere in the midst of these interactive cycles. For mixed-race people, racial identity development is conspicuous because they can choose to identify as black, white, or biracial. The way in which they resolve their identity is strongly influenced by the validation and/or rejection they experience from others. The more they are able to accept the fact of their mixed-race ancestry, cognitively and emotionally, then the greater their overall health.

In the chapters that follow, we focus on applying the COBI model to different contexts within which mixed-race children are embedded (please see model 2.1 for an illustration). We start by examining how the historically

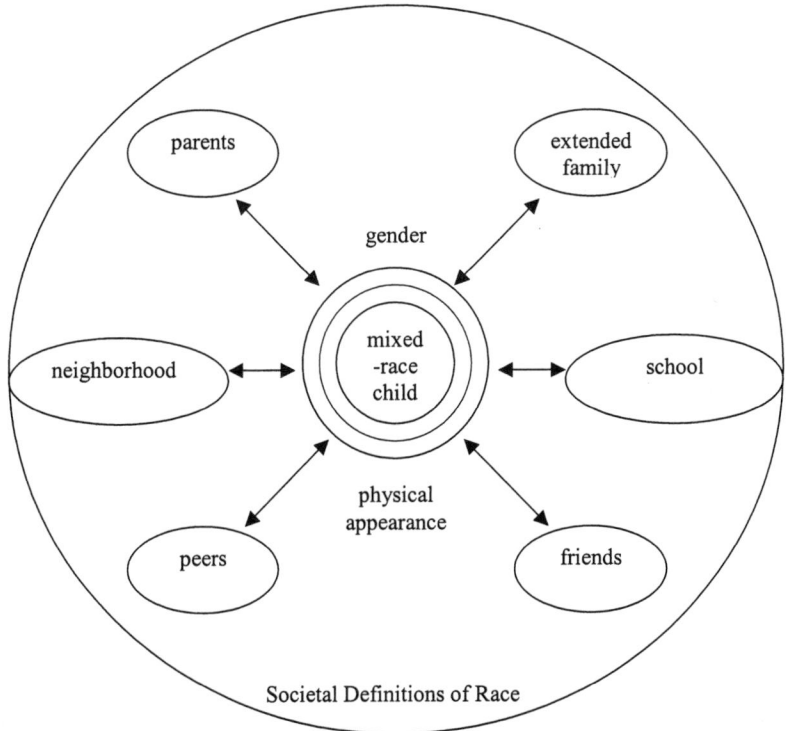

MODEL 2.1
Systemic Model of Biracial Identity Development

grounded macro level definitions of race set the parameters for individual identity construction. In successive chapters, we consider the interactions that occur within families and communities. We also devote attention to the salient role that physical appearance plays in mediating identity development. Finally, we explore the impact that gender has on how girls experience validation and rejection around their racial identity.

NOTES

1. Kerry Ann Rockquemore and David Brunsma, *Beyond Black: Biracial Identity in America* (Thousand Oaks, Calif.: Sage, 2002); Maria Root, "Resolving 'Other' Status: Identity Development of Biracial Individuals," *Women & Therapy* 9.1–2 (1990): 185–205; Maria Root, "The Multiracial Experience: Racial Borders as Significant Frontier in Race Relations," in *The Multiracial Experience: Racial Borders as the New Frontier*, ed. Maria Root (Thousand Oaks, Calif.: Sage Publications, 1996); Debbie Storrs, "Whiteness as Stigma: Essentialist Identity Work by Mixed-Race Women," *Symbolic Interaction* 22.3 (1999): 187–212. For a description of multiracial people choosing a white racial identity, see Kerry Ann Rockquemore and Patricia Arend, "Opting for White: Choice, Fluidity, and Black Identity Construction in Post–Civil Rights America," *Race & Society* (forthcoming).

2. F. James Davis, *Who Is Black? One Nation's Definition* (University Park: Pennsylvania State University Press, 1991); Rainier Spencer, *Spurious Issues: Race and Multiracial Identity Politics in the United States* (Boulder, Colo.: Westview Press, 1999).

3. Lisa Jones, *Bulletproof Diva: Tales of Race, Sex, and Hair*, 1st ed. (New York: Doubleday, 1994); James McBride, *The Color of Water: A Black Man's Tribute to His White Mother* (New York: Riverhead Books, 1996); Judy Scales-Trent, *Notes of a White Black Woman: Race, Color, and Community* (University Park: Pennsylvania State University Press, 1995); Barak Obama, *Dreams from My Father* (New York: Random House, 1995); Gregory Howard Williams, *Life on the Color Line: The True Story of a White Boy Who Discovered He Was Black* (New York: Dutton, 1995).

4. Lynn Norment, "Lenny Kravitz: Brother with a Different Beat," *Ebony* (1994): 29.

5. France Winddance Twine, "Brown Skinned White Girls: Class, Culture, and the Construction of White Identity in Suburban Communities," *Gender, Place, and Culture* 3.2 (1996): 205–24.

6. Michelle's case was drawn from Rockquemore and Arend, "Opting for White: Choice, Fluidity, and Black Identity Construction in Post–Civil Rights America."

7. See Mary C. Waters, *Ethnic Options: Choosing Identities in America* (Berkeley: University of California Press, 1990).

8. Gloria Anzaldúa, *Borderlands/La Frontera: The New Mestiza* (San Francisco, Calif.: Spinsters Aunt Lute, 1987); Dorcas Bowles, " Bi-Racial Identity: Children Born to African American and White Couples," *Clinical Social Work Journal* 21.4 (1993): 417–28; Philip Brown, "Biracial Identity and Social Marginality," *Child & Adolescent Social Work Journal* 7.4 (1990): 319–37; G. Reginald Daniel, "Black and White Identity in the New Millennium: Unsevering the Ties That Bind," in *The Multiracial Experience: Racial Borders as the New Frontier,* ed. Maria P. P. Root (Thousand Oaks, Calif.: Sage Publications, 1996), 121–39. Lynda Field, "Piecing Together the Puzzle: Self-Concept and Group Identity in Biracial Black/White Youth," in *The Multiracial Experience: Racial Borders as the New Frontier,* ed. Maria Root (Thousand Oaks, Calif.: Sage Publications, 1996), 211–26; Jewelle Taylor Gibbs, "Biracial Adolescents," in *Children of Color: Psychological Interventions with Culturally Diverse Youth,* eds. Jewelle Taylor Gibbs and Larke Nahme Huang (San Francisco, Calif.: Jossey-Bass, 1998): 305–32; Christine Hall, "The Ethnic Identity of Racially Mixed People: A Study of Black-Japanese," Doctoral Dissertation, University of California, Los Angeles, 1980; Roger Herring, "Developing Biracial Ethnic Identity: A Review of the Increasing Dilemma," *Journal of Multicultural Counseling & Development* 23.1 (1995): 29–38; Deborah Johnson, "Developmental Pathways: Toward an Ecological Theoretical Formulation of Race Identity in Black-White Biracial Children," in *Racially Mixed People in America,* ed. Maria Root (Thousand Oaks, Calif.: Sage Publications, 1992): 37–49; Christine Kerwin, Joseph G. Ponterotto, Barbara Jackson, and Abigail Harris, "Racial Identity in Biracial Children: A Qualitative Investigation," *Journal of Counseling Psychology* 40.2 (1993): 221–31; George Kitahara Kich, "The Developmental Process of Asserting a Biracial, Bicultural Identity," in *Racially Mixed People in America,* ed. Maria Root (Thousand Oaks, Calif.: Sage Publications, 1992): 304–17; W. Carlos Poston, "The Biracial Identity Development Model: A Needed Addition," *Journal of Counseling & Development* 69.2 (1990): 152–55; Kerry Ann Rockquemore, "Between Black and White: Exploring the 'Biracial' Experience," *Race & Society* 1.2 (1998): 197–212; Rockquemore and Brunsma, *Beyond Black: Biracial Identity in America;* Root, "Resolving 'Other' Status: Identity Development of Biracial Individuals"; Barbara Tizard and Ann Phoenix, "The Identity of Mixed Parentage Adolescents," *Journal of Child Psychology & Psychiatry & Allied Disciplines* 36.8 (1995): 1399–410.

9. Rob Parker, "Jeter Doesn't Choose Sides," *Newsday* (1998): 44.

10. Jayne was a client in a supervision group that Laszloffy consulted.

11. Samantha's case is drawn from Rockquemore and Arend, "Opting for White: Choice, Fluidity, and Black Identity Construction in Post–Civil Rights America."

12. See also Marion Kilson, *Claiming Place: Biracial Young Adults of the Post–Civil Rights Era* (Westport, Conn.: Bergin & Garvey, 2001); Kisten Renn, *Mixed Race Students in College: The Ecology of Race, Identity, and Community on Campus* (Albany: State University of New York Press, 2004); and Kendra Wallace, *Relative/Outsider: The Art and Politics of Identity among Mixed-Heritage Students* (Westport, Conn.: Ablex, 2001).

13. Jayson was a participant in the Survey of Biracial Experiences, an interview study of black/white biracial college students from Michigan, Connecticut, Massachusetts, and Alabama.

14. Kendra Wallace, *Relative/Outsider.*

15. While empirical research documents the existence of the transcendent identity option, it is difficult to find a single multiracial celebrity that has chosen this identity. Several possibilities exist to explain the absence. First and foremost, black-appearing multiracial celebrities may choose a transcendent racial identity; but because they are assumed to be black by the media, they are never explicitly asked about their racial identity. The same could be said for white-appearing multiracial celebrities who are assumed to be white, but in fact, have chosen a transcendent identity. Another possibility is that there are multiracial celebrities who feel social and economic pressure to either declare border or black identities, and do so, not as a reflection of their own self-understanding, but to protect their celebrity statuses.

16. John's case was drawn from Rockquemore and Brunsma, *Beyond Black: Biracial Identity in America.*

17. Peter is an acquaintance of Laszloffy.

3

Racism in America: What Parents Need to Know

Having presented a systemic model of racial identity development, we begin with the most abstract component: societal definitions of race. In this chapter, we explore how societal definitions of race and the realities of racism shape the lives of mixed-race children. This may be the most difficult component of the model for some readers because it forces us to reconcile what we *want to believe* about our society with what *actually exists*. While many of us wish that we lived in a colorblind society, that racism was long dead, and that race no longer mattered in our daily lives, that idealized notion is inconsistent with the empirical reality of racial inequalities. Understanding racism can be especially challenging for white parents of mixed-race children who, until they had a child of color, may have been largely oblivious to the omnipresence of racism in the United States.

The primary purpose of this chapter is to provide an overview of existing racial inequalities for caregivers and service providers who may be unclear about how race is woven into the fabric of our institutions and impacts the daily lives of people of color. To that end, we explore the three most common manifestations of racism (ideological racism, institutional racism, and individual racism) and consider how they impact mixed-race children. This frank discussion of how racism shapes social relations within the United States is a necessary part of understanding the environment within which mixed-race children exist because it directly impacts how they are perceived by others and how they experience the world around them. Throughout this chapter, we

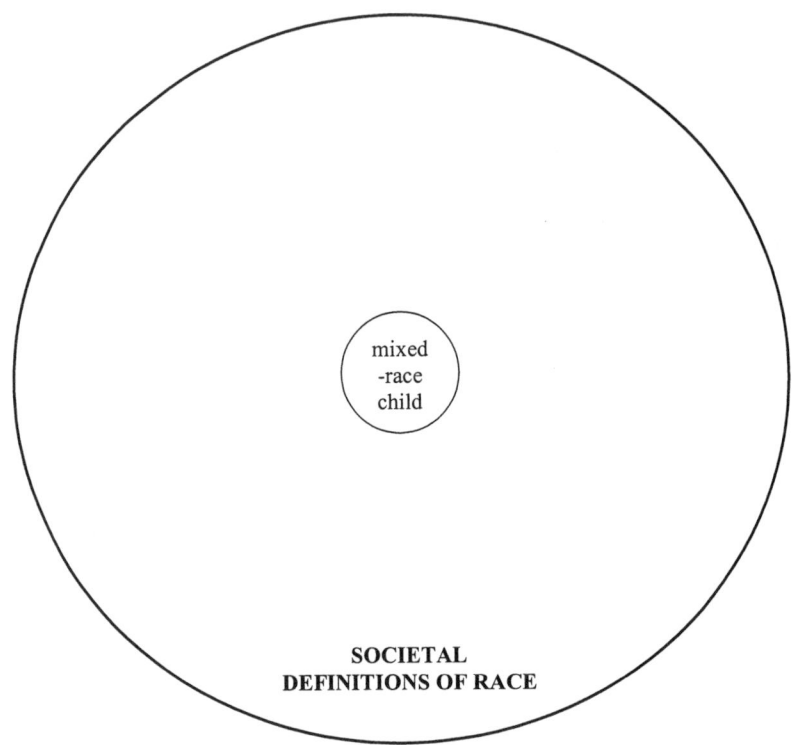

MODEL 3.1
Structural Parameters of Racial Identification

encourage parents and practitioners to reflect on how their own attitudes and behaviors may unconsciously reproduce racism. Readers who are familiar with the history of race relations in the United States and the interconnections between ideology, institutions, and identity may wish to skim this chapter and/or move directly to chapter 4.

PAST PROBLEMS AND PRESENT REALITIES

In the United States, all citizens are socialized to believe in a general set of principles that are collectively held dear and believed to be uniquely American. Primary among them is the principle stated in our Declaration of Independence that "all men are created equal." While Americans recognize the history of slavery and the explicit segregation that followed, many believe that the Civil Rights movement rectified the vast majority of past wrongs and, as a result, racial groups today have equal opportunities. In short, many believe that racism has been eradicated in our public institutions and only rears its ugly head in isolated incidents of individual aggression.

While the Civil Rights era did result in important legislation that reduced some structural barriers for African Americans, today the United States remains a racially stratified society, where blacks and whites differ dramatically on almost every important measure of success and opportunity. Table 3.1 illustrates that even in 2002, whites in the United States have higher educational attainment, higher socioeconomic status, and more power than African Americans.

While we rarely stop to consider it, most Americans live highly segregated lives, and this separation underpins vast differentials in access to opportunities and quality of life. The fact is that most of us live in neighborhoods where people look like us, our children attend public schools that are racially homogenous, and our Sunday mornings are spent in churches that are racially segregated.[1] While this may not seem to be a problem for those who are interracially married, we must also recognize the rarity of such unions. In 2000, interracial marriages still only accounted for 2.9 percent of all marriages in the United States. When we step back and examine the macro level reality of racial inequalities today, we have to ask: How is it that so many Americans live amidst separation and inequality, yet persistently believe that racism is an artifact of the past? To understand this collective dissonance requires a nuanced and multifaceted conceptualization of the way that race organizes our lives.

EXPLORING RACISM

The very word "racism" engenders strong emotional responses. It is a potent and potentially inflammatory word. It's a word that precludes the possibility

Table 3.1. Comparing Blacks and Whites in 2002

	Whites	Blacks
Percent with four-year college degree	29.4%	17%
Percent living below poverty level	7.8%	22.7%
Percent of children living below poverty level	9.5%	30.2%
Percent earning $75,000 or more per year	35.3%	15.9%
Percent unemployed	5.1%	10.8%
Percent of U.S. senators from the group	100%	0%
Percent of CEOs in Fortune 500 companies	98%	0.8%

Source: U.S. Census and Fortune magazine

of neutrality because it positions people in extremes as either victim or victimizer. By definition, racism refers to any attitude, belief, behavior, or institutional arrangement that favors one racial group over another.[2] Beyond this broadest definition, racism becomes more complicated because it occurs at various levels and manifests in different ways. Here we focus on three types of racism: 1) ideological racism, 2) institutional racism, and 3) individual racism. As we discuss each of these different types of racism, we use the public education system as an example. We do so because it clearly illustrates the interconnected nature of ideological, institutional, and individual racism, and because it is central to most children's lives.

Ideological Racism

One of the most abstract, yet critically important types of racism is *ideological racism,* which refers to beliefs in the biological, intellectual, and/or cultural superiority/inferiority of different racial groups. Understanding ideological racism is important because beliefs about the superiority of one racial group over another have historically been used to justify existing exploitation of one group by another. In the United States, the entire system of slavery was built on the pervasive ideology of white supremacy, or a belief that whites are superior to all other races. That belief justified the enslavement of human beings because of the color of their skin, while also supplying a rationalization of why that system was correct and morally just. Black people were deemed to be subhuman, animal-like creatures best suited for manual labor. Because their intellectual capabilities were believed to be limited, they were considered unable to care for themselves, so enslavement was deemed benevolent. The ideology of white supremacy made slavery possible, while simultaneously justifying its continuation. In short, that uniquely American principle that "all men are created equal" actually emerged at a time when blacks were not considered "men," and women were not considered at all. So "all men" really meant "all landowning white men" are created equal.

After the demise of slavery, a period of explicit segregation followed. While this new set of social relations differed from slavery, it was still an inherently unequal and exploitative system guided by the same ideology of white supremacy. Believing that whites were pure (while everyone else was impure) created a need for different facilities for black and white people in all sectors of life. Swimming in the same pool, eating at the same restaurant, or sitting

next to one another on the bus was simply unthinkable. But more importantly, separate institutions were created so that blacks and whites would not
attend the same schools. This social and institutional separation was necessary
because whites were considered fundamentally different than blacks and
would be contaminated by their presence. The unequal quality of the schools
was also justified by white supremacist beliefs because whites' superiority le-
gitimated higher quality facilities for white children. While segregation represented a different social system than slavery, it was built on the same set of
racist beliefs, and it was precisely those beliefs that discouraged dismantling
the system.

White supremacy, as a racist ideology, not only supported unequal social
arrangements, but was also elevated to "scientific theory" during the late-
nineteenth and early-twentieth centuries as scientists developed elaborate typologies of the human races.[3] They set out to document racial differences to
show that biological variation between racial groups explained their unequal
status in society. Black people were deemed to be less intelligent than whites
because they were *biologically incapable* and, therefore, innately inferior. Interestingly, these studies always defined the race of the scientist (who was
white) as superior while supporting existing social inequalities and exploitation of other races.

Over time, scientific theories of racial difference have been disproven and
the Human Genome Project has put to rest any lingering sense that human
beings can be neatly divided into four separate and mutually exclusive categories (although many people continue to hold onto biological notions of
race). Sociologist Rainier Spencer describes the demise of biological concep-
tions of race in the following way:

> It is now recognized as a mistake to assume that all members of a particular
> socially-defined race are alike, either in their cultural orientations or their phys-
> ical structures. There are no biological criteria we can apply consistently that
> will yield the traditional racial groups that Americans have as a society estab-
> lished. It is the racist history of the United States and the continuing popular be-
> lief in biological race that allow people to accept uncritically the racial
> structures still operating in the country.[4]

Researchers today understand race as a *social* category that serves as a basis
of power relations and group position. Races, as biologically distinct and

identifiable groups, do not exist, but the *idea* that races are distinct groups with specific behavioral traits and characteristics does exist. In other words, race is real insofar as people believe it is real, and that it has real consequences for people's life chances and opportunities.[5]

Ideological racism has not dissolved over time, but has merely changed, evolved, and mutated along with historical circumstances. While some hold on to beliefs in white supremacy as a biological fact (despite the mountain of evidence against it), belief in white superiority is much more commonly expressed today as *cultural superiority*. This type of ideological racism asserts that blacks are inferior because of deficient values, attitudes, manners, morals, language, aesthetic, and leisure activities.

Although the idea of *ideological racism* may seem difficult to grasp, it is important to understand that our country was built on the foundation of white supremacy. The social world that we live in today emerged from a very specific and problematic history of black/white relations, and those beliefs continue to haunt our institutions and ways of thinking today. Understanding ideological racism is also necessary for any discussion of institutional or individual racism because both have deep historical roots that are tied to problematic beliefs about black and whites.

Institutional Racism

The core institutions in American society—long-established structures such as the state, the education system, the economic system, the media, and the criminal justice system—have each played a role in the creation and perpetuation of the racial inequalities that exist today. Institutional racism refers to the practices, policies, procedures, and culture of social institutions that deprive racially identified groups from equal access, opportunities, and treatment. Louis Knowles and Kenneth Prewitt argue that: "Institutional racism is more subtle, less visible, and less identifiable but no less destructive to human life and human dignity than individual acts of racism."[6]

Understanding the history of institutions and the context in which they were created is imperative because most were designed for a homogenous group. For example, the public school system in the United States was originally created for whites only. Educating slaves was considered useless (as they were intellectually deficient) and dangerous (because it might give them rebellious ideas). In many Southern states, teaching a slave to read was a criminal act. After legal slavery was abolished, black children were allowed to receive an education, but the conditions under which it occurred were markedly inferior to white children.

Refusing to educate blacks during slavery and the legal requirements that mandated school segregation after slavery are examples of conscious and deliberate institutional racism fueled by a clear and undeniable belief in white supremacy. These explicit policies allow us to see how a particular institution (public education) was created on a foundation of inequality fueled by ideological racism. However, institutional racism is not always deliberate. At times, institutions evolve and progress, yet their policies and procedures continue to result in unequal treatment of blacks and whites.

In 1954, the landmark Supreme Court ruling in *Brown v. the Board of Education* determined that the doctrine of separate but equal was fundamentally flawed because the very basis of separation assumed inequality. Separate would always involve unequal access to legitimate educational opportunities. In this case, deliberate institutional racism was recognized, declared illegal, and mandated for change. In the years following this critical decision, some immediate integration was achieved, and certainly many generations of African American children have received vastly improved educations as a result. Yet, upon closer scrutiny, there are still numerous ways in which institutional racism continues to deny black children access to an equal and quality education, albeit in unconscious and indirect ways.

Fifty years after the Supreme Court mandated desegregation, public schools remain largely segregated, especially in large urban school districts and the suburbs surrounding them.[7] Continued inequity occurs despite *Brown* and the existence of court-mandated busing plans. Public schools are racially segregated today because of the prevalence of residential segregation. Most people live in racially homogeneous neighborhoods and, as a result, most children attend racially segregated schools. In other words, where housing is segregated, a neighborhood school system amounts to a segregated school system.[8] Moreover, because public schools are funded largely by property taxes, and because African Americans are disproportionately poor, a large number of African American children reside in largely poor black neighborhoods where they attend inadequately funded and functionally inferior schools.[9] As a result, "separate and unequal" remains the reality of American education.

School systems that serve communities of color almost always have inferior facilities, a lack of appropriate resources, some of the most poorly trained teachers, and, as a result, extremely dismal records of academic achievement. In *Savage Inequalities,* Jonathon Kozol graphically demonstrates how public education in the United States remains separate and unequal on the basis of race and class.[10] His investigation of elementary schools in major U.S. cities revealed a pattern of inequality. Within predominantly low-income black communities, children attended rotting schools that were poorly staffed and inadequately funded, and that grossly failed to meet children's basic educational, physical, and psychological needs. Meanwhile, in adjacent communities that were predominantly white and middle to upper income, a dramatically different reality existed because more money was spent per pupil as a result of higher property values. The result was a systematic pattern where white children received a higher quality, state-of-the-art education that produced all the corresponding high-achievement outcomes.

Unequal school funding and residential segregation produce de facto segregation in the public school system even after formal barriers have been dismantled. But even *within* schools, we find policies and procedures that systematically disadvantage black children. The clearest example is ability grouping—or tracking—which is the practice of placing students of similar ability in groups or classes together to optimize learning, a practice used in the vast majority of public schools in the United States. Researchers have found that race influences placement in groups so that minority students are often placed in the lowest tracks. Once students are placed in a low track, they tend to stay in that track for the remainder of their public school career, setting their future educational trajectory by limiting their opportunity to enter higher education, regardless of their ability.[11] A vicious cycle is set in motion, whereby the effects of institutional racism in school during the early years undermines black children's academic success, which affects high school graduation rates, as well as the likelihood of pursuing higher education. In turn, this greatly impacts future job opportunities, earning potential, and opportunities for career advancement.

When we consider the fact that the public school system was built on the foundation of white supremacy and the separation of races, we should not be surprised to find schools today that are a product of that history. Deliberate institutional racism in the past created and reproduced racial inequalities, but today unconscious and nondeliberate institutional racism perpetuates those inequalities.

Individual Racism

In addition to the ideological and institutional levels, racism occurs most tangibly and painfully at the individual level. It is at this level where it is most necessary to emphasize the distinction between *intentional* and *unintentional* racism. Intentional racism is what most people think of when they hear the word "racism." It is associated with overt behaviors where the objective is clearly to deny someone access to an opportunity or resource, or to hurt and defile someone on the basis of race. Intentional racism conjures up images of Jim Crow segregation, KKK rallies, and more recent acts of racially motivated violence in East Jasper, Texas, when three white men brutally murdered James Byrd, an African American, by dragging him to death with a pickup truck. While these are indeed examples of intentional racism, most present-day racism tends to be of the unintentional variety.[12] In cases of unintentional racism, the person committing the discriminatory act is unaware of the ways in which racist ideology is organizing his/her behavior.

At the core of individual racism is a belief that a person or group is "less than" on the basis of race, producing negative emotions toward a person or group. For those who behave in a racist manner toward people of color (irrespective of their race), this often reflects either a conscious or unconscious internalization of white supremacy. Because the ideology of white supremacy resides at the heart of most American institutions, it is virtually impossible to live in the United States and be immune to the numerous ways that notions of white supremacy are reflected in the attitudes and practices that shape our society. We inevitably absorb and internalize white supremacist ideology to varying degrees. Moreover, because our actions often are a product of our beliefs and attitudes, the internalization of these ideas shapes our behaviors. In this way, people of all races are prone to behaving in ways that discriminate against people of color in some form.

Individual racism in education is most commonly illustrated by differential teacher expectations. Researchers have focused on teacher expectations intensely since the publication of *Pygmalion in the Classroom,* a study that described a now-famous experiment on teacher expectations.[13] A researcher tested children in an elementary school classroom at the beginning of the school year. Teachers were told that the test was to identify "academic spurters," students whose achievement would greatly improve during that academic year. In reality, the test was a basic IQ test. Twenty percent of the students were identified to teachers as "academic spurters" even though they were actually randomly selected. At the end of the year, the spurters improved their IQ scores by ten to fifteen points more than the other children. Why? Because the teachers *expected* them to do better, *treated* them differently, and the children *responded* to those heightened expectations.

Researchers continue to find that teacher expectations influence student performance. Unfortunately, many teachers' expectations are formed at least partly on the basis of race and class, so black children are significantly more likely than white children to be diagnosed with a learning disability and sent to remedial or special education classes.[14] Among black and white children engaging in similar types of behaviors, black children are more likely to be singled out for disciplinary action and treated more harshly than their white counterparts. These experiences with being labeled "bad kids" or "poor learners" disrupt the quality of the educational process for too many African American children.

Because racism at the individual level tends to occur in indirect ways, it is often beyond the conscious awareness of the transgressor. Below we offer a variety of examples of individual level racism. These examples are intended to illustrate how people of any race can behave in a discriminatory manner. Some of the examples below reflect intentionally discriminatory behaviors, while others reflect unintentional acts of discrimination. In either case, all of these examples reflect behaviors that are inherently damaging because they perpetuate racial divisions and inequality.

- Using racially derogatory language
- Locking car doors when driving through a predominantly black neighborhood
- Administrators hiring blacks for low-level, low-wage positions in spite of the ways that applicants' experience may qualify them for higher-level positions
- Teachers having lower academic expectations of black students than white students, and therefore challenging and encouraging them less

- Guidance counselors and teachers discouraging black students from taking classes and establishing career goals that would prepare them for higher paying jobs
- Real estate agents showing black clients fewer homes than white clients and steering them to predominantly black neighborhoods
- Bankers denying mortgages to black customers more often than to white customers of similar income levels, and charging higher interest rates of black customers when loans are granted
- White families assuming that their property values will decrease when black families move into their neighborhoods, and therefore moving out and/or failing to create a welcoming environment
- Customer service representatives displaying a less receptive, friendly, and helpful demeanor when assisting black customers versus white customers
- Airline ticket agents or flight attendants automatically assuming that African American passengers are ticketed in the economy class
- Department store security agents tracking and suspecting black customers of crime more frequently than white customers
- Parents discouraging their children from forming friendships with children of particular racial groups
- Parents becoming concerned or even angry when they learn that their son or daughter is dating someone of another race

All of the examples demonstrate ways in which individuals can behave in discriminatory ways, whether intentional or unintentional. In many cases, those who commit such acts can be persons of any racial group, which is consistent with the definition of individual racism.

IMPLICATIONS FOR INTERRACIAL FAMILIES

Racism, in all its various manifestations, poses any number of challenges for parents who are raising mixed-race children. When a belief in the superiority of whiteness informs our beliefs, subtle expressions of racism are inevitable, yet the idea that racism is wrong makes it hard for many people to recognize and acknowledge their own capacity to act in a racist way. When this disconnect occurs, too many parents, teachers, and social service providers retreat into the rhetoric of color-blindness. They insist that they "do not see color" and, therefore, are incapable of harboring a prejudicial thought in their mind, much less acting in a discriminatory way. Of course, it is impossible to live in the United States and not learn that race exists, that people are fundamentally different according to their racial group, and that racial groups are hierarchically related to one another. Protestations that a person "doesn't see race" are usually a way of saying "I believe all people are created equal." It is an affirmation of an egalitarian value. The problem is that "not seeing race" all too often means turning a blind eye to racism and refusing to critically examine one's own beliefs and behaviors. We especially want to caution parents and caregivers not to confuse the way they wish the world could be and the way it really is. Insisting on a color-blind reality may literally blind a person from the reality of racism at multiple levels. We believe that a vital part of raising healthy mixed-race children involves understanding how racism manifests and using this insight to act in ways that will counteract its potentially damaging effects.

Ideological Racism

The major implication of ideological racism, and more specifically, the ideology of white supremacy, is that it teaches mixed-race children to overvalue whiteness and devalue blackness. For parents, this translates into a need to directly confront this ideology and counteract the influence it has on how mixed-race children are classified, understood, and treated by others, and how they come to think and feel about themselves racially.

The most tangible example of how ideological racism influences the lives of mixed-race people is the perception of available options for racial identification. During slavery, white supremacist ideology gave birth to the "one-drop rule," which was used to determine who was black (and who was white). Blacks were believed to be subhuman; therefore, even one drop of black blood was believed to "contaminate" an individual, eliminating the possibility of being "purely" white. Because social norms at the time made it impossible for a white slave master to have a black child, mixed-race children were considered to be both black and slaves.[15]

The one-drop rule, while rooted in slavery, survived its demise and became a matter of law in order to maintain segregation. It uniquely precludes the possibility of alternative group membership no matter how far removed generationally an individual is from that one-drop, and irrespective of their physical appearance. Because of this long-standing pattern of racial categorization, multiracial individuals have been considered black throughout most of American history, and still are in many communities throughout the United States. As F. James Davis argues, the one-drop rule is so pervasively embedded in American society that it has, until very recently, been almost universally accepted by both blacks and whites alike and has been most vigorously defended in recent years by African Americans.[16]

While our society today seems to be far removed from slavery, we continue to use the one-drop rule, something that was born directly of white supremacist logic, to categorize multiracial people. To be sure, if mixed-race children phenotypically look black, they will experience the world as black people. However, we see the continued use of this racist norm most clearly among mixed-race people who do not appear black but have black parentage. When filling out institutional forms or needing to identify themselves to someone, the one-drop rule dictates that the only available identity is black. Many thought this norm had been officially dismantled when the 2000 Census directed citizens to mark "all that apply" for their racial category. On the surface, it seemed that mixed-race people could now check both black and white. However, behind the scenes, the data is pulled back into the traditional categories so that the person who checked off both black and white becomes solely "black."[17]

Once again, we see the pattern of white supremacist ideology informing state policy on racial group membership, which is enforced and reproduced by institutional and individual practices. Parents will be asked to designate their child's race on school forms (as well as other institutional forms), and they must make informed and conscious decisions about how to respond. Here again, thinking of oneself as "color blind" is of little help in the face of a racialized social world. In this case, ignoring the fact that schools and other government agencies demand categorization is a form of denial that will be rectified by teachers, staff, or administrators who complete blank information on their own or who force children into the existing scheme. For example, Maria Barner recalls the following incident:

> When I was in the fifth grade I had a teacher, and I hated her so much. She was always mean. We had one of those tests and I had to fill out my racial category. I think I put "other." I just put something different—other than "black." And she really went off. She was like, "Why did you do this?"

I said, "'Cause my mom's white and my dad's black."

She said, "Change this to black. You're black because your father's black, and you have his last name so you're automatically black. So just forget the white side." She said that black dominates. She was black.[18]

We recommend that parents take a proactive role in discussing the ideology of white supremacy with their children and in helping kids recognize that other ways of understanding race are possible. Parents also need to guide their children in identifying the specific institutional polices and practices as well as individual attitudes and behaviors that result from this ideology. In particular, we encourage parents to assist their children in understanding how white supremacy limits the perception of options for how to define oneself racially. As part of resisting ideological racism, parents must support a broad range of options for how their children may come to racially self-identify. While white supremacy may only "allow" for certain choices, and while institutions and individuals may reinforce this constraint through their behaviors, numerous self-understandings are possible, and seeing this range of options is a vital step in resisting ideological racism.

Institutional Racism

With regard to racism at the institutional level, parents must be ever-mindful of the ways that organizations may discriminate against mixed-race children on the basis of race, particularly in cases where children's phenotypic characteristics suggest they are black. Parents who are wise to the realities of racism in America are better able to prepare their children to negotiate these realities because they recognize how our social institutions perpetuate white supremacy rather than dismantle it. They are better able to help their children identify, understand, and respond to the unique challenges that people of color face related to education, housing, employment, and their representation within government, industry, and media.

Recognizing how institutional racism shapes American society is a valuable tool for parents of mixed-race children to possess because institutional racism perpetuates racial inequality on a broad scale. It is important for children to learn to identify how racism organizes institutional policies and practices, and to see models of appropriate action to resist it. One way to do this is by having explicit conversations in the presence of children about the role that racism plays in the underrepresentation of blacks and other people of color as senators, congressional representatives, governors, and in the "White" House, as well as CEOs and upper management in the private sector, as professional sports team owners and head coaches, and as media moguls. As children are exposed to adult conversations, they indirectly learn how to see and understand the ways that institutional racism shapes life in America. Gradually, parents can talk more directly with children about these issues, inviting them to offer racially based critiques of what they see in the world around them, including using current events as a basis for guiding these discussions.

Another way for parents to address institutional racism is by taking targeted actions that are designed to confront it. Attesting to the importance of proactive engagement, Beverley Tatum offers the following metaphor:

> I sometimes visualize the ongoing cycle of racism as a moving walkway at the airport. Active racist behavior is equivalent to walking fast on the conveyor belt. The person engaged in active racist behavior has identified with the ideology of White supremacy and moving with it. Passive racist behavior is equivalent to standing still on the walkway. No overt effort is being made, but the conveyor belt moves the bystanders along to the same destination as those who are actively walking. Some of the bystanders may feel the motion of the conveyor belt, see the active racist ahead of them, and choose to turn around, unwilling to go to the same destination as the White supremacists. But unless they are walking actively in the opposite direction at a speed faster than the conveyor belt—unless they are actively antiracist—they will find themselves carried along with the others.

For parents, assuming an active antiracist stance when faced with an existing institutional policy that is racially discriminatory is an important way to model both how to recognize the effects of institutional racism and how to confront these forces in their own community. Children learn important lessons from this type of modeling, directly and indirectly. This social action may include individual intervention, as well as working collectively with parents of black children and/or a multiracial family coalition. Appendix A lists national and state organizations as a resource.

Individual Racism

Within contemporary society, overt expressions of racism are considered socially unacceptable because our culture espouses equality and rejects differential treatment based on race. As a result, most of us are raised to believe that it is morally reprehensible to hold racist beliefs and behave in racist ways. At the same time, the specific messages many of us receive about race often conflict with the broad general ideas we have about equality. However, most of us are unaware of how our own internalized values conflict. We may see ourselves as people who are committed to values like equality, while failing to recognize deeply held racial beliefs that contradict these more noble ideals. And because these deeply held beliefs tend to shape our behaviors, it is not uncommon for many of us to commit subtle discriminatory acts without realizing it and without recognizing the contradictions between our own behavior and the broader ideals we hold about justice and morality.

Subtle, indirect expressions of racism reflect a person's unconscious racial beliefs and ideology. Yet most of us fail to fully recognize our own biases, especially when they contradict other values we also embrace. While most of us learn that "all people are created equal" and "racism is wrong," we simultaneously exist within a society that teaches us to overvalue whiteness and devalue blackness. Many of us embrace a general commitment to equality while also harboring beliefs about the inherent superiority of whiteness. These deeply engrained beliefs tend to manifest themselves in specific discriminatory behaviors that are indicative of individual-level racism.

For parents of mixed-race children, addressing individual-level racism involves a two-prong focus on self and others. The focus on others requires recognizing and (where appropriate) constructively confronting individual acts of racism by others, especially among those who fulfill institutional roles such as teachers, social workers, health care professionals, and so on. Since individual-level racism often occurs subtly and indirectly, parents must be tuned in to the nuances. They must possess the capacity to think and interpret reality in terms of race. By developing their "racial radar," parents can routinely consider the possible role that race may play in situations where underlying motives seem ambiguous. For example, Janet is the (white) mother of an eight-year-old son named Eric.[19] She and her husband Peter (black) became worried when Eric was placed into a remedial reading group. They were unaware that Eric had difficulties with reading, so this placement took them by surprise. In discussing their concern with his teacher, Mrs. Simon, who was white, they were told about Eric's difficulty during reading lessons. She explained that he had difficulty concentrating and she believed he needed specialized attention to compensate for his learning difficulties. Both Janet and Peter perceived Mrs. Simon as genuinely concerned about their son and interested in helping him. They trusted her good intentions. But they also were wise to the realities of racism and how it often subtly shapes teacher's perceptions and assumptions in ways people may not even realize. Janet said:

> I know that it's not uncommon for teachers, especially white teachers, to expect less from students of color. I don't believe that Eric is having trouble with reading. I know how he reads and I would say he is advanced for his age. I suspect he's bored in his reading group and his lack of focus is because he's not being challenged enough, rather than because of some disability. I think Mrs. Simon isn't able to see this because her prejudices are getting in the way. I can't prove this, but I know her conclusion about Eric is dead wrong, and I know enough of what happens to black kids in schools, and Eric looks black. So this is my opinion of what's happening, and it just reminds me that I have to be extra vigilant and watch out for my son. Even with people who are well-intentioned, and I believe Mrs. Simon is, hidden prejudices can get in the way.

In addition to tuning in to the ways in which others' racism may affect their children and families, parents of mixed-race children also need to be mindful of their own potential racism. As an example, we often hear both black and white parents claim that they "don't see race" while simultaneously favoring their light-skinned children over their darker-skinned children. If they did not see race, then they would not call curly hair "good hair," they would not refer to hazel, blue, or green eyes as "pretty eyes," and they would not behave differently toward their children based on these characteristics. Each of these common expressions reveals an internalized sense of good and bad, pretty and ugly, and worthy and unworthy based on a white beauty standard.[20] The fact that light-skinned blacks not only receive preferential treatment from other black people but also have higher social mobility reveals the racial reality that there is a hierarchy of appearance, that distinctions are made among people of color, and that rewards accrue to those who appear closest to whiteness.[21] While this all may occur at the unconscious level, the insistence that we are "color blind" is particularly problematic because it represents a false assessment of our attitudes, a refusal to acknowledge that we all harbor prejudicial beliefs as a result of living in America, and it provides a convenient pass for not doing the hard work of critically evaluating our own beliefs and behavior.

We all reside within a society built on white supremacy and as a result each of us has learned to devalue blackness. The challenge is to recognize our own racism and understand the ways in which it may shape our own attitudes and behaviors. While it is easy to assume that the greater burden is on white parents to understand their racism, black parents need to be equally vigilant. In some cases, black parents may harbor strong negative feelings toward whites that can result in individual-level racism that is hurtful to their children. In other cases, black parents may harbor feelings of internalized oppression that can lead to expressions of racism toward other blacks. Again, this can send powerfully damaging messages to children.

In the final analysis, parents of mixed-race children should be aware that racism influences *every* aspect of their child's environment, right down to the way their child is perceived by others and how they understand themselves. The one-drop rule, because it is so rationally illogical, provides a perfect illustration of the way that ideology informs identity, and how the problems of the past persist and are perpetuated into the present. Understanding how racism at the institutional and individual levels organizes our society and social interactions should arm caregivers to better identify and challenge it. Because this is the broad context within which mixed-race children and families exist, parents are faced with the challenge of being ever-mindful and aware of how it acts on and influences their children's emerging racial identities.

NOTES

1. Andrew Hacker, *Two Nations: Black and White, Separate, Hostile, Unequal* (New York: Ballantine, 1992); Michael Emerson and Christian Smith, *Divided by Faith: Evangelical Religion and the Problem of Race in America* (New York: Oxford University Press, 2000).

2. Tracey Laszloffy and Kenneth V. Hardy, "Uncommon Strategies for a Common Problem: Addressing Racism in Family Therapy," *Family Processes* 39.1 (2000): 35–50.

3. Tukufu Zuberi, *Thicker Than Blood: How Racial Statistics Lie* (Minneapolis: University of Minnesota Press, 2001).

4. Rainier Spencer, *Spurious Issues: Race and Multiracial Identity Politics in the United States* (Boulder, Colo.: Westview Press, 1999), 35.

5. Michael Omi and Howard Winant, *Racial Formation in the United States: From the 1960s to the 1990s*, 2nd ed., (New York: Routledge, 1994).

6. Louis Knowles and Kenneth Prewitt, *Institutional Racism in America* (Englewood Cliffs, N.J.: Prentice Hall, 1967).

7. Gary Orfield and Chungmei Lee, *Brown at 50: King's Dream or Plessy's Nightmare?* (Cambridge, Mass.: Civil Rights Project, 2004).

8. John E. Farley, "Housing Segregation in the School Age Population and the Link between Housing and School Segregation," *Journal of Urban Affairs* 6.4 (1984): 65–80.

9. Orfield and Lee, *Brown at 50: King's Dream or Plessy's Nightmare?*

10. Jonathan Kozol, *Savage Inequalities: Children in America's Schools* (New York: Crown, 1991).

11. Adam Gamoran, "Is Ability Grouping Equitable?" *Educational Leadership* (October 1992): 11–17; Adam Gamoran, "The Variable Effects of High School Tracking," *American Sociological Review* 57 (1992): 812–29.

12. See Eduardo Bonilla-Silva, *Racism without Racists: Color-Blind Racism and the Persistence of Racial Inequality in the United States* (Lanham, Md.: Rowman & Littlefield, 2003).

13. Robert Rosenthal and Lenore Jacobson, *Pygmalion in the Classroom: Teacher Expectation and Pupils' Intellectual Development* (New York: Holt, Rinehart and Winston, 1968).

14. Dan Losen and Gary Orfield, *Racial Inequality in Special Education* (Cambridge, Mass.: Harvard Educational Publishing Group, 2002).

15. F. James Davis, *Who Is Black?: One Nation's Definition* (University Park: Pennsylvania State University Press, 1991); Rainier Spencer, *Spurious Issues: Race and Multiracial Identity Politics in the United States* (Boulder, Colo.: Westview Press, 1999).

16. Davis, *Who Is Black?: One Nation's Definition.*

17. U.S. Census, *Guidance on Aggregation and Allocation of Data on Race for Use in Civil Rights Monitoring and Enforcement* (Washington, DC: Office of Management and Budget Bulletin, No. 00–02, 2000).

18. Barner's case is drawn from Pearl Fuyo Gaskins, *What Are You? Voices of Mixed-Race Young People* (New York: Henry Holt, 1999), 58.

19. Janet and Peter are parents who participated in research conducted for Laszloffy's doctoral dissertation. See, Tracey Laszloffy, "An Exploratory Study of Family Therapists Working as Consultants to Address the Interaction Between Race and Education in an Elementary School," Doctoral dissertation, Syracuse University, 1997.

20. Kathy Russell, Midge Wilson, and Ronald E. Hall, *The Color Complex: The Politics of Skin Color among African Americans* (New York: Harcourt Brace Jovanovich, 1992).

21. Verna Keith and Cedric Herring, "Skin Tone and Stratification in the Black Community," *American Journal of Sociology* 97.3 (1991): 760–78; Margaret Hunter, "Light, Bright, and Almost White: The Advantages and Disadvantages of Light Skin," in *Skin Deep: How Race and Complexion Matter in the "Color-Blind" Era*, eds. Cedric Herring, Verna Keith, and Hayward Derrick Horton (Urbana: University of Illinois Press, 2004): 517–35.

4

Starting at Home: Families and Racial Socialization

Families play a pivotal role in children's development. The importance and impact of families in the lives of children cannot be emphasized strongly enough. Families are the places where children receive some of the most powerful and lasting messages about their own identities and the world around them. Ideally, when families are healthy, they not only teach children how to become responsible and caring human beings, but also provide comfort, support, and protection for children as they face life's trials and tribulations.

While the process of raising children is daunting for all parents, there are particular challenges faced by parents raising mixed-race children. We have argued in the previous chapter that within our racially polarized society, race shapes virtually all aspects of life. From the womb to the tomb, race matters, especially when one is faced with the responsibility of raising a child of color.[1] Because of the power of race, parents raising mixed-race children have a responsibility to engage in a process of racial socialization that will prepare their children to understand and effectively negotiate the complexities of race relations.

For decades, psychologists, sociologists, and family scientists have studied the phenomenon of racial socialization within families of color, especially African American families.[2] Traditionally, racial socialization refers to the ways in which black parents teach their children about the realities of race. Racial socialization includes preparing them to manage situations where racial discrimination occurs, and fostering positive beliefs about their racial identity to counter societal devaluation. The research literature suggests that

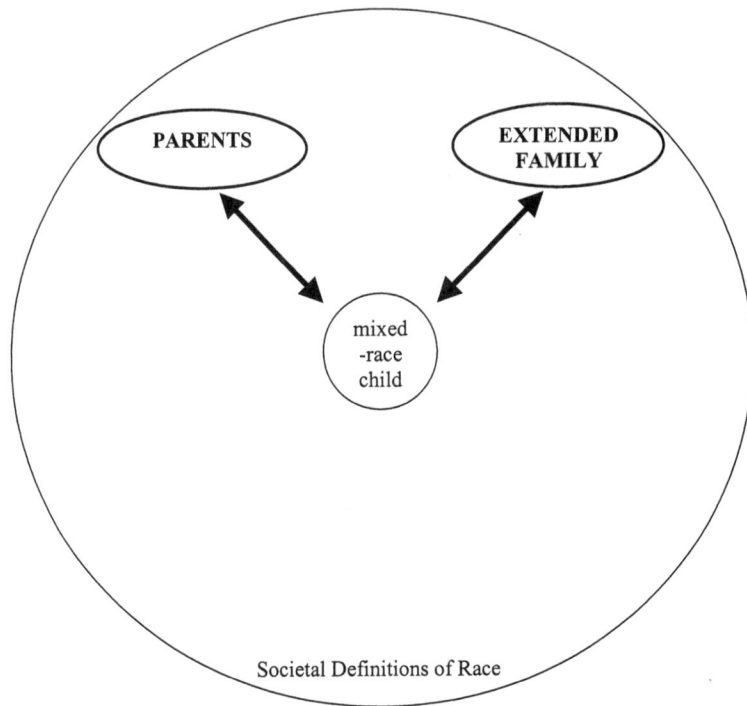

MODEL 4.1
Family Influences on Racial Identity Development

most black parents engage in some process of racially socializing their children. Moreover, the more actively parents racially socialize their children, the more likely children are to develop a stronger sense of self-esteem, have higher rates of academic achievement and lower rates of disciplinary problems, and appear to be more psychologically well adjusted overall.

We utilize the concept of racial socialization more broadly than the way it has been traditionally conceptualized and applied. Because race powerfully shapes social reality for all people, we emphasize that *all parents* teach their children specific racial attitudes, beliefs, and behaviors.[3] It's not only black parents who racially socialize their children, but white parents as well. All parents, directly or indirectly, consciously or unconsciously, for better or worse, send their children messages about how to view and respond to matters of race and how to understand themselves racially. Given that, we recognize that within most black families, there is a consciousness of race that tends to be absent in most white families. While race shapes family life and parenting practices in both black and white families, these influences tend to be more overt and deliberate in black families.

The nature of white privilege is such that few white people ever consciously consider the role that race plays in their lives.[4] Because it is often difficult for white parents to recognize the influence of race in their lives, the extent of their racial awareness is limited to the few occasions when they may find themselves in a situation where they are the racial minority.[5] White privilege affords the opportunity to live one's life without having to think about how one's race may be an advantage or disadvantage in various contexts. Despite this general lack of consciousness, most white parents do indeed racially socialize their children. Though indirect, unintentional, and invisible, white parents teach their children how to "be white," how to think about race, how to locate themselves racially within the world around them, and how to view and treat others on the basis of race.[6]

Two unique factors complicate racial socialization for parents of mixed-race children. First, the politics of race in our society are such that mixed-race people exist along the margins where there is no clear community of mixed-race people or a clearly developed ideology of the mixed-race experience that can be used to guide their racial socialization in a positive, cohesive manner. Second, unlike most single-race children, mixed-race children have no parent with whom they can directly identify with as a mixed-race person. In other words, unless one's parent is also mixed-race, the majority of mixed-race children are learning about race from one or more adults who have not directly experienced their racial reality. These adults usually have a view of race that is informed by their own racial identity and the racial socialization they received while growing up. This means that with few exceptions, most mixed-race children do not have the luxury of being raised by a parent whose own racial identity and racial socialization are similar or relevant to the realities of their multiracial experience. For these and many other reasons, raising mixed-race children can be a complicated process. To assist parents and practitioners working with interracial families, we outline several factors that influence the racial socialization of mixed-race children within families. We follow that discussion with strategies caregivers can use for healthy racial socialization.

FACTORS THAT SHAPE HOW PARENTS
APPROACH RACIAL SOCIALIZATION

There are a three important factors that shape how parents racially socialize their children: 1) individual parental factors, 2) the quality of the relationship between parents, and 3) how parents respond to their children's physical appearance. In this section, we present each factor using examples to illustrate the ideas. We then provide two case studies so that readers can be clear about how these factors play out in actual families.

Individual Parental Factors

How parents of mixed-race children approach racial socialization is heavily informed by the experiences they have had with race in their own biography. Specifically, the way that they were racially socialized as children, how they define and relate to their own racial identity, and the nature of their experiences with people of varying races all impact how individual parents racially socialize their children. We discuss each in turn.

The Racial Socialization Parents Received When They Were Children

The way that parents approach the racial socialization of their own children is informed by the socialization they received while growing up. In general, this socialization differs between blacks and whites. Many black parents raise their children to understand themselves racially as black people and to be aware of how race shapes institutional and interpersonal dynamics. In contrast, most white children are socialized to not think about matters of race, unless there are people of color involved. They are not raised to think about their own whiteness and the ways in which their whiteness shapes their life experiences.

The ultimate manifestation of privilege is not having to be aware of your privilege. It allows for a state of blissful ignorance. As members of the racially privileged group, most whites are not compelled to consider what it means to be white and the benefits they derive as a result of their racial privilege. They are, in a sense, "clueless" about the reality and complexity of race.[7] According to theorists on racial identity development, this cluelessness is characteristic of the primary stage of white identity development in which an individual lacks any conscious self-understanding as a white person and how whiteness shapes their life. For whites who are at this primary level of racial consciousness, when their attention is drawn to issues of race, more often than not the focus is centered on people of color, with little consideration of their whiteness. As a result, the vast majority of white children are implicitly socialized to associate "race" with "people of color," and therefore they don't learn to think of themselves as members of a race, nor do they learn to recognize the many ways in which their racial identity influences their lives. This creates a challenge for white parents of mixed-race children because most were raised with a limited awareness of the realities of racial stratification. Consequently, most lack a clear model for how to approach parenting in ways that actively address racism.

In some less common instances, white people are raised in families where active attention was devoted to addressing and explaining race, and where children are encouraged to assume an antiracist stance. In such families, children learn the meaning of their whiteness and they learn to critically challenge notions of white supremacy. Those who were raised in this way are advantaged in raising mixed-race children because they are conversant with issues of race and have a model for how to approach parenting in a way that explicitly acknowledges the omnipresence of race in daily life.

When white parents have not been socialized to be tuned in to race, they may not be knowledgeable about racial inequalities or lack sensitivity to the perspectives of people of color. Such parents tend to orient their children to identify as mixed-race with an emphasis on whiteness or to identify as white. In some instances, they may even orient their children to disavow race altogether, which in many ways, is synonymous with white socialization. White parents who received a more antiracist racial socialization are more likely than not to encourage their children to identify as mixed-race with an emphasis on their blackness, or to identify as black. White parents' racial socialization is especially important because most heterosexual black/white interracial couples consist of a white mother and a black father. Mothers are frequently the primary caregivers and are largely responsible for racially socializing their children. Therefore, most mixed-race children are raised in families where they receive the majority of their direct care and racial socialization from white mothers.

In contrast to the ways in which most white children are raised, most black children are raised to be mindful of race and how it shapes reality. They grow up knowing and understanding that they live in a racially divided and unequal society where they have membership in a racially devalued group. Most black parents devote some attention to fostering the development of skills and strategies for negotiating the pressures of living within a racially oppressive environment. Whether overtly or covertly, consciously or unconsciously, most prepare their children to cope with the challenges they may face in society. Consequently, more often than not, black parents of mixed-race children possess some understanding of the realities of race and have a model for how they can approach racial socialization in a deliberate manner.

While most black families engage in some form of active racial socialization, there are important variations in how this process is approached. One of the factors that affects how black parents approach racial socialization is the particular stance parents have in response to conditions of oppression. Not all black people experience racial oppression and devaluation in the same way, nor do they respond to and cope with these experiences in a monolithic manner. For example, some learn to cope with racism and discrimination by developing a *one-down stance*. This consists of avoiding confrontation with a would-be oppressor and behaving in ways that are designed to soften potential aggression. Black people who assume this stance do not see themselves as having the power to challenge white people. They see themselves in a subjugated position and accept as a reality that they must assume a deferential posture as a means of survival.

In contrast to the one-down stance, there are those who adopt a *resistance stance*. Black people who adopt a resistance stance are acutely aware of the racial indignities and injustices that white people have inflicted on blacks, and they position themselves to challenge racial inequalities and prejudice. There are varying degrees to which one may engage in acts of resistance, but those who assume a resistance stance share a conscious recognition of racial inequality and an intentional commitment to push against it in their daily lives. In some cases, this resistance may be overt, as in the case of a social activist who openly calls attention to racial injustice and directly strives to challenge it. In other cases, the resistance may be covert. In such cases, one may appear on the surface to be assuming a one-down stance, but beneath that surface, such a person is keenly focused on challenging the inequalities or injustices they are faced with, albeit in an indirect and subtle manner.

Another possibility is the stance of *internalized oppression*. Such persons internalize negative attitudes and beliefs about black people and they survive by (consciously or unconsciously) colluding with the white power structure. In some cases, these black people may appear to have a strong sense of racial pride, but this is based on a narrow definition of what it is to be black. In other words, they categorically reject any black person who does not fit their particular definition of "what it means to be black." They tend to utilize stereotypically "white standards" to judge other black people, and are harshly critical to those who do not conform. In this way, they reinforce the rules of oppression and domination rather than resisting them. Black people who adopt an internalized oppression stance align themselves with whiteness and reject blackness, or they reject a liberatory, multidimensional view of blackness. Because of their identification with whiteness, they often find ways to rationalize the subtle racism of white people and give whites the benefit of the doubt, even when it is undeserved.

How black parents of mixed-race children approach racial socialization is strongly tied to the stance they have in response to racial oppression. Black parents who assume a one-down stance are most likely to orient their children to identify as black, or to encourage their children to identify as mixed-race, but with an emphasis on their blackness. In contrast, black people who assume a stance of resistance are likely to orient their children to identify as black and to assume an intentional stance of resistance against racial injustices. Black parents who assume an internalized oppression stance are apt to encourage their children to identify as mixed-race, but with an emphasis on their whiteness. They may also orient their children to identify as exclusively white or to reject notions of race altogether.

The Nature of Parents' Racial Experiences

The ways in which parents approach racial socialization are also guided by the types of experiences they have had with both white and black people throughout their lives. Both the frequency of their contact with members of each group, and the quality of this contact are important. In terms of *frequency*, both blacks and whites are likely to have extensive experiences interacting with whites because white people make up the majority of the U.S. population. Most black people are likely to have had numerous opportunities to interact with and relate to other black people, but few whites can claim the same frequency. Certainly, there are some black people who have had limited interactions with other blacks. Those who were raised by parents of another race or who grew up in predominantly white communities may have had few interactions with other black people. Moreover, some white people have lived in communities, attended schools, and/or were raised in families where they have had extensive interaction with black people. Frequency of contact is important because this creates the opportunity to learn about others, and ultimately to learn about one's self in relation to others. There simply is no substitute for experience.

In addition to frequency of contact, the *quality* of the experiences one has had with whites and blacks is also critical. It should go without saying that the more positive the experiences are with members of both groups, the more open parents will be to exposing their children to members of these groups. Consider two black people who grew up in predominantly white communities. In the first case, the person had a largely negative and hostile experience with whites, while in the second case, the person felt completely accepted by and respected by whites. The qualitative differences in their experiences leads to variation in their comfort level and feelings about white people overall. The same can be said for whites interacting with blacks. Hence, the frequency and quality of the interracial contact parents have had shapes how they think and feel toward members of different racial groups.

How Parents Define and Relate to Their Racial Identity

The way that parents define themselves racially and understand their own identity also plays a key role in how they raise their children. Parents who have consciously reflected on their racial identity, who recognize the ways in which it shapes their perceptions of reality, and are at peace with their identity are better equipped to racially socialize their children in healthy ways. Parents' own racial identity reflects a developmental process whereby some may be at earlier stages while others are at more advanced stages. The stages of development have similarities and differences for both blacks and whites.

According to models of white identity development, individuals initially operate at a primary level of racial development that consists of an unconscious identification with whiteness and unquestioned acceptance of stereotypes about racial minorities.[8] As racial identity development progresses, they enter a conflict stage during which time awareness of racial issues grows and they are challenged to consider their whiteness. At this stage, individuals are conflicted between wanting to conform to majority norms while also wanting to support ideals of social and racial justice. This conflict is associated with feelings of guilt, anger, and depression that may lead to either feelings of anger toward white culture and adopting a strong prominority stance, or to defensive retreat into the "white world." If an individual advances to the highest level of racial development, he or she experiences a redefinition of whiteness. This involves taking responsibility for maintaining racism while simultaneously identifying with a white identity that is nonracist. One sees both the opportunities and obstacles and is open to learning from their own and other racial groups.

Since few whites are raised to think about their whiteness consciously, they often operate at the primary level of racial development. Few white people are ever challenged to think of themselves as having a racial identity, so they do not progress to higher levels of racial consciousness. As a result, they spend little time considering what it means to be white, which can easily result in the erroneous conclusion that "whiteness" does not exist as a specific orientation, in much the same way that "blackness" does.

The "invisibility of whiteness" can easily lead white parents to assume that racial issues do not concern them. They may believe that the impact of race is an individual choice, and if they only choose to avoid talking about race and not make "an issue of it," then no race-related challenges will arise. White parents who operate at the primary level of development may expose their children to specific experiences and values that they perceive as "neutral" or "raceless" without seeing the "whiteness" that these experiences reflect. For example, particular ways of dressing, certain types of foods, holiday rituals, decisions about how to spend family vacations, and approaches to discipline all reflect particular cultural orientations. For whites who are in the primary stage of racial identity development, it can be difficult to recognize how their whiteness reflects a specific orientation that is aligned with the values of the dominant culture.

For white parents of mixed-race children, it is especially important to move beyond the primary level of development by confronting, struggling, and coming to terms with their whiteness so they can provide a positive model of whiteness for their children. In practical terms, this would lead to a white person being able to talk frankly about how whiteness shapes his or her life, including acknowledging the oppressive aspects of this identity. To do this effectively, it is important to have worked through one's emotions as a way of moving beyond defensive anger or debilitating levels of guilt. Those who come to peaceful, constructive terms about their whiteness are able to own this identity, account for the unearned benefits they derive from it, and commit to positive social action whereby they *use their power to lose their power.*

Most black people have some awareness of themselves as racial beings and some idea about how race shapes their daily lives. However, like whites, black people vary in their stages of racial identity development. According to black identity models, the primary level of development is the pre-encounter stage. This stage is characterized by a superficial understanding of race and a tendency to identify with the norms and values of white culture.[9] In the extreme, one manifests a level of self-hatred that consists of a deep sense of internalized oppression. More often that not, black people encounter racism, leading to an immersion stage where one's understanding of race and the black experience within a racist society leads to a deeper engagement with one's self as a black person. Often, there is a corresponding rage toward white culture and a rejection of all that whiteness represents. It is possible to become stuck at this level of development, although ideally a person would continue to progress by embracing a black identity that is characterized by a clear understanding of what it means to be black within a white society. In the final stage, individuals feel a sense of pride about blackness, while at the same time being able to critically evaluate whiteness. They are able to differentiate between individual white people and the broader systems of white oppression.

Dana was a twenty-year-old African American woman who exhibited the characteristics associated with the pre-encounter stage of black identity development.[10] As a light-skinned woman, she rejected darker-skinned black people. Most of her friends were either light-skinned blacks or whites, and she routinely made critical comments about black people in the presence of whites, as if to buy some piece of approval she imagined she might gain from them.

After taking a course called *African American Identity,* Dana had an encounter experience that jolted her into more critically evaluating her relationship with both blackness and whiteness. As she started to see the strains of internalized racism she suffered from, she was able to begin tearing it apart. She also started to understand how she had overidentified with whiteness in ways that were hurtful to her sense of integration as a black person. With her emergent awareness, she was able to gradually move closer to other black people who she had previously rejected. At the same time, she found herself feeling increasingly angry with white people, to the point that she said she hated all white people. Eventually, Dana was able to make another shift whereby she still felt justified anger toward white oppression, but she no longer generalized to the point of rejecting all white people. Moreover, she became more grounded in a deeper understanding and love of herself as a black person.

Whether you are black or white, and irrespective of your stage of racial identity development, everyone internalizes some aspects of societal messages that overvalue whiteness and devalue blackness. The extent to which such messages are either deconstructed and rejected, or absorbed and integrated, shapes how a person comes to think and feel about their racial identity. Certainly, the more developed each person's racial identity, the more likely they are to have worked through the meaning of blackness and whiteness and understand their feelings about blackness and whiteness. Parents of mixed-race children who have interrogated their racial identity and have progressed beyond primary levels are in a better position to provide positive modeling for their children.

Quality of Relationship between Parents

In the previous section, we examined how individual factors influence racial socialization for parents of mixed-race children. We now move to the more complicated issue of the interactional factors between parents, and how the quality of their relationship shapes racial socialization. More specifically, we examine how conflict and tension within couple relationships indirectly affect children's racial socialization.

All couple relationships are complex and difficult, and even the best relationships involve struggle. Communication is difficult, intimacy is complicated, and few of us have the benefit of being taught specific skills for how to develop and maintain healthy couple relationships. In an ideal world, both of a child's parents would share an open, honest, and caring relationship, and would be united by a common philosophy about how to raise their children that would include active, healthy approaches to racial socialization. Real life rarely works this way. More often than not, parents of all children struggle in their relationships. These struggles, in turn, affect parenting. When we add the dynamics of race within interracial relationships, creating and maintaining a healthy relationship becomes even more challenging.

When couples experience conflict, strife, and tension within their relationship, this creates the perception of "sides," which children have to negotiate between. The challenge children face is that in supporting one parent, they may feel disloyal to the other. In fact, the other parent may also see the child as disloyal. This contributes to feelings of guilt and a sense of being caught between warring parties where the child is damned no matter what choice he or she makes. In other instances, children may gladly align with one parent out of anger toward the other. Whatever the particular scenario may be, within interracial families, conflicts between parents often become racialized and have profound overt and covert effects on children.

In the case of overt effects on children, one or both parents may racialize whatever conflict exists between them. Take, for example, Frank (a white male) and Michelle (a black female), who had been married for twelve years and had three children.[11] After Michelle learned of Frank's affair (with a white woman), they were divorced. The children lived with their mother and, following the divorce, they faced a dramatic reduction in their income. Michelle worked two jobs, yet there was barely enough to make ends meet. Their hardships were deepened by the fact that Frank was a "deadbeat dad" who often failed to make child support payments on time and rarely spent time with his children. To make matters worse, he was engaged to the woman with whom he had had the affair. Michelle had feelings of deep resentment and anger toward her exhusband, and she did not hide these feelings from her children. Since the children also felt abandoned by their father, both mother and children were united in their shared rage toward him.

Race reared its ugly head when Michelle racialized the interpersonal conflict between her and Frank. She did so by frequently commenting on how he had left her because he preferred a white woman. Her sense of betrayal and hurt was shaped by racial dynamics and she was overt about these. She spoke openly about how white people could not be trusted, how they always stuck together, how they used black people and then threw them away. For the children in this family, the impact of the overt messages they were receiving about race were shaped by the dynamics in their parents' relationship. The conflict between their parents and the disintegration of their relationship, coupled with the fact that the children felt abandoned by their father and viewed their mother as the only parent they could depend on, all added weight to the overt race-based messages Michelle conveyed. In light of the family dynamics, the children were strongly aligned with their mother and estranged from their father, which included adopting their mother's views on race.

In the case of covert messages, parents do not directly link their conflicts to race, but on an indirect level, children infer racial meanings. For example, Derrick is a black father who raised his two children as a single parent.[12] The children's white mother left them with Derrick when they were only two and three years old because she was not ready for motherhood and did not love Derrick anymore. She claimed that she needed to pursue her own dreams or else she would never feel fulfilled. Derrick never made any racialized comments about the children's mother and, in fact, rarely spoke of her at all. However, the children understood that he, like they, felt betrayed and abandoned by her. Indirectly, the children were internalizing feelings about whiteness and blackness based on what had occurred between their parents. Because their father was the caregiver, they saw him as the only parent on whom they could rely, and they developed a strong attachment to their blackness. Conversely, because of the ways their mother had hurt them and their father, they distanced themselves from all aspects of her, including the whiteness she represented.

Parents' Responses to Their Children's Physical Characteristics

Another powerful factor that shapes racial socialization is a child's physical appearance. How parents respond to a child's physical characteristics sends the child direct and indirect messages about race. For example, consider a family with two girls who are only a year apart in age. One of these girls is light-skinned with light brown eyes, wavy, sandy-colored hair, and narrow lips and nose. The other is dark-skinned with brown eyes, tight, curly, black hair, full lips, and a broad nose. These types of physical differences often result in differential treatment within families. Given the racial hierarchy that organizes society in the United States, the nature of the differential treatment is to favor lighter-skinned, "whiter-looking" children over darker-skinned, "blacker-looking" children. Not only does this send powerful messages about race and what is considered valuable, it also creates complicated, often painful dynamics among siblings.

Sibling rivalry is as old as Cain and Abel and it is an inevitable dimension of family process. The typical tensions and competitions that exist between siblings are often compounded and made more painful when race becomes part of the equation. Children find themselves competing for the affection and approval of parents who may be basing their preferences on physical characteristics. When this occurs, children internalize powerful messages about race, what is valued and devalued, and, in turn, these implicit messages impact their self-understanding and relations with others.

The impact that physical appearance has on family dynamics and racial socialization within interracial families is also linked to how families are perceived outside of their home. Interracial families are all too familiar with strangers assuming that parents and children with differing racial characteristics are not related. For example, at an airport, Tracey observed a situation where a security agent was assigning passengers to one of several security check lanes. There was an interracial family in line composed of a white man, a black woman, and two biracial children. The security agent assumed that the white man was coupled with a nearby white woman and that the black woman and two children were a family unto themselves. Based on this assumption, he tried to send the family in two different directions. His behavior revealed the erroneous yet common assumption that families are made up of people with similar skin color and physical characteristics.

It is not just that people make assumptions about who may (or may not) be related based on physical appearances but that particular meanings get attached to specific physical appearances. For example, in conversations with interracial families where the mother is black and the children appear white or are light-skinned, time and time again these families tell us how others assume that the mother is the children's nanny. Yet we have never encountered a family where a white mother reported that she was mistakenly assumed to be the nanny of her children who are either mixed or black in appearance. The differences here speak to the power of racial stereotypes that depict black people in the role of "servants" of white people. When children and parents have discrepant physical appearances, it often leads to an array of misperceptions on the part of strangers regarding who is (and is not) related, and how they might be connected. Depending on how much experience parents have had with these matters, their understanding of the underlying dynamics, and comfort in handling such situations, public misperceptions can become a source of great strain and frustration within interracial families.

Multiple factors influence how parents racially socialize their children. Model 4.2 provides a visual illustration of the interconnectedness and dynamic nature of the structural, social, and emotional factors at work in this process. Each factor shapes the messages that are sent to children about race, racism, and racial identity. What should be clear by looking at the model is the high potential for

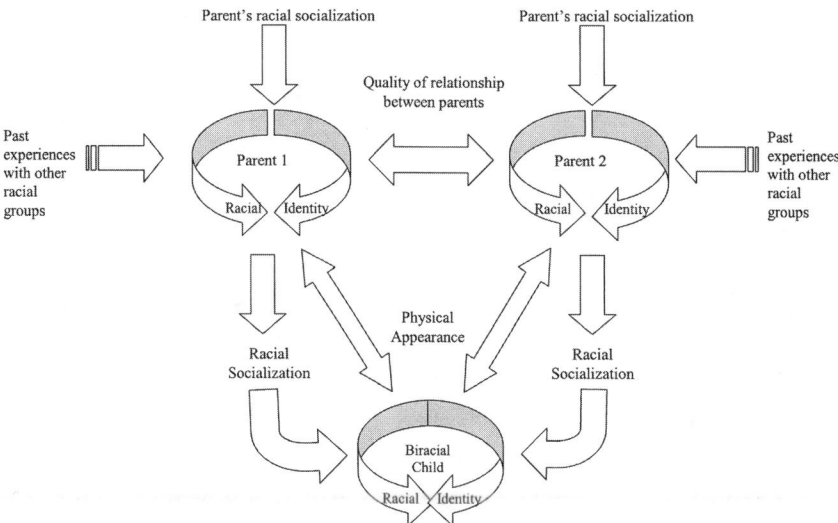

MODEL 4.2
Parental Factors That Influence Racial Identity Development for Biracial Children

conflicting messages between parents who have different racial backgrounds, experiences, socialization, and understandings of the world. It also is important to bear in mind that in some family systems, other adults besides parents may play a role in raising children. Stepparents, grandparents, aunts, uncles, cousins, or people not related by blood or marriage can influence children's socialization, thereby increasing the potential for children to receive conflicting messages about race and feel trapped between competing loyalties.

PULLING IT ALL TOGETHER: CASE STUDIES

To illustrate some of the concepts previously described, we now provide two case studies. Our goal is to demonstrate how parents' individual factors (e.g., how they were racially socialized, the nature of their racial experiences, their own racial identity development), the quality of the relationship between parents, and how they respond to their children's physical characteristics shape and influence racial socialization within two interracial families.

Case #1: Chris and Gina

Gina is a white woman who grew up in a white family, lived in a white neighborhood, and attended a predominantly white elementary school in

Lafayette, Indiana.[13] Gina's parents openly advocated for racial equality and social justice. When she was thirteen, her family moved to Chicago, where their new neighborhood and local school were racially mixed. Gina's two best friends were African American girls, and when she was fifteen, she started dating her first boyfriend, Tarek, who was African American. Gina and Tarek broke up when Gina left home to attend college where she dated several young men of varying races. When she was twenty-one, she met Chris, an African American man, and they fell in love.

Chris grew up in a black family, lived in a black neighborhood, and attended racially mixed schools in Chicago. His parents actively socialized him and his two brothers to understand the existence of racism in America and to develop a positive sense of themselves as black men. Chris socialized with a group of racially mixed friends, although his best friend was African American. Throughout high school, he dated mostly black girls, with the exception of two white girls in his senior year. In college, he dated a black woman for two years and, after they broke up, he did not date for a year until he met Gina and they fell in love.

Two years after Chris and Gina graduated, they married with the full support of both of their families. They moved to Atlanta where they were both employed by a black-owned and operated real estate firm. A year later, they had their first child, Kia.

Both Gina and Chris are close to their respective families and intimate circle of friends, who are mostly black. The couple lives in a predominantly black neighborhood and they are active members of the local NAACP chapter. When Kia is ready to start school, it is their intention to send her to a racially diverse school.

Chris and Gina's background and their current lifestyle choices speak to their shared racial ideology that affirms blackness. They also have a positive relationship with their respective racial identities. Having been raised to recognize racism, to love blackness, and to work for racial justice, Chris is solidly grounded in his identity as a black person. At the same time, he has had close, positive relationships with white people and this contributes to his ability to make distinctions among white people and remain open to those who are progressive in their racial ideology—people like Gina.

Because Gina was raised to think and act in terms of racial equality, and because her early experiences involved extensive crossracial contact, Gina's racial ideology closely matches Chris's. Moreover, because of her extensive crossracial experiences, Gina has had opportunities to interrogate her whiteness and come to terms with her identity as a white person. She acknowledges the privileges she has as a white person and is committed to using these in socially progressive ways on behalf of racial justice. It is the advanced level of their own racial identity development that enables them to embrace both whiteness and blackness, and to be proactive in their affirmation of blackness, all of which provides a strong foundation for racially socializing Kia in healthy ways.

In terms of their couple relationship, the relatively happy and stable relationship Chris and Gina share protects Kia from having to manage competing messages about race that might otherwise be reflected in conflicts within her parents' marriage. Because they are united in their racial ideology, Kia receives consistent messages in the home about her racial identity. Both Chris and Gina are raising Kia to identify as a mixed-race person who emphasizes her blackness. While Kia's physical appearance is such that her racial identity is ambiguous, the socialization she receives from her parents affirms that she is a mixed-race person. They are able to support her in developing a sense of comfort with this sense of self, in spite of the numerous times she is questioned and even challenged about her identity.

Case #2: Peter and Pam

Pam, who is white, had virtually no interracial interaction growing up. Her family was white, she always lived in a white neighborhood, and she attended predominantly white schools in Johnstown, Pennsylvania.[14] Although she had little crossracial contact growing up, her family espoused the importance of "treating everyone as an individual and not being prejudiced." In spite of this, Pam's father was known to make comments about "niggers" and "spics." Pam dated only white males until she was twenty-two, when she met Peter, a twenty-four-year-old African American man.

Peter grew up in a black family, lived in a neighborhood where his family was one of only two black families, and attended racially diverse schools in a suburban community outside of Pittsburgh. As the youngest of eight children, Peter received very little direct socialization from his parents about many things, including race. He had many friends growing up, most of whom were white. In high school, his first girlfriend was black, but thereafter, all of the girls he dated were white.

Peter and Pam met while they both worked in the sales department of a telecommunications firm. They dated for three years before marrying. One month later, Pam was pregnant with their son, Josh. Both Pam and Peter are connected with their families, but there are mild tensions on both sides. One of Peter's sisters has expressed some irritation about Peter's choice of a white partner. Although Pam's family accepts Peter as a "great guy," their marriage has not altered the racial ideology that leads her father to continue using the term "nigger" when talking about black people other than Peter. Currently, Pam and Peter reside in southwestern Pennsylvania. They live in an all-white neighborhood and plan to send their son to an almost exclusively white private school.

Pam and Peter's backgrounds and current lifestyle choices suggest that they are highly oriented toward whiteness. While Peter has more comfort and experience interacting with black people than does Pam, they both seem to prefer socializing within mostly white circles. Both Pam and Peter share a racial ideology that espouses a superficial commitment to seeing all people as equal, but beneath the surface they both harbor unchallenged negative views toward blacks. While they reject the use of racial slurs and see these as racist, they share a variety of negative attitudes toward blacks that reflect an internalization of white supremacist ideology. They are especially hostile toward poor black people whom they say "make excuses" and "don't do more to advance the race."

Pam and Peter are at a primary level in their own racial identity development. Pam is oriented exclusively toward whiteness, which she has never interrogated in order to understand the privileges she derives from it, the ways in which is it oppressive, and how it shapes her view of the world. Peter struggles with his blackness. He has many negative feelings about being black and is critical of most black people. While he acknowledges that white racism is responsible for many historical ills toward blacks, his behaviors and life choices illustrate a white orientation.

As a couple, Peter and Pam share a stable, satisfying marriage. They do not have serious conflicts between them that could get racialized. When combined with the fact that they are matched in terms of their respective relationships with their racial identities and their racial ideologies, it places them on the same page in terms of how they approach Josh's racial socialization. However, because they both possess an uncritical valuation of whiteness and devaluation of blackness, their shared orientation is lacking in balance and perspective. Consequently, while Peter and Pam say they are raising Josh to be mixed-race in his self-identification, in practice they are socializing him to be exclusively white, and, importantly, *not* black. One of the challenges this may eventually pose for Josh is that his physical appearance clearly reflects his mixed-race identity. Because he looks like a light-skinned black person, he will never be fully accepted by the group with whom he most identifies, and he will likely encounter rejection from black people who will be turned off by his inability to relate to them.

STRATEGIES FOR HEALTHY RACIAL SOCIALIZATION OF MIXED-RACE CHILDREN

Healthy socialization involves talking honestly, openly, and directly with children about how race shapes everyday life. It is also based on allowing children the freedom and opportunity to be curious, to ask questions, and to share their observations and views without fear of reprisal, disapproval, or punishment. It entails challenging racial views, attitudes, and beliefs that perpetuate racial inequalities. It involves fostering the acquisition of skills for negotiating situations where, as mixed-race people, children may be racially isolated, targeted, and maligned. It requires parents to provide children with information, examples, and role models that will offer positive representations of black people and mixed-race people, as well as examples of how whites and blacks can work together to achieve racial justice and harmony. Healthy socialization involves creating an environment that nurtures a sense of racial self-love, and the fortitude to draw on this love under adverse conditions.

Honest Education about the Realities of Race

Healthy racial socialization must include honest, open education about the realities of race. When parents are able to talk directly with their children about race and discuss how race shapes daily life, children not only acquire a cognitive understanding of the complexities of race, but they also develop a sense of comfort and ease in talking about racial issues.

For most black people, educating children about race is a necessary part of childrearing. This is not a skill that needs to be learned later in life, but rather a way of being in the world, and survival strategies are passed from generation to generation. Most black parents educate their children about racism from the time they are very young. While parents vary in the extent to which they emphasize and educate their children about race, most do so to some degree because they recognize that this is an instrumental aspect of preparing their children to survive within a hostile environment.

In contrast, race education is not an integrated aspect of how most white parents raise their children. Because white privilege precludes the necessity of white people needing to understand race as a survival skill, most do not. While some progressive white parents actively educate their children about race, this is the exception and not the rule. For white parents of mixed-race children, teaching their children how to identify, understand, and respond to racism can be difficult because these were not lessons they were exposed to during their own upbringing. It may require some white parents to first deepen their own education on race relations, and to practice how to communicate these understandings with others as preparation for doing this with their own children.

In some cases, simply entering into an interracial relationship exposes white partners to the particular realities of race that they otherwise would not have experienced. They may come to realize in a personal way the depth of racism that exists. This exposure often comes in the form of facing criticism and scorn from other whites because of their relationship, or having opportunities to observe up close how their partner is treated. While there is no way for white partners to truly grasp what it feels like to be black, the disapproval and rejection they encounter from others comes close. And with this opportunity comes the possibility of expanding their awareness of racism.

In other cases, white people may learn about racial inequalities through their interactions with black people (above and beyond their spouse). Through sharing space with black people, it becomes possible to listen to how they perceive reality. Listening to conversations among black people discussing race relations and talking directly with black people about racial issues provides a fertile ground for learning about how race shapes daily life for people of color. In some instances, white partners may be confronted by black people who mistrust their motives and intentions. They may question the depth of the white partner's racial "knowing" and authenticity, and may treat the white partner with guardedness and possibly even scorn. This, too, is a learning opportunity. Through such encounters, white partners have a chance to hear and learn about black perspectives more deeply, including learning about some of the specific issues that shape contemporary race relations from the point of view of different black people.

Practicing the Art and Skill of "Talking Race"

"Talking race" is an art and a skill because there is a specific vocabulary and grammar that define "race talk." Learning how to talk race effectively requires extensive practice within diverse racial contexts. The more one talks race, and the greater the diversity of people with whom one communicates, the greater the fluency he or she will develop. Talking race can be difficult, especially in crossracial settings. Even among those who share close relationships, it is often hard to surmount the societal taboos that prohibit open, direct conversations about race. This remains such a loaded and emotionally charged topic that even good friends and family members avoid the topic rather than risk the discomfort and possible alienation that may ensue if the subject is broached. This is especially the case during crossracial interactions. Anxiety on both sides constrains the possibility of direct discussion. For white people, there is the fear that if they raise the topic of race, they may "say the wrong thing" and be deemed a racist. For black people, there is the fear that if they raise the topic, their views and feelings will be rejected, invalidated, and dismissed by whites who may accuse them of being too sensitive, too hostile, or wanting to make excuses and "play victim." Finding opportunities to "talk-race" is often difficult, even among those who share close relationships.

Christina, a white woman, had a close friendship with an African American woman named Sarah for over twenty years.[15] She considered Sarah one of her dearest friends and yet, it was only after completing a course in multicultural therapy that Christina realized she and Sarah had never discussed race. This amazed Christina because it never even crossed her mind as a topic of conversation. After becoming conscious of the omission, she decided to discuss it with Sarah. Not surprisingly, Sarah was not only aware of the fact that they had never discussed racial issues, but purposely avoided the topic because she assumed their friendship might be threatened if it ever came up. Christina was shocked; she could not believe that Sarah was so threatened by the possibility of discussing racial issues that she purposely avoided the topic in conversation.

As they continued the dialogue, Sarah eventually told Christina about her experiences in life as a black person. Sarah described the multitudinous ways she felt devalued and mistreated as a black woman, and of the various humiliations she endured in silence because she didn't believe she would be supported by any of the white people she knew. Christina was horrified and saddened to learn what life had been like for Sarah, but she also felt ashamed that she never realized any of her friend's pain before this discussion.

Christina said:

> I was so upset when I started to see all of this at last. I also for a moment was angry with Sarah because I wondered why she had never spoken to me about these things. Then I became angry with myself because I realized my role in all of this. It's not that I was ever racist in any way, but I was racially insensitive. I never thought about what life was like for Sarah as one of the only black people in this mostly white community. I never initiated discussions of race, I never asked her about her experience, I never said anything that even hinted that I had any idea of what she might be experiencing. She had no reason to trust I would want to hear or that I could even understand her.

Recognizing Sameness and Difference

Both black and white parents must realize that while they may share many vital things in common with their children, their racial experiences are different. The uniqueness of their child's experience is significant. This point may be harder for black parents to wrestle with than white parents because they share in common the fact that both they and their children are people of color. This creates a bond, a basis for a shared understanding about what it means to have membership in a racially devalued group. At the same time, mixed-race children have an even more marginalized experience because they often do not "fit" into totalizing categories of either whiteness or blackness, which places them at risk of being rejected by both groups, and of never feeling as if they truly belong anywhere.

The challenge for parents is to simultaneously connect with children around the ways in which they have a shared experience, while also recognizing and acknowledging their differences. As part of this, it is helpful for parents to explicitly affirm to their children that they are aware of these similarities and differences. Parents need to convey that they see how their children's mixed-race status provides the benefit of being able to relate to both whiteness and blackness, and the challenge of never feeling completely a part of either world.[16]

Affirming Blackness

We live in a society where blackness is categorically devalued while whiteness is treated with reverence. For this reason, parents need to make a conscious effort to push against the tide of negative messages about blackness and introduce children to the many strengths of blackness. Some of the ways parents can do this is by exposing children to the many positive achievements of African American people, providing them with examples of the diversity of black life by helping them see role models who represent a range of backgrounds, and showing them loving examples of blackness.

Part of affirming blackness involves providing children with opportunities to interact with and relate to black people. This is a vital part of the healthy socialization of mixed-race children. Most mixed-race people will have contact with and exposure to whites because they are the numeric majority in the United States. Therefore, their ability to interact with whites is unlikely to be much of a concern. However, more questionable is whether they will have sustained contact with and the ability to relate to black people. If mixed-race children do not learn how to relate to black people early in life, they are at risk of being ostracized by black people who will sense their discomfort and awkwardness. Providing children with opportunities to interact and relate with black people early in their lives can help offset any potential rejection they may encounter later in life if they do not possess an understanding of and comfort with black culture and black people.

Providing Positive Representations

Healthy racial socialization of mixed-race children demands that parents provide exposure to positive representations of black and mixed-race people. Whenever we make this point during public presentations, we often are asked by a white person in the audience, "Why don't you also say it's important to include positive representations of white people, after all, these kids are half white?" Our answer here is simple: Children of all races are bombarded with numerous positive representations of whiteness. In fact, the need to make a point of exposing children to positive representations of black and mixed-race people is a reaction to the dominance of whiteness in our society, and the systematic way in which white supremacy advances positive notions of whiteness while conveying negative notions of blackness.

Our society abounds with negative messages about blackness and what it means to be black. For example, common phrases such as "blackmail," "black market," "black sheep of the family," and a person's "dark side," to name a few, all equate blackness or darkness with something that is bad. The media ignores the diversity of black experience and opts to focus a disproportionate amount of attention on the worst aspects of black life. At other times, black people are simply ignored altogether, which also sends a message of devaluation. "Whether the issue is a painful color caste system in black life or violent actions used by whites against blacks (denigrating speech, physical aggression, dehumanizing representation), every day all black people encounter (as does everyone else) some expression of hatred toward blackness, whether we recognize it or not."[17] Therefore, the work for black people around identity involves challenging negative valuations of blackness.

The overvaluation of whiteness and the devaluation of blackness is a phenomenon that parents of mixed-race children must actively work to balance. Ideally, children should be exposed to balanced representations of whiteness and blackness, but in this society the scales are tipped in such a way that blackness is rarely represented in positive ways. To provide children with a more balanced view, parents need to make a purposeful effort to introduce children to black and mixed-race people of all walks of life who are making constructive contributions to their families, communities, and society. They can introduce children to books written by black and mixed-race authors and that address themes that are relevant in the lives of people of color. They could expose children to magazines that cater to black and mixed-race readership, and make a point of taking kids to see movies that depict black and mixed-race people in multifaceted and nonracist ways. In situations when children see a movie, commercial, television ad, or music video that depicts black and mixed-race people in stereotypical and negative ways, it is important to initiate follow-up conversations that provide for some critical analysis of the problematic nature of these depictions.

Preparing Children for Encounters with Racism

Mixed-race children are members of a racially stigmatized and marginalized group. As such, they will inevitably encounter racism and rejection at varying points in their lives. Healthy racial socialization requires parents prepare their children for the harsh realities of prejudice and discrimination and teach them specific strategies for how to respond to racism. Derek Salmond is a black-appearing, mixed-race fifteen-year-old.[18] He explained the importance of being prepared to respond to racism in the following way:

> There was a girl on my water polo team. We had started going out and doing stuff together with groups of friends. She told her father about me and he just wasn't going to have it. He didn't want his daughter to hang out with someone of another ethnicity.
>
> I was stunned at first, but I always knew it was going to happen eventually. It's something that both of my parents had prepared me for. They always made me aware that there is racism out there and that I was definitely going to stand out because I'm of a different ethnicity. In many cases, it was just my dad telling me about encounters he had had. And when I started seeing girls, he reminded me that I was different and that girls may decide not to like me because of that, or that their parents may have problems with that. And that just made it easier for me to cope. When it came about, it wasn't as striking a blow for me as it may have been for others who wouldn't have been prepared for it.

Because mixed-race people are both white and black, but not entirely white or black, they are at risk for being targeted by both white *and* black people. Parents must talk with their children to help them understand that they very likely will encounter such experiences on both sides of the fence. Talking with children about these possibilities helps prepare them so that if they have such encounters, they are not caught off guard. Moreover, by introducing children to these possibilities, parents have the opportunity to help them understand the dynamics associated with the prejudices of white and black people. They also can help their children understand that if they are subjected to such indignities, these tend to say more about the offender than it does about them. This way, the offense will not be internalized, chipping away at their sense of self.

When to "Talk Back" and When to "Pull Back"

A critical aspect of helping prepare children to deal with racism involves helping them make distinctions between when to "talk back" and when to "pull back." This involves learning how to critically evaluate a situation to assess the costs and benefits of either talking back or pulling back. With practice, it becomes easier to formulate rapid assessments of a situation to ascertain when it is feasible to confront an expression of racism, and when it is best to simply step back.

"Talking back" involves having the capacity to call attention to an expression of racism and hold the offenders accountable. To talk back, one must possess a clear, strong voice and feel some comfort with the inevitable tension that arises when challenging racism. To help children develop this capacity, parents need to give their children "voice lessons." This begins with parents creating opportunities within the home to practice asserting their voices. Parents should create space for kids to exercise their voices by asserting their views, challenging various points of view, and advocating on their child's behalf. These are the skills they will need outside of the home to stand up effectively to experiences with racism, so it is best to begin cultivating these within the home, where there is greater safety and freedom to experiment and learn through trial and error.

"Pulling back" is based on the idea of "picking your battles." While there is much to be said for challenging racism and standing up for one's self, there are times when it is best to just let things slide. In a situation where talking back may result in some physical harm, "pulling back" may be a better course of action. As part of giving their children voice lessons, parents need to teach their children how to control and modulate their voices, including not asserting themselves in certain situations. For example, in school, a child who has a teacher who has been racially insensitive may want to talk back, but there are reasons why it is more prudent for the child to pull back and not antagonize the teacher. If the teacher seems like the kind of person who cannot receive feedback openly, if there is reason to believe he might be punishing the student, or if the offenses have been mild enough, it may be in the child's best interests to pull back.

Nurturing Self-Love

One of the most powerful resources parents can cultivate within their children involves teaching them how to love and value themselves racially, even when they are faced with people, situations, and circumstances that may denigrate, dismiss, and devalue them. Supporting children in learning ways of valuing themselves is a most powerful strategy for combating the inevitable tide of devaluation they will encounter as members of a racially marginalized group. As bell hooks states: "Love is profoundly political. Our deepest revolution will come when we understand this truth. Only love can give us the strength to go forward in the midst of heartbreak and misery. Only love can give us the power to reconcile, to redeem, the power to renew our weary spirits and save lost souls. The transformative power of love is the foundation of all meaningful social change. Without love our lives are without meaning. Love is the heart of the matter. When all else has fallen away, love sustains."[19]

Self-love is hard to achieve, but is especially difficult for mixed-race people. The challenge facing mixed-race people is that if they embrace their blackness, they are embracing a part of self that is profoundly devalued in society. Conversely, if they embrace their whiteness, they are embracing a part of themselves that opens them up to rejection from whites who continue to operate according to the politics of the "one-drop rule," and rejection from blacks who will interpret their embrace of whiteness as a de facto rejection of blackness. Those mixed-race people who claim their mixed-race identity as a third and unique dimension of their racial self also risk rejection. "Biracial" is not a category of identity that is widely understood or accepted, so this identification places one at risk of being rejected by all single-race people who simply do not grasp the meaning of this identity, understand the contours that define it, and view those who claim it as truly marginal. This creates a conundrum for mixed-race people around how to embrace and love the different parts of themselves.

Those who feel as if some or all parts of their ancestry are a basis for rejection and scorn from others will struggle with self-love. To love one's self is to fundamentally accept one's self and feel worthy of affirmation and love from others. Yet self-acceptance and feeling worthy of being loved and cared for by others can be difficult when an individual has endured a litany of painful rejections and has been exposed to a web of messages that inherently devalue and denigrate the parts that comprise the self.

Achieving self-love is an intentional process. It requires a person to push against the stream of negative, critical messages about the various part of his or her self that others fail to understand or accept. To resist these messages, it is helpful to understand where they come from within those who convey them. All too often, these rejections say more about the rejecter than the rejected. For example, when a black person condemns a mixed-race person for claiming his whiteness and/or mixed-race identity, this condemnation often stems from the pain this black person has felt around the devaluation and rejection of his blackness. While this does not justify their mistreatment, it does help to explain it, and can soften the impact of the rejection. The mixed-race person can realize that the scorn is more about the other person's pain than it is about some flaw within himself. If a white person rejects a mixed-race person for claiming her blackness, whiteness, and/or mixed-race identity, this reflects the white person's conditioning within a white supremacist society and the racist devaluation of blackness she internalized. Understanding this locates the problem within the accuser and allows the mixed-race person to externalize the problem as opposed to viewing their existence as the problem.

For parents raising mixed race children and for professionals working with this population, it is important to understand the central role families play in shaping mixed-race children's racial identity development. We have explored how individual parental factors, parents' responses to their children's physical characteristics, and the quality of the relationship between parents shape the racial socialization of their children. Clearly, parents and extended family members are not the only people who exert a socializing force in children's lives. Therefore, we turn now to focus on community factors that shape the racial socialization process.

NOTES

1. Kenneth Hardy and Tracey Laszloffy, "Deconstructing Race in Family Therapy," *Journal of Feminist Family Therapy* 5.3/4 (1994): 5–33; Cornel West, *Race Matters* (Boston, Mass.: Beacon Press, 1993).

2. See Diane Hughes, "Correlates of African American and Latino Parents' Messages to Children about Ethnicity and Race: A Comparative Study of Racial Socialization," *American Journal of Community Psychology* 31.1–2 (2003): 15–33; Michael Thornton, Linda Chatters, Robert Taylor, and Walter Allen, "Sociodemographic and Environmental Correlates of Racial Socialization by Black Parents," *Child Development* 61.2 (1990): 401–19.

3. See Debra Van Ausdale and Joe R. Feagin, *The First R: How Children Learn Race and Racism* (Lanham, Md.: Rowman & Littlefield, 2001).

4. Peggy McIntosh, "White Privilege: Unpacking the Invisible Knapsack," in *Re-Visioning Family Therapy: Race, Culture, and Gender in Clinical Practice*, ed. Monica McGoldrick (New York: Guilford Press, 1998), 147–52.

5. Ruth Frankenberg, *White Women, Race Matters: The Social Construction of Whiteness* (Minneapolis: University of Minnesota Press, 1993).

6. Amanda E. Lewis, *Race in the Schoolyard: Negotiating the Color Line in Classrooms and Communities* (New Brunswick, N.J.: Rutgers University Press, 2003).

7. Janet E. Helms, *Black and White Racial Identity: Theory, Research, and Practice* (New York: Greenwood Press, 1990).

8. Helms, *Black and White Racial Identity: Theory, Research, and Practice.*

9. William Cross, Thomas Parham, and Janet Helms, "The Stages of Black Identity Development: Nigrescence Models," in *Black Psychology*, 3rd ed., ed. Reginald L. Jones (Berkeley, Calif.: Cobb & Henry Publishers, 1991), 319–38.

10. Dana was Laszloffy's undergraduate advisee.

11. Michelle came to see Laszloffy for therapy in response to the difficulties she was having coping with her divorce.

12. Derrick is an acquaintance of Laszloffy.

13. Chris and Gina are friends of a colleague of Laszloffy.

14. Peter and Pam are clients Laszloffy worked with in therapy. Their presenting complaint was marital stress related to Pam's struggles to adjust to recently diagnosed chronic illness.

15. Christina was a student in a graduate course taught by Laszloffy.

16. Donna Nakazawa, *Does Anybody Else Look Like Me? A Parent's Guide to Raising Multiracial Children* (Cambridge, Mass.: Perseus, 2003) is an excellent resource for age-appropriate ways to talk about race with children.

17. bell hooks, *Salvation: Black People and Love,* 1st ed. (New York: William Morrow, 2001).

18. Derek's case is drawn from Pearl Gaskins, *What Are You? Voices of Mixed-Race Young People* (New York: Henry Holt, 1999), 120.

19. hooks, *Salvation: Black People and Love.*

Beyond the Family: Community Influences on Racial Identity Development

Just beyond the proverbial front door lies a broader community that plays a vital role in the socialization of mixed-race children. Schools, neighborhoods, religious organizations, and youth clubs are places where children are exposed to implicit and explicit messages about race and their racial identities. Each of these settings has a particular racial climate that can send positive or negative messages about race. An important challenge facing parents of mixed-race children is to be aware of the various ways that their children experience the broader community, monitor those settings, and intervene in situations where necessary.

While communities are made up of many different institutional contexts and social relationships, in this chapter we focus on two that are among the most salient. First, we focus on how mixed-race children are racially socialized within the educational system. Second, we consider how children's racial socialization is reinforced in their relationships with peers and friends. We also offer specific guidelines to help those working with mixed-race children identify potential problem areas. The purpose of this chapter is to make visible the often invisible forces that shape and differentiate children's experiences in institutional settings.

FACTORS THAT SHAPE RACIAL SOCIALIZATION WITHIN SCHOOLS

Schools are one of the most important socializing agents in the lives of children. Outside of families, they may be the most important. While the primary

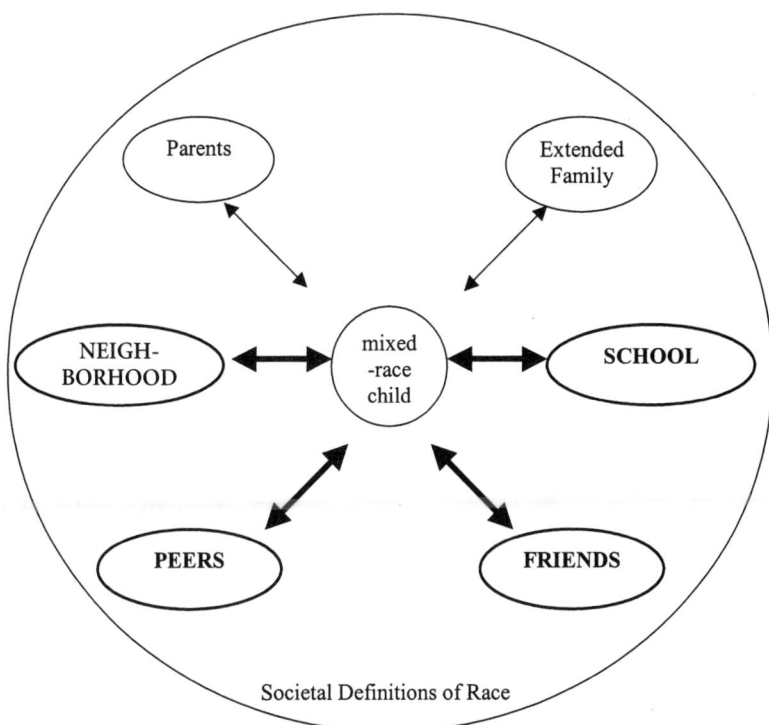

MODEL 5.1
Community Influences on Racial Identity Development

and overt function of schools is to teach academic skills and content, their secondary function is to teach children about themselves, and how to interact effectively with other people. One of the ways schools teach children how to relate is along the dimension of race. Schools, like families, convey powerful messages about race. Sometimes called the "fourth R," children learn lessons about race in their school experience that last a lifetime.[1]

In far too many instances, the racial lessons that schools convey tend to support white supremacy, white power, and white dominance in relationships. There are cases, of course, where schools make a conscious, purposeful effort to counteract this orientation and to promote racial awareness and sensitivity throughout all layers of the system. In such environments, children are actively socialized to understand and deal with racial issues in direct, honest ways that promote inclusiveness, and challenge dynamics that maintain historically based patterns of inequality.[2]

The overall racial climate in any particular school shapes the degree to which it is likely to be attentive to the unique challenges that mixed-race children face. Oftentimes, mixed-race children are likely to have an "outsider status" in schools. The nature of this "outsider status" is such that on one hand, the one-drop rule precludes them from being completely accepted by whites. On the other hand, unless mixed-race children are able to distance themselves from whiteness in terms of their appearance and identification, they may be rejected by blacks who view any affiliation with their whiteness as an expressly antiblack sentiment. Therefore, mixed-race children may be faced with the dilemma of having to reject one part of themselves or modify their behavior, identification, and self-presentation to gain acceptance. Those who have a blended identity are at risk of isolation and rejection from both blacks and whites. Whether or not school systems recognize these potential social difficulties and work to promote a racially inclusive climate for all children greatly affects how mixed-race children are racially socialized within their school environment. We focus now on three components of the racial climate within schools and how they influence mixed-race children's racial socialization. These factors include: 1) the racial composition of the school, 2) the racial awareness and sensitivity of a school's leadership, and 3) teachers' attitudes and behaviors.

The Racial Composition of the School

The experiences that mixed-race children have in schools are largely mediated by the racial composition of the student body, faculty, and staff. In schools where the student body is mostly white, faculty and staff are likely to be predominately white as well. As is often the case in mostly white institutional settings, issues of race are rarely considered, poorly understood, and infrequently addressed.[3] Any focus on race is generally limited to a specific incident involving a student, or perhaps a teacher of color. In schools where the student body is either racially diverse or predominantly black, the faculty and staff composition most often reflects the students'.[4] In such schools, teachers are more likely to be aware of race, although they are not necessarily more sensitive.

The point here is very simple. When children exist within a largely homogenous environment, they become oriented toward the group of people with whom they interact regularly. In other words, they become comfortable among those who they see and interact with daily. Whether it is a white child in a black environment or a black child in a white environment, children adapt to their surroundings.

Researchers have found that the racial composition of children's social networks influences racial identification.[5] Children who grow up in predominantly black environments are more likely to identify as black, while those who grow up in predominantly white environments are more likely to identify as biracial. Because this "choice" exists, their environments tend to be even more important because something as simple as the racial composition of their school can have a profound impact on whether they come to identify more with whiteness or blackness, or some combination of the two.

Racial Awareness and Sensitivity of Schools' Leadership

Racial awareness can be defined as "the ability to recognize that race exists and that it shapes reality in inequitable and unjust ways. . . . Concomitant with the onset of racial awareness is the ability to distinguish between one's beliefs about how things should be, versus the ways things really are in the present."[6] Those who possess racial awareness have a cognitive understanding of how race structures differential access to opportunities, and they have insight into the ways in which perceptions of reality differ depending on one's racial identity. While it is possible to have racial awareness without racial sensitivity, the reverse is not true. Those who are racially sensitive can translate their awareness into action because they possess the capacity to anticipate how others may think and feel, and adjust their behavior accordingly.

Within schools, there is a direct link between the degree of racial awareness and sensitivity of a school's leadership team and the overall climate. Irrespective of the race of a school's principal, those who are in positions of power set the tone for how the system at large understands and responds to race relations and racial inequalities. Since the best way to demonstrate this point is through examples, we offer two cases for illustration.

Principal Maclin

Diana Maclin is a white principal at an elementary school where 35 percent of the student body is African American, 60 percent is white, and the majority of teachers are white.[7] Principal Maclin has a well-developed knowledge of the history of racial injustice within the United States as well as the contemporary realities of race and racism within America. Although she grew up in a white family and within a predominantly white community, she attended a university with a large population of students of color. During that time, she had numerous personal and academic experiences that heightened her racial sensitivity by exposing her to racial inequalities. She became convinced that education played the most important and potentially transformative role in addressing this social problem. Her conviction led her to become an educator, and later a school administrator with the goal of using her power to challenge racial inequalities. Principal Maclin created an environment that acknowledges the ways that schools unconsciously reproduce racial inequalities (via tracking and differential expectations) and proactively worked to dismantle those policies and procedures.

In her eleven-year tenure as the principal of an elementary school, Principal Maclin has remained committed to the goal she developed in college. She remains aware of, and sensitive to, the subtle ways that teachers can inadvertently designate students of color for more severe disciplinary action, and she takes steps to challenge her teachers to resist falling into this trap. She routinely invites outside consultants to examine the schools' racial climate and recommend how she and the teachers can enhance their racial sensitivity. She organizes annual open dialogues with her faculty and between the faculty and parents. She actively recruits and works to retain minority faculty, and seeks to make the overall school more supportive of students and faculty of color. She also encourages her faculty to address race in their classrooms, both in the curriculum and in student relations.

Because of Principal Maclin's programs, students and faculty regularly discuss racial issues in an open and direct manner. A spirit of active engagement exists within the school around identifying and responding to racial inequalities. Everyone doesn't always agree, discussions can get heated, and all parties are not always satisfied. However, black and white students thrive academically and socially in her school. In other words, Principal Maclin has a high degree of racial awareness and sensitivity that promote candor about issues of race and a spirit of inclusiveness for all students.

Principal Jackson

Ralph Jackson is an African American principal of an elementary school where 20 percent of the students are black, 80 percent are white, and most faculty members are white.[8] Principal Jackson grew up in a black family who resided within an otherwise all white community. Outside of his own family, he has had limited contact with other black people, and in fact tends to be uncomfortable around other blacks. During his childhood, Jackson often heard his parents make derogatory comments about black people, suggesting that most were not successful because they lacked personal motivation and discipline. He learned to think of his own family as "exceptional" because they were committed to hard work and success. Principal Jackson does not believe that racism exists in contemporary U.S. society, but that it is largely an excuse that blacks (and other people of color) use to distract from their personal failures. He cites his own family's success story as proof that minorities are capable of achieving as long as they are willing to work hard.

In his role as an elementary school principal, Jackson believes that all children, irrespective of race, have an equal opportunity for success. Therefore, he believes that a color-blind approach to education works best and that discussion about race should be minimized so as to not stigmatize black students. When black parents complain about potentially discriminatory behavior against their children, Principal Jackson becomes irritated and dismisses such allegations as unfounded. Moreover, he views the fact that black students are disproportionately sent to see him for disciplinary action and have lower rates of academic achievement (compared to white students) as evidence of the failure of black students and their families, and not of structural inequalities within the school. Hence, Principal Jackson's lack of racial awareness and sensitivity shapes the overall school climate by discouraging open conversation about race, overlooking racial inequalities, and failing to foster an environment of racial inclusiveness.

In the two examples presented here, the racial ideology and level of racial awareness and sensitivity of Principals Maclin and Jackson set the tone for their school's racial climate. Each principal's awareness and sensitivity greatly influence the degree to which racial issues are openly acknowledged and discussed within the school, the level of understanding teachers and staff have about racism, and the extent to which the school fosters a climate that actively challenges racial inequalities and promotes racial inclusiveness. It is not hard to imagine that the experiences of mixed-race children would vary in schools with principals who possess such dissimilar levels of racial awareness and sensitivity.

Teachers' Attitudes and Behaviors

Teachers are as potent a socializing force within schools as parents are within families. As a result teachers' attitudes and behaviors have a profound impact on the classroom environment they establish and how they racially socialize all students, especially mixed-race students. Most teachers have good intentions where their students are concerned. They become teachers because they care about children and want to make positive contributions to their lives. Yet, once race is factored in, even the best intentions are sometimes derailed by subtle attitudes and behaviors rooted in unconscious biases. For example, teachers who accept the one-drop rule are likely to assume that mixed-race children of ambiguous appearance are black. This may contradict how a child understands herself and/or the identity that parents have encouraged in the home. Teachers may also harbor unconscious racism that leads them to privilege lighter-skinned students while overlooking, underestimating, or punishing darker-skinned students. Researchers have demonstrated that teachers are more likely to favor white and light-skinned children. Several studies have documented that early in the school year, both black and white teachers have a tendency to "ability group" children in their classes using criteria unrelated to ability. In one study, children who are light-skinned or white-appearing end up in the high ability groups, had the highest expectations placed on them, and, therefore, learned the most by the end of the year.[9]

Teachers' attitudes and behaviors toward mixed-race children are mitigated by their physical appearance and racial self-presentation (i.e., their racial identity, clothing choice, affective expression style, and language usage). Mixed-race children's physical traits may range from appearing white, to ambiguous, to black.[10] These appearances, coupled with children's behaviors and how they present themselves racially, interact with the attitudes, beliefs, and biases that teachers bring to the classroom and may result in differential treatment.

For example, a child whose appearance is ambiguous but possibly white, and presents himself as white, will engender different reactions from a teacher depending on that teacher's particular set of attitudes, beliefs, and biases. In general, a white teacher is more likely to accept and even prefer a mixed-race child fitting this description. In the case of black teachers, again, it depends on the teacher's particular attitudes, beliefs, and biases. A black teacher who is closely identified with whiteness may relate favorably to this child, while a black teacher who is closely identified with blackness may perceive this child as rejecting blackness and may feel some mild irritation or even hostility toward him.

In cases where teachers favor a child's appearance and racial presentation, they are more likely to respond positively to the child, and thereby reinforce the child's racial identification and behaviors. Conversely, teachers who feel uncomfortable with a child's appearance and racial presentation are more likely to respond negatively. This can challenge and undermine a child's racial identification and self-understanding. Hence, a complex interaction occurs between mixed-race childrens' physical appearance, their behavior (which includes how they present themselves racially), and teachers' particular attitudes, beliefs, biases, and responsive behaviors. The interplay of these factors plays a powerful role in the racial socialization process mixed-race children encounter in schools.

How children behave in school, including how they present themselves racially, reflects the nature of the racial socialization they receive at home in their families. Conflicts may arise in cases where the messages about racial identity are different at home than at school. Here is where the child's agency becomes significant. For example, consider a mixed-race child who has been socialized at home to think of herself as black and who therefore presents this way in school. Problems can arise if she attends a predominately white school where there is pressure for her to modify her behavior. How she responds to such pressure will depend on the types of punishments and rewards she perceives in each context for any given behavior. She may adjust her behavior at home and at school to satisfy the demands of each context, or she may assert whatever identity feels most genuine, even if it means defying pressures within school (or possibly home) to act a certain way.[11] However the child adapts, her behavior will influence how others, including teachers, respond to her.

Teachers' attitudes and behaviors about race can either contribute to or undermine healthy racial socialization. Therefore, teachers need to be mindful of how their attitudes and behaviors, especially those that are subtle, may influence how they relate to their mixed-race students. When asking teachers to consider how their attitudes guide their behavior toward mixed-race students, we often hear, "I treat all my students the same way. I don't see color. Race does not influence what I do." While claims of "color-blindness" are almost always well intentioned, they are too often misguided. As discussed in chapter 3, it is impossible to not see race. Not only do all sighted people literally see variations in skin color, we have all learned to attach meanings to physical differences and categorize people by these differences. We make personal choices every day that are driven by our awareness of race, including choices about friends, dating and marital partners, where to live, where to eat, what to do for fun, and even where to sit on public transportation, in restaurants, and at the movies.

When people claim to not see color, what they are really saying is that they do not consciously discriminate on the basis of color. While they literally see race, they want others to know that they treat everyone the same in spite of race, which is a noble and admirable objective. Unfortunately, claims of color-blindness confuse admitting that we see race with whether or not we discriminate on the basis of race. These are two separate issues. It's possible to admit to seeing and being influenced by race without this translating into treating people unequally because of it. In fact, those who can own up to seeing race are less likely to discriminate because their openness and honesty about the subject act as a buffer against the type of covert, unintentional racism many people commit.

Teachers whose attitudes and behaviors encourage healthy racial socialization for their mixed-race students are the most likely to avoid claims of color-blindness. Instead, they are able to openly consider issues of race, possess high levels of racial self-awareness, and are comfortable interacting with racially diverse people. Conversely, the lower teachers' racial awareness is, the less likely they are to promote healthy racial socialization among their mixed-race students.

SCHOOL-FOCUSED STRATEGIES FOR PARENTS

Parents have a responsibility to monitor their children's experiences in school and to intervene in situations where their children may be struggling. There are several dynamics that may make it difficult for parents to assume this role. Depending on the type of experience parents had in school when they were children, they may find walking through the front doors of their child's school or calling the teacher on the phone to be intimidating prospects. Also, in situations where parents' are not in the majority in terms of the overall racial composition of the school, or are a different race than their child's teachers, they may struggle to address racial issues with school personnel. For example, a black parent may feel uncomfortable approaching her son's white teacher about incidents she believes reflect racial insensitivity. She may expect the teacher to be defensive and dismiss her concerns, and if the school administration is mostly white, this may reinforce her fear that she will not be heard. She may also worry that if she offends or angers the teacher, he may retaliate against her child.

Nonetheless, whatever qualms parents may have, it is their responsibility to advocate on their children's behalf. Parents of mixed-race children must be prepared to intervene in school situations where their children's healthy identity development may be compromised. To assist parents in assessing and, where necessary, intervening with teachers and schools around racial issues, we present the following strategies.

Normalizing Talks with Children

Having regular conversations with children about their day at school provides parents with a window into possible areas of concerns their children may be facing in school. While most conversations will not reveal problem areas, having regular discussions will normalize the open dialogue. If problems do arise, the mechanism is already in place for parents to converse directly with their children.

It is also helpful if parents routinely raise racial issues for discussion as another way of creating a net to catch information that might reveal concerns that need to be addressed within school. Parents who invite candid discussions about race as a normal part of everyday conversation will make it easier for their children to share racially based questions, concerns, or issues they may be experiencing in school.

Sometimes with the best of intentions, parents keep silent around issues of race, not realizing that their silence communicates a message in and of itself. Silence about racial issues communicates that they are nonexistent or illegitimate topics for conversation. Maria Root argues that avoiding discussion about racial identity confuses children.[12] Mixed-race adults, when reflecting back on their childhood, often tell us that their family "never talked about race." When asked how they interpreted that silence, they most frequently assumed that racial issues (like sex or money) should not be discussed openly. As a result, they felt uncomfortable sharing racial incidents or problems with their parents and kept those concerns locked up inside. Even more directly, Marion Kilson characterizes the mixed-race experience as replete with "silent struggles." She describes the problem of silence in the following way:

> Many [respondents] never discussed their feelings about race with anyone as they were growing up; some did not know how their own racial experience differed from their siblings' encounters, because they had never discussed such issues together; others were silent about racial identity issues in adolescence, whereas they had discussed them with their parent earlier in childhood or with friends and parents in adulthood. Some have grappled with their families' denial of their racial identity.[13]

When parents encourage open, regular conversation about race at home, it provides children with a vocabulary, conversational skills, and a general comfort in addressing a complex, often difficult-to-discuss topic. Normalizing discussion is especially valuable for mixed-race children who, by virtue of their marginal racial status, may be faced with situations in school (and beyond) where they will need to be able to address racial matters with skill, ease, and clarity. Having had the opportunity to practice discussing these matters at home provides necessary preparation for being able to handle such conversations competently, both in school and in other venues. By inviting children to openly discuss race and the myriad of complex issues surrounding this topic, parents of mixed-race children can provide critical tools that will likely assist them in addressing racial issues outside of the home.

Establishing Relationships with Teachers before Problems Arise

One way to reduce the anxiety that might accompany having to confront a teacher about race-related concerns is to establish a positive relationship with the teacher early in the school year. Parents will have the greatest position of strength if they introduce themselves to teachers without having a problem define their first encounter. Then, in the event a problem or concern arises, they already have an established foundation to build on.

Vanessa Williams, a single black mother of a seven-year-old mixed-race son named Jason, made a point to go to his school prior to the first day and introduce herself to his new teacher.[14] Vanessa believed getting to know her son's teacher, Mrs. Stanowski, would help Jason make the transition from his old school to the new school. She approached Mrs. Stanowski in a friendly and engaging manner, and made a point to stress that she wanted Jason to have a positive experience in his new school, and hoped his new teacher

taking. Friends can pressure children, directly or indirectly, into violating their own ethical standards and even engaging in illegal behavior. In cases of unhealthy friendships, they can lead children to question aspects of their reality to the point that they grow insecure and afraid, and adopt ways of being that ultimately may sabotage their psychological health.

Both peers and friends play an influential role in children's racial socialization. We encourage caregivers to examine how the racial composition of friendship groups, the racial messages conveyed by peers and friends, and underlying racial tensions between friends may affect racial identity development.

The Racial Composition of Friendship Groups

The racial composition of children's friendship groups substantially influences children's racial socialization and racial identity development.[15] Moreover, the interaction between the degree of control children have over the racial composition of their friends and the choices they make suggests a great deal about how they see themselves racially and what they believe about race. Where children exist within racially homogeneous environments, they have limited choice over who they select as friends. However, when mixed-race children are embedded in diverse environments where there are children of all races, their choice of friends indicates who they most identify with and are using as a reference group. Ideally, all children, and mixed-race children in particular, would have access to a racially diverse group of peers. A diverse peer group allows greater opportunity to develop a multifaceted view of race and expands children's options in terms of their own racial identity.

Friendships are important because children's racial orientations tend to match their friends' with whom they have the highest regard. Mike, a fifteen-year-old boy whose mother was white and father was black, grew up in a predominantly white community and attended predominantly white schools.[16] Within this social network, his friendship choices were limited to mostly white children. His closest friend in school was a white boy named Paul, but he was also very close with his older sister's boyfriend, Kaleel, an eighteen-year-old African American man. Mike and Kaleel spent many hours together playing video games, listening to music, and watching sports on television. Through Mike's friendship with Paul, and with his peers at school, he was oriented toward whiteness. However, through his friendship with Kaleel, Mike began to accept and value his blackness. Because Mike looked up to Kaleel and aspired to be like him, this friendship encouraged him to more strongly embrace his blackness. Mike found a way to remain comfortable with Paul and with his own whiteness while simultaneously valuing blackness. However, he needed the relationship with Kaleel to balance the overwhelmingly white orientation of his environment.

Racial Messages Conveyed by Peers and Friends

The messages mixed-race children receive from peers and friends about race in general, and their racial identities in particular, shape their sense of who they are and where they fit in the world. If peers and friends understand a child's racial identity in one way and affirm it, the child is likely to embrace this view of self and build on it. Conversely, if peers and friends reject or criticize a child's racial identity, the child is more likely to reject or modify this self-definition and strive to develop an identity that will garner greater social approval.

To illustrate the effect that the messages conveyed by peers can have, consider Tasha, a mixed-race woman of ambiguous physical appearance.[17] Though she is now a grown woman, Tasha recalls a painful incident that occurred when she was eleven. Tasha attended a public school that was about 30 percent black and 70 percent white. One day, she accidentally backed into a black girl who was standing behind her in the lunch line. The girl, who Tasha had never seen before, snapped at her, "Watch where you're going white girl." To this Tasha replied, "I'm not white, I'm biracial." The girl rolled her eyes and said, "Oh yeah, you could have fooled me. Maybe you should look again." At that point, several of the people in line (all of whom were black) laughed.

For Tasha, this experience was traumatic. She felt that the black girl who made the comment and the others who laughed had collectively invalidated her blackness and she felt humiliated by the encounter. She concluded that she was "too white" in terms of how she appeared to others and needed to work harder at representing her blackness, especially while around black people. As a result, she began to make a conscious effort to more overtly assert her blackness in an effort to thwart black people from questioning her. As an adult, this incident remained deeply embedded in her psyche, providing an example of how treatment by peers, even those who are not friends, can play a powerful role in the racial socialization process.

While peers' responses to mixed-race children are influential, those conveyed by friends are even more potent. Joanne, a mixed-race woman who appears white, had three friends she was extremely close with while growing up, all of whom were white.[18] As an adult, Joanne does not recall race ever being addressed directly, except for one time when she was ten years old. On this occasion, one of the girls made a derogatory racial joke about a black girl in the lunchroom and the other girls laughed. Joanne immediately felt uncomfortable, and while she laughed to distract from her discomfort, she realized that this incident revealed two things. First, that her friends saw her as white. Second, that they held negative views toward blacks. The feeling it aroused in her was not anger, but fear that if they ever saw her as black, they would reject her. Joanne concluded that she needed to be as distant as possible from her blackness if she were to be accepted by her friends.

The physical appearance of mixed-race children plays a pivotal role in how peers and friends view and respond to them. For example, Darryl is a thirteen-year-old mixed-race boy who appears black.[19] Throughout his life, he had racially mixed groups of friends, although most people saw him as black. In an interview, Darryl explained that while most people assume he is black, he prefers to think of himself as biracial. He said, "My mother is white and my father is black, so I'm both black and white. I'm biracial even though people think I'm just black." When questioned further about his racial identification, Darryl went on to say: "If I don't acknowledge both my black and my white sides, it's like I'm not acknowledging both of my parents, and that's not right. But it is hard 'cause, like I said, most people assume I am just black, even my friends act that way when they know better."

While Darryl wants to blend both his blackness and whiteness, over time, the way he is perceived by his friends may lead him to emphasize his blackness more intensely, and to eventually suppress or even abandon his desire to have a more balanced racial self-identification. This is what happened to Darryl's sister, Alicia. "My sister also looks black. When she was growing up, she always insisted that she was biracial, but when she got to high school, that changed. In high school, she just started saying she was black. Her friends all treated her that way and she said it was just easier to go along with that." Darryl and Alicia illustrate how their friends' reactions to their physical appearance affects the way they identify. Peers and friends have the power to accept or reject their racial identities. In this way, they can either reinforce or undermine the racial socialization children receive at home.

Racially Based Tensions within Friendships

Even among good friends, it is not uncommon for tensions to develop that have racial undertones. We live in a society that organizes people hierarchically by race. Since there is no vaccine to protect any of us against internalizing this hierarchy and the associated messages that overvalue whiteness and devalue blackness, each of us, to some degree, carries these notions within us. As a result, the messages that affirm lightness and degrade darkness often infiltrate relationships, even very close friendships, creating an assortment of interpersonal strains.

Ben, who is mixed-race, has an ambiguous appearance with a light complexion, green eyes, and wavy hair. His best friend, Lamar, who is African American, is dark-skinned with brown eyes and tightly curled black hair.[20] Both boys are fourteen and have been friends since they were nine. While they get along well, there has always been an unacknowledged tension under the surface of their relationship. As Ben stated, "Sometimes Lamar gets moody and edgy and it's hard to be around him when he's like that, but overall, we get along great."

Lamar explained the same tension in the following way: "Ben is my friend and we go way back, but sometimes it makes me mad the way people treat him better because he's lighter. Girls are always asking me about my cute friend, the one with the good hair and pretty green eyes. That does make me mad, but I know it's not his fault."

Both boys were aware of the tension that their different appearances generate, but they never speak about it directly. As Lamar said, "It's not really Ben's fault, so what's the point of saying anything? It would just make things harder. But it does get to me inside." And according to Ben, "I know he feels bad because he's darker than me, and people tend to like lighter more than darker. I feel guilty about that. But we try not to let it get in the way because we can't do anything about it, but it's always there."

Lamar and Ben's comments reveal how racial dynamics can infiltrate close relationships and create underlying strains, even between longtime friends. In this case, both boys are aware of the unspoken conflict and the basis for it, yet they don't discuss it with each other for fear that it might exacerbate the problem. The tension Ben and Lamar experience is related to how others extend preferential treatment toward Ben because of his light skin. This makes Ben feel guilty and Lamar angry and resentful. In some cases, the tension within a friendship reflects racially biased views and values that are held by the friends themselves. For example, Kelly and Resha, who are each fifteen, have been friends for three years.[21] While they describe their relationship as close, there is an underlying racial tension that stems from their unexamined color complex.

Kelly is mixed-race but appears black, while Resha is black but light-skinned and appears racially mixed. Because of their appearances, Resha often receives better treatment from others than Kelly, but this is not the major source of the strain between them. According to Kelly, "She pisses me off sometimes because she thinks she is better than me 'cause she's lighter. Just sometimes I hate how she acts so cute." According to Resha, "I know it bothers Kelly that I'm light and I have nice hair and pretty eyes." Interestingly, Resha's reference to "nice" hair, "light" skin, and "pretty" eyes reveal an underlying belief that light skin, green eyes, and curly hair are more attractive than dark skin, brown eyes, and kinky hair. In other words, Kelly was not imagining that Resha believes she is prettier. Some of the tension in their relationship reflects their shared views about the relative worth of lightness and darkness, views that are learned over time and reflect racist beauty standards. As Kelly acknowledged, "I guess I kinda feel like Resha thinks she's better than me 'cause she's lighter and that makes me feel bad about myself. I wish I weren't so dark. I know that's bad to say, but it's true." Underlying racial tensions in friendships both reflect and reproduce broader societal messages about race but, more importantly, they influence how children learn to think and feel about themselves.

STRATEGIES FOR MANAGING CHILDREN'S RELATIONSHIPS WITH FRIENDS AND PEERS

Parents are the front line when it comes to monitoring, and when necessary, intervening in children's relationships with friends and peers. This is a huge responsibility. When race is factored in, the task becomes even more challenging. To assist parents in this area, we present several strategies that they can employ to enhance the positive effects and minimize the negative effects that friendships can have on children's racial identity development.

Conduct a Racial Assessment of Children's Friendships

Before parents can decide whether to intervene in their children's friendships, they must assess the quality of these friendships and the possible role that racial issues play in shaping them. Below is a list of several questions parents can ask themselves to begin the process of evaluating their children's friendships and the role race may play.

- Does your child seek out relationships with a racially diverse group of friends?
- How much open dialogue occurs between your child and her/his friends about race? What is the overall theme and tone of the dialogue? If no such dialogue occurs, why?
- How dependent does your child seem to be on receiving approval or validation from her/his friends? How might matters of race be related to this?
- Do your child's friendships (either overtly or covertly) discourage them from acknowledging and expressing any parts of their racial identity?
- Are you aware of any tensions in your children's friendships that may be racially based? If yes, how are these tensions handled?
- Have you noticed sudden shifts in your child's moods and behaviors that may indicate some underlying distress (e.g., becoming unusually sullen, quiet, withdrawn, angry, moody, irritable, and/or distracted, a drop in grades, marked changes in daily routines and/or personal care activities, a sudden, noticeable decrease or increase in interactions with friends)? If yes, what types of factors might explain the changes? Could racial issues be related to this at all?
- Do the parents of your child's friends make racist or racially insensitive comments, expressing racially biased attitudes? Do they behave in racially biased ways?

The purpose of the assessment questions is to encourage parents and caregivers to think about children's friendships through a critical lens. These questions should help in formulating an overall picture of how race may shape children's friendships. If parents identify potential sources of strain, distress, or insecurity for their children related to issues of race and their relationships with their friends, they should devise constructive ways of intervening. While we cannot offer a cookbook approach for handling the myriad of potential situations caregivers might need to address, we offer several general strategies that can be used to guide such interventions.

Talking Directly with Children

Sometimes a direct approach is the best approach. In other words, if parents are concerned about racial issues between children and their friends, simply talking directly with their children about their concerns may be all that is required. Talking directly means identifying the issue in a straightforward and clear way. It is important to not confuse directness with harshness. While it is useful to speak honestly and openly, it also is important to express one's views with gentleness and sensitivity to minimize the potential for arousing defensiveness, shame, or anxiety. Because children's friendships can be delicate, we recommend several tips to guide parents in approaching such conversations.

Be Curious

Rather than assuming to know what's going on in children's lives with their friends, it's helpful to be curious and invite children to share their experiences and perceptions of their friendships. While they may sometimes need assistance verbalizing certain ideas or feelings, at least initially, we recommend that parents create space for them to express how they view their relationships with others.

James Bedford is an African American father of ten-year-old Wesley, who is a mixed-race child of ambiguous appearance.[22] He noticed that Wesley hid his violin under his bed whenever his best friend, Jamar (who is African American), came over. Mr. Bedford suspected this was tied to discomfort Wesley had about playing the violin and feared rejection from his black friend. More specifically, he wondered if any part of this had racial overtones for Wesley. He recalled that his son once asked him not to play any classical music on the radio when Jamar was over, and yet he had never made that request when his white friend Rob visited their home. Mr. Bedford decided it was necessary to have some "straight talk" with Wesley. He started the conversation in a way that affirmed Wesley, rather than in a way that was critical:

> I've noticed that whenever Jamar comes over, you hide your violin under the bed. Now that I think of it, I don't recall you ever telling him you play the violin. And I know that you don't want me to play classical music when Jamar is

over, but you never asked me not to play it when Rob's over. So I am just won-
dering if you could talk with me about this and help me understand what you
might be worried about?

Mr. Bedford, while being direct with Wesley, did not assume to know the
reason behind the behavior he had observed. Instead, he expressed curiosity
and asked Wesley to help him understand. By creating this space, Wesley had
the freedom to say for himself what the issue was. He told his father, "Jamar
wouldn't think it's too cool that I play the violin. Classical music is more of a
white thing."

Offer Balanced Feedback

Once parents have some idea of what the issues are, it is important to provide balanced feedback. In other words, their feedback should emphasize both
the advantages and disadvantages of their children's position. Mr. Bedford, to
his credit, did so effectively when he responded to Wesley by saying:

> One of the things I really like about what you are saying is that you're telling me
> it's important to you that you get along with black people. That's a good thing.
> At the same time, it's also important to you to be true to yourself, so if you think
> someone won't like something about you, that's their problem, not yours. As for
> classical music, I guess there are some black people who don't care for it, but
> that's true of some white people too.

Mr. Bedford's comment reflected balanced feedback because he both affirmed
and challenged his son's position in a nonreactive way.

Recognizing Roots of Underlying Reticence

In some cases, children will not respond when parents try to talk with them
directly. They may shut down and remain silent or give evasive responses designed to avoid dealing with the issues their parents are trying to discuss. It is
useful for parents to try to understand what may be contributing to their children's evasiveness and distance. Perhaps a child fears a certain response from
a parent. In such situations, the parent must be careful not to exhibit the behavior the child fears (e.g., yelling or becoming agitated). It is incumbent on
parents to be sensitive to the role they play in their children's reluctance to
speak. At the same time, it is important for parents to be persistent and not get

discouraged. Persistence, especially a gentle form of nonaggressive persistence, is essential to encouraging children to open up and talk.

Talking to the Parents of Children's Friends

At times, it may be necessary for parents to intervene by contacting the parents of their children's friends. If they have reason to believe a friend's attitudes or behaviors are harmful in some way, or if they become aware of ways in which another child's parents have said or done something worrisome, intervention may be required. As we have suggested elsewhere, the best way to approach such an interaction is in a nonblaming way by using "I" sentences and avoiding accusations. This strategy makes it possible to address potentially volatile issues in civil ways, which may lead to positive resolution.

Carly Cavello is a white woman who had been divorced six years from her husband, Ronald, who was black.[23] They had three daughters who all lived with Carly. One afternoon, Carly overheard her daughter, Jessica, talking with her white friend Lisa. She became concerned when Lisa stated, "My mom wouldn't want me to come over here if she knew your father was black. It's a good thing he doesn't live with you." Carly knew she needed to talk to Jessica about this, but she also decided she needed to talk with Lisa's mother as well.

Carly approached her conversation with Lisa's mother, Eileen Simon, by sharing what she had heard and waiting for Eileen to respond. It was significant to her that Eileen did not deny that this was, in fact, her position. Instead, she said, "I think Jessica is a wonderful girl and I don't mind her visiting your home." Carly responded by saying, "I appreciate this, and I also think Lisa is a wonderful girl. It is important to me, however, to find out what your views are about interracial relationships. Even though Jessica's father and I are divorced, it has nothing to do with race. And I try to teach my kids to not use race as a gauge for evaluating people, especially since they are both black and white. These issues are important to me and since Jessica and Lisa spend so much time together, it's important to me to know what your views are as well."

Carly's statement began with an affirmation of Eileen's daughter. From there, she used "I" messages to assert her views and explain what was important to her. She followed by seeking information from Eileen. At no point did Carly accuse Eileen. She left her complete latitude to define her position on the topic of interracial relationships without assuming to know it. In other words, Carly took responsibility for her position and left Eileen room for her position, whatever it was. When approached in this manner, even the most difficult conversations have a greater likelihood of progressing constructively.

Eileen revealed that she did not approve of interracial relationships, and she would not want her daughter to ever be in one. At that point, Carly had to decide if she wanted Jessica to remain friends with Lisa, given her mother's views. While she could have decided to disrupt the friendship, she concluded that Jessica needed to learn to deal with people who harbored these views. She did not discourage the friendship, but she did speak directly with Jessica about the views Eileen held and what she was teaching Lisa. She also used the situation to talk with Jessica about how to handle similar situations in the future when she was confronted with another's racism.

Exposing Children to Racially Diverse Peers

Ideally, children should have the opportunity to interact with children of varied racial backgrounds. This creates the greatest sense of openness and the richest opportunities for learning about matters of race and who they are in relation to others. While children who attend racially homogeneous schools are limited in terms of who they can develop friendships with at school, children can gain exposure to more diverse peer groups through other venues. If children attend a racially homogenous school, we encourage parents to be proactive about exposing them to environments where they will be able to interact with a racially diverse group of peers. Community centers, summer camps, dance classes, theater groups, sports, or youth clubs can create opportunities for children to meet and develop friendships with children of different races.

We frequently encounter parents who are raising mixed-race children in entirely white communities where they have no regular contact with black people (aside from their black parent). These thoughtful and considerate parents want to know why their children are uncomfortable around black people, a situation that is especially problematic for black parents. Seeing their own children shy away from black children in diverse settings or expressing dislike for black children is often a wake-up call that some aspect of the child's social network needs attention. It should not come as a surprise that children feel uncomfortable around people with whom they have limited contact. Assuming that their children will fit in with and feel comfortable around other black children by virtue of their skin color ignores the most basic elements of childhood socialization: Children feel comfortable around people with whom they have regular positive contact.

Similarly, we hear parents express shock that their children are inarticulate around racial issues, especially in their responses to the "what are you" question. Another variation of this concern is that parents didn't realize that their children had "issues" about their racial identity until they were adults and finally felt comfortable discussing it with them. When we ask how often these parents discussed race in the home, they respond that it just never came up. The fact is that what seems very simple and straightforward—talking about race in an interracial family—often does not occur. The silence effectively communicates that race is not a legitimate topic for discussion. Regrettably, the failure to normalize conversation about race has consequences that may not be realized until much later in a child's development.

We encourage caregivers and those who work with biracial children to be purposive about their racial socialization and fearless about discussing race, the single most important factor that organizes their child's life experience. Beyond families, the experiences mixed-race children have in their broader communities shape how they understand race relations and their own racial identity. While we have focused on two dimensions of community in this chapter (schools and relationships with peers and friends), the use of a critical lens to view institutional policies and relationships can be expanded to any other community institution. By offering specific strategies parents and social service providers can use to support healthy racial socialization of mixed-race children within schools and the context of their peer and friend relationships, we hope to raise consciousness around the fact that there are many socializing forces in children's lives that send varied and potentially contradictory messages about race. The clearer parents are about community influences on their children's racial identity development, the better they can help their children process those mixed messages.

NOTES

1. Amanda Lewis, *Race in the Schoolyard: Negotiating the Color Line in Classrooms and Communities* (New Brunswick, N.J.: Rutgers University Press, 2003).

2. David P. Levine, *Rethinking Schools: An Agenda for Change* (New York: New Press, 1995).

3. Alice McIntyre, *Making Meaning of Whiteness: Exploring Racial Identity with White Teachers* (Albany: State University of New York Press, 1997).

4. Kofi Lomotey, *Going to School: The African American Experience*, (Albany: State University of New York Press, 1990).

5. Kerry Ann Rockquemore and David L. Brunsma, "Socially Embedded Identities: Theories, Typologies, and Processes of Racial Identity among Biracials," *Sociological Quarterly* 43.3 (2002): 335–56.

6. Tracey Laszloffy and Kenneth Hardy, "Uncommon Strategies for a Common Problem: Addressing Racism in Family Therapy," *Family Processes* 39.1 (2000): 35–50.

7. Diana Maclin was the principal of an elementary school located in a midsize Northeastern city. Laszloffy met Maclin during a regional school administrator's conference where she was presenting a racial sensitivity training seminar.

8. Ralph Jackson was a principal of an elementary school located in the same region as Diana Maclin. He also attended the racial sensitivity training seminar at the school administrator's conference.

9. Ray Rist, "Student Social Class and Teacher Expectations: The Self-Fulfilling Prophecy in Ghetto Education, " *Harvard Educational Review* 40.3 (1970): 411–51.

10. David Brunsma and Kerry Ann Rockquemore, "The New Color Complex: Appearances and Biracial Identity," *Identity* 1.3 (2001): 225–46.

11. Note that we see some evidence of this phenomenon in nationally representative data sets, such as the Adolescent Health data set, where some mixed-race children reported one racial identity at school and a different racial identity at home. See David R. Harris and Jeremiah Joseph Sim, "Who Is Multiracial? Assessing the Complexity of Lived Race," *American Sociological Review* 67.4 (2002), 614–27.

12. Maria Root, *Love's Revolution: Interracial Marriage* (Philadelphia, Pa.: Temple University Press, 2001).

13. Marion Kilson, *Claiming Place: Biracial Young Adults of the Post–Civil Rights Era* (Westport, Conn.: Bergin & Garvey, 2001), 76.

14. Vanessa Williams and Mrs. Stanowski participated in the research conducted for Laszloffy's dissertation. See Tracey Laszloffy, "An Exploratory Study of Family Therapists Working as Consultants to Address the Interaction between Race and Education in an Elementary School," Doctoral dissertation, Syracuse University, 1997.

15. Melissa Herman, "Forced to Choose: Some Determinants of Racial Identification in Multi-Racial Adolescents." *Child Development* 75.3 (2004): 730–48.

16. Mike is the son of an acquaintance of Laszloffy.

17. Tasha was a member of a students' of color focus group that Laszloffy led at a university located in the Northeast.

18. Joanne was a student in a graduate course Laszloffy taught that focused in multicultural issues in therapy.

19. Darryl was Laszloffy's client who attended family therapy sessions on the recommendation of his school social worker who was concerned about problem behaviors he had been exhibiting in school.

20. Ben and Lamar were panelists at a diversity workshop held as part of a residence life training day at a midsize university located in the Northeast.

21. Kelly is the daughter of an acquaintance of Laszloffy's and Resha is her close friend.

22. James Bedford was a participant in the research conducted for Tracey Laszloffy, "An Exploratory Study of Family Therapists."

23. Carly Cavello participated in the research conducted for Tracey Laszloffy, "An Exploratory Study of Family Therapists."

6

More Than Skin Deep: Appearances and Mixed-Race Identity

Our systemic model of racial identity development suggests that in addition to the structural and relational factors that influence children, their physical appearance is an important determinant of racial identification. Thus far, we have outlined the primary structural factors (societal definitions of racial categorization) and relational factors (family socialization and community relations). In this chapter, we approach the much more delicate issue of how children's physical appearance shapes their racial identity development.

It is critically important to consider phenotype in the racial identification process because physical appearance is the primary cue for racial group membership in the United States and remains the greatest factor in how mixed-race children are classified by others. At the same time, it bears repeating that race is a social and not a biological reality. Therefore, our discussion of racial phenotypes rests on the understanding that what we refer to as "black" and "white" physical features are those we have been socially conditioned to notice as different, meaningful, and associated with particular racial groups. In short, we remind readers that racial group classification is a product of historical circumstance. Nonetheless, because particular physical features are commonly understood as markers of group membership, and because they differentiate mixed-race children's social experiences, it is necessary to openly address them.

First and foremost, multiracial children vary greatly in their physical appearances. Some look white, some look racially ambiguous, and others look black.

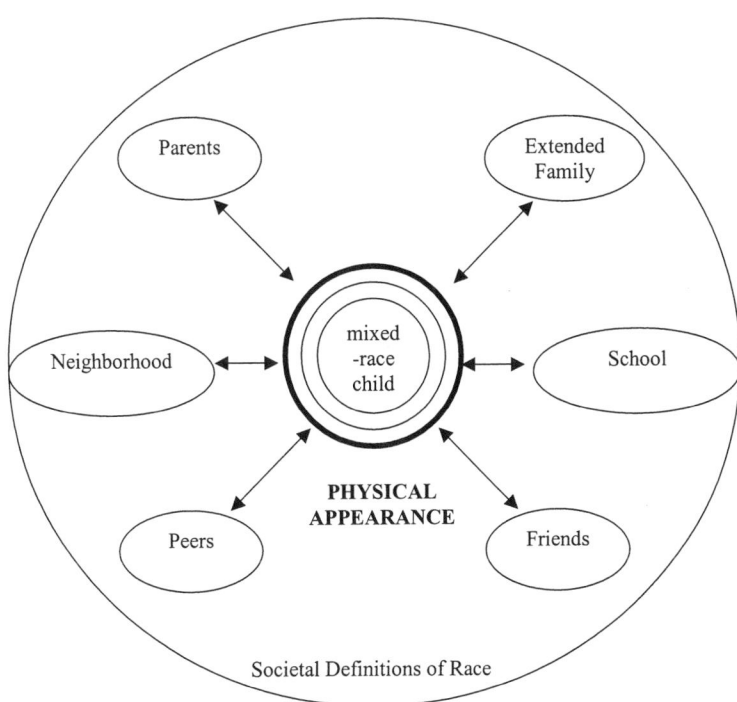

MODEL 6.1
Phenotype and Racial Identity Development

Clearly, even children within the same family can have radically different physical appearances. While the relationship between physical traits and racial identity may seem to be straightforward and direct, the reality is more complicated. In other words, a child's physical characteristics do not directly and exclusively determine their racial identity so that those who look black identify as black, those who look white identify as white, and those who look somewhere in the middle identify as biracial. The multiracial experience is far more complex. It is not uncommon to find a mixed-race person who appears white yet identifies as black. Nor is it uncommon to find a mixed-race person who appears black yet identifies as biracial. So we must start with an understanding that racial identity and physical appearances are not always perfectly correlated.

As we have argued throughout this book, to understand the rules of racial categorization operating today, we have to look back at the historical circumstances from which they emerged. Therefore, we start with a brief historically

grounded discussion of the link between physical appearance and racial identification. We then consider how appearances affect identity choice among
mixed-race individuals, highlighting case studies that illustrate various places
on the COBI model. Finally, we suggest ways caregivers can address rejection
around physical appearance that has the potential to cause emotional distress
in children.

RACE AND PHYSICAL APPEARANCE: MORE THAN MEETS THE EYE

Our physical appearance provides basic information to others about who we
are before we ever engage in any interaction. The way we look informs others
how to categorize, understand, and behave toward us. We look at other people and immediately know if they are old or young, male or female, black or
white. Each of these factors then triggers a whole set of meanings we have
learned to associate with that status, which informs us about the person and
influences our behavior. If we encounter an elderly white woman, we assume
different things about her and behave in different ways toward her than we do
if we see a young black man.

This instantaneous identification is possible because our physical bodies
represent a collection of cultural meanings. Thus, skin color, hair texture, and
facial features are not simply construed as value-neutral bodily features, but
carry symbolic meanings. Our physical characteristics act as inescapable sig-
nifiers used by others to define and situate our identities as well as imply various meanings about our attitudes, values, and moral character. The ability to
immediately categorize others is possible because we are all operating on
shared understandings of social categories. We each understand the difference
between young and old, male and female. In order for us to achieve an identity, the way we appear to others must match their understanding of us. If this
mutual identification does not occur, then our presented identity is challenged and cannot be realized. For example, a woman can say she's a man.
However, if her appearance fails to elicit identification from others as "male,"
her identity as a man fails. While age and sex are somewhat clearly defined categories, when it comes to "black" and "white," the line is much hazier.

In a racially stratified society, race functions as a master status, or a primary
identification that subsumes all other types of identities. For example, during
slavery, the one-drop rule emerged as the classification norm because the economic system necessitated a way of clearly defining who was black or white.

Even mixed-race people who physically looked white were considered black because black group membership was determined by ancestry (or that one very powerful drop). After emancipation, the one-drop rule remained the primary means of classification, so people with a broad range of physical characteristics and ancestries continued to be considered black. The point is that because race is socially constructed, arbitrary rules have to be put in place to determine who is black. Those rules simply mirror existing hierarchical beliefs about the relative status of each group and are not always directly related to what people physically look like. We see the absurdity of these rules most clearly when we look on the margins because that is where the prevailing myth that race is determined by skin color falls apart. Instead, it becomes clear that race is determined by historically rooted rules grounded in white supremacy.

Even today, the one-drop rule remains intact. It is readily challenged, and at times discredited, but by and large it remains the guiding norm by which both blacks and whites understand who is black in the United States. However, because the one-drop rule is increasingly questioned, alternative racial identifications have emerged and are considered legitimate in particular contexts. This classification confusion exacerbates the ambiguity between appearance and identity and opens the space for mixed-race people to have choices about their racial identification. While their "choices" are not fully unconstrained, more options exist than have previously been available. Yet, identity choice is most directly constrained by physical appearance so that people whose phenotype most closely approximates whites have the greatest number of choices. They can identify as black, biracial, or white. However, those who appear black have little or no identity choice other than black.

Because race supercedes other identities and appearances communicate racial group membership, it is difficult to claim a racial identity that does not match one's physical appearance. The fact that those who look black have difficulty claiming an identity other than black, while someone who looks white can claim a black identity illustrates the purity we continue to associate with whiteness and the stigma of blackness. It also illustrates the way that societal categorizations constrain individual self-understanding. The bottom line is that physical appearance does affect racial identity development among mixed-race children, but that occurs in a highly *contextualized* manner.

Given that identity is a socially validated self-understanding, an identity must be true to our own self-understanding *and* validated by others. It is our sociocultural environment that influences how we understand ourselves and how we are understood by others. Thus our skin color and physical characteristics have a personal and a social component: We understand our own skin color, but we also interpret our appearance through the "eyes" of others within any given interaction. *If a mixed-race child is to construct a racial identity other than that dictated by the historically rooted one-drop rule (i.e., as black), that alternative identity must be: 1) considered legitimate in their social context and 2) validated in their interactions with others.* With these two considerations in mind, we turn now to a discussion of how appearance and identity are interlinked at different places along the COBI model.

Appearance and Singular Identities

Among those who have formed a singular identity as black or white, their conception of what it means to be "black" (or less commonly "white") is inclusive of a wide range of appearances. Moreover, unless the person is at the extreme end of the identity continuum, those with singular identities are still able to acknowledge their mixed parentage. In contrast, those at the extreme ends of the continuum usually do not acknowledge the existence of their opposite-race parent. For them, having a parent of another race is not salient to their self-understanding as exclusively black (or white), and may not be offered as identifying information unless directly requested.

John is a twenty-year-old college student who self-identifies as white.[1] His case, while rare, is worthy of further consideration because it directly challenges the one-drop rule and illustrates the interaction between phenotype and environment in identity development. John was raised by his white mother and white stepfather in an affluent white suburb in the Midwest. He was not told that his biological father was black until he was eighteen, which did not change his racial self-understanding whatsoever. In part, John's failure to consider the race of his father as necessitating a modification of his racial identity is due to the negative association with the circumstances of his conception (his mother was raped). It is also partly due to his physical appearance and the fact that other people assume, without question, that he is white. John learned to understand himself as "white" without knowing that his biological father was African American. His white identity was validated throughout his childhood because of his appearance and social environment. When it was revealed to him that his biological father was black, he was unable to reconcile that fact with his own self-understanding as white. He did not modify his racial identity to incorporate the truth of his interracial parentage, but instead continued to consider himself a white person who happened to have a black parent.

John falls at the edge of the COBI model because of his exclusive identification as white and his denial of blackness. As discussed in chapter 2, while mixed-race people may make various choices about their identity that represent different levels of blending, we consider any identity choice that is grounded in denial as unhealthy. Importantly, John is not entirely to blame for the problematic resolution of his mixed-race status. His mother and stepfather hid the truth from him for eighteen years, communicating through the silence of secrecy that both his conception and his blackness were shameful. They also failed to recognize his refusal to integrate the new information into his self-understanding as a red flag. While John's white identity may continue to be validated by those in his environment, he will face a continual need to resolve his racial identity as he progresses through his life.

In John, we have a case of an individual who looks white and has developed a white racial identity. This is possible because he appears white and is both classified and accepted by others as white. It is helpful to contrast his story with an individual who looks white and identifies as black, thereby illustrating the complex link between physical appearance and racial identity. Gregory Howard Williams tells the story of his childhood racial identity development in the critically acclaimed book *Life on the Color Line: The True Story of a White Boy Who Discovered He Was Black*. This same title could apply to John's story, except that Greg's resolution of his racial identity turned out very differently.

Greg, like John, had one black and one white parent and physically appeared white. Because his father passed for white, he also believed he was an ordinary white boy with two white parents, until he was ten. At that time, Greg's mother left the family and his father loaded the kids on a bus to return to his hometown of Muncie, Indiana. During the bus ride, Greg's father informed him and his brother that he was, in fact, black, and that when they got off that bus in Indiana, the boys would also be black. Despite numerous trials and tribulations, and his white appearance, Greg developed a black identity. He did this because in his social context (unlike John's), everyone knew that his father was black, and everyone was operating on the assumption of the one-drop rule. Those two facts made Greg black and he grew to accept that identification.

When we consider more deeply the juxtaposition of Greg and John, what is clear is that while physical appearance typically corresponds with racial identification (you look white, others assume you are white, and you develop a white identity), the direct link between appearance and identity is *profoundly mediated by social context.* Here we see that having a white appearance is meaningless if you have a black biological parent, if others know about that parent, and if having a black parent precludes others from validating a white identity (Greg's experience). If others don't know about your black parent and/or having a black parent does not discredit a white identity, then appearance and identity can be directly connected (John's case). Therefore, appearances alone do not solely dictate racial identity for mixed-race people; instead, they interact with historically rooted cultural norms of identification and the assumptions others have about racial group membership.

Singular identities rely heavily on a combination of: 1) physical characteristics and 2) the local availability of identity options. In many communities, "biracial" is simply not an available option for racial identification, either because others do not hold that category to be meaningful or an individual's phenotype suggests adherence to traditional categories of racial grouping. In a recent study of mixed-race college students, most of the participants who identified as black reported that they appear black to others.[2] People regularly assumed they were black because there was nothing ambiguous about their phenotype that would hint at interracial parentage. One respondent named Norm identified himself as black, described his own appearance as black, and said he was assumed to be black by others. There was no ambiguity about his physical appearance that would lead others to inquire about it or ask him about his racial background. Norm's identity and appearance were perfectly matched, causing little difficulty in mutual identification or racial identity development. When multiracial people are assumed to be black by others and exist in a predominately black social network, constructing and maintaining a black identity is a common occurrence.

Like Norm, John has a straightforward relationship between his appearance and his racial identity, only in the opposite direction. He understands himself as white and is assumed by other people to be white. Predictably, the identity he puts forward and others' categorization of him are both white and the mutual identification process occurs quickly, efficiently, and without incident. In contrast, Greg looks white but was assumed black by other people because they knew his father was black and they believed in the one-drop rule. In these three cases, we can see how appearances are *linked to* identity, but do not exclusively *determine* identity because of the way that racial identity is influenced by historical, cultural, and contextual factors.

Appearance and Blended Identities

The link between physical appearance and racial identity choice is the most difficult for those whose self-understanding falls closer to the center of the COBI model than those at the singular ends. In order to flesh out that linkage, it is again necessary to further consider the contextual nature of racial identification.

Across research samples, those who self-identify as "biracial" tend toward a common set of social experiences. Because many samples are drawn from college campuses, participants tend to be middle class, raised in (predominantly white) suburban areas, and have mostly white friendship groups in childhood and adolescence. They may have been the only (or one of few) nonwhites within their schools and communities. Their socialization experiences are similar to their white peers, resulting in comparable behavioral strategies, consumption patterns, and cultural tastes. The only differences between these individuals and their peers are that they have a black parent and most physically appear to be people of color. In short, many look black but have white cultural frameworks.

In the minds of their white peers, these mixed-race people are more like them than different and, therefore, don't fit into their stereotypical and media-derived conception of "black." The result is that mixed-race adolescents repeatedly hear from their peers (in a complimentary fashion), "Well, I don't really think of you as 'black,'" implying: 1) the speaker has a specific perception of what "black" is, 2) "black" is something different from the speaker (not "white"), and 3) the mixed-race person does not fit into that category because they are more like the speaker than their understanding of "black" (which is negative). The mixed-race person fails to fit into either cognitive category "black" or "white" so both parties tacitly agree to a new identity—"biracial"—where biracial means, for both, something between black and white.

Even though "biracial" may be validated in some contexts, it is not universally accepted as a legitimate category of racial identification. When a child claims "biracial" as their racial identity, that claim may be accepted as a meaningful and validated, directly challenged, or rejected outright. When operating within a local network, children can learn to respond to challenges or rejection by either renegotiating their identification with others or remaining in a nebulous, marginal, and unresolved state with regard to their racial identity. Mixed-race children are not fully constrained by others' definitions of them in daily interactions. They have agency to the degree that they can choose how they respond to others. This is important because mixed-race children (particularly those who understand themselves as biracial) must develop the interactional skills to push back against categorizations that fail to reflect their self-understanding. They can challenge others about their insistence on categorizing them in accordance with the one-drop rule or in mutually exclusive categories, thus pushing back against attempts to constrain them. The only option other than resistance is for the individual to reconsider their racial identity.

We are often asked what difference appearances make in the development of a fully blended (or "biracial") identity, and if there are phenotypic differences between those who have a biracial identity validated by others versus those who do not. This is critical because there is great potential for rejection among children who assert "biracial" as their racial identity. Those who develop a black identity are adopting that which has been historically deemed acceptable according to the one-drop rule, so they will receive little resistance to that identification. In comparison, those who construct a biracial identity are on shakier ground because they are defying the structurally imposed mandate of blackness and the assumption of mutual exclusivity that underlies it. For various political, ideological, historical, and traditional reasons, the assertion of biracial identity may be challenged most strongly by African Americans and within predominately black communities.[3] While "biracial," as a racial category, is acceptable in some communities and in some geographic areas, it is not legitimate in others, and may be interpreted as an antiblack sentiment, an effort to distance oneself from the black community, or a signifier of deeply internalized racial self-hatred. Therefore, children who identify as "biracial" may be negatively described as "uppity," "confused," and/or as "thinking they are better" than black people. Alternatively, biracial may be a meaningless identity in some white communities where people are operating on the assumption of the one-drop rule, so that any individual with a black parent is considered black irrespective of their physical appearance.

Because validation by others is at the heart of racial identity development, conflict arises when individuals cannot be placed immediately and unconsciously into a specific racial group. Racial categorization is particularly difficult when: 1) bodily features are ambiguous, 2) the classifier has information about the individual that complicates categorization based on appearance (such as knowing that a person has one black and one white parent), or 3) the individual's secondary and tertiary cues (language and dress) do not fit into the other's preconceived ideas about members of a particular racial group. Any one or a combination of these factors can introduce difficulty. Physical ambiguity and the confusion it causes is most frequently resolved when others directly ask: "What are you?"[4]

It is the micro-level negotiations over racial identification that explain how children construct racial self-understandings regardless of their bodily appearances. Mixed-race children who develop a biracial identity can physically appear black. However, their white parentage, socialization in a white community, and self-presentation allow them to understand themselves, and be validated by others, as "biracial." Biracial identifiers also include children whose physical characteristics are ambiguous (but not white) with similar socialization experiences. Finally, children who are "light enough to pass" (or look white) and share social experiences similar to their white peers may come to understand themselves as biracial. In sum, regardless of a child's bodily characteristics, their racial identification as biracial derives from the environment they are in and their ability to negotiate a meaningful identity with others. The situation is entirely different for those who do not possess the interactional tools to negotiate and challenge those who reject them. Here, the process of mutual identification is bypassed and the individual is assumed to be black (or in some instances, assumed white) by others. Those who understand themselves as biracial, but fail to have their self-understanding validated by others are trapped in the gray area between the one-drop rule and the Multiracial movement, both of which have worked to define their racial identities in opposing directions.

Appearance and the Transcendent Identity

Mixed-race people who refuse any racial identification (what we call "transcendents") have appearances that run the full phenotypic spectrum. That said, it is clearly far easier to transcend race when you look white, as opposed to looking black. Mike, a college student in the Midwest, is typical of white-appearing transcendents.[5] He is assumed by most people to be a white male, although if asked, he acknowledges his mixed ancestry and has a strong and clearly articulated explanation of his transcendent identity. Mike's presentation of self is intentionally raceless because he doesn't consider himself to have any racial identity. In his case, a raceless self-presentation is the functional equivalent to presenting a white identity. In fact, built into his every interaction is the anticipation that others will assume he is white. When Mike enters into an interactional context, his physical features communicate a white identity. He does not use any cues to signify blackness, such as speaking in black vernacular or wearing clothing that would cue black group membership. Because he looks white, others assume he is white, and he allows miscategorization in order to facilitate and prioritize his nonracial identities.

Mike's transcendent identity developed over time and is a result of his white appearance and his family racial socialization, where his parents stressed the inaccuracies and ideological problems inherent in racial categorization. Due to his physical whiteness, he can go for long periods of time with his nonracial identities at the forefront of his self-definition (as a function of white privilege). However, when Mike went to college, his transcendent identity was unacceptable because his campus was racially polarized. There, racial identity indicated group membership and served as a signifier of where he was supposed to stand on social issues, whom he should befriend, and the range of others considered acceptable to date. On his campus, the raceless stranger was not an available possibility, so Mike responded to this new context by reluctantly accepting categorization as black in accordance with the historical social norm of the one-drop rule. While Mike did not develop a black *identity*, he did develop acceptance of using the *label* "black."

Mixed-race people who physically appear white can maintain a "color-blind" worldview, where racelessness is possible because their phenotype bestows on them the privileges of whiteness. The privileged racial group does not have to be aware of race and how it shapes daily reality for people of color. For example, unless white people find themselves in predominantly black environments where they are the numeric minority, they never have to see or acknowledge how race influences their life experience and the world around them. Mixed-race people who look white and are white-identified can experience the world as white people. This includes the privilege of having a raceless identity. In other words, like many white people, they can argue that "people are just people," that they "don't see" race, and that they have "transcended race"—all of which are positions commonly taken by whites in post–Civil Rights America.[6]

While a transcendent self-understanding is facilitated by a white appearance, it is not exclusively the domain of white-appearing individuals. In fact, it is developed by those who vary widely in skin color and appearance. However, the more an individual appears to be a person of color, the more negotiation and interaction work that must be done to sustain a transcendent identity. Steve, a black-appearing transcendent, must constantly contest and challenge others' categorization of him, whereas Mike's white privilege (via phenotype) does not require any such interaction skills.[7] In the vast majority of interactions, racial categorization is unspoken, so Steve is assumed black without any opening for renegotiation. When he hails a cab, shops in a store, or walks down the street, strangers see him as a black person. Only when racial categorization is overt can he offer an explicit verbal challenge to the racial reasoning of others. Even then, his nonracial identity is only likely to be validated at an abstract level. Steve can often convince others intellectually that race is less a biological reality and more a problematic social construct, a conversation that results in validation of his identity. Because he is highly persuasive and because many people are committed to the stance of color-blindness, they readily accept his transcendent identification.

STRATEGIES FOR CHALLENGING REJECTION AROUND APPEARANCE

We have argued that physical appearances significantly influence how others categorize and respond to mixed-race people. If a child appears white, others understand her as white and respond accordingly. The same is true in instances where a child appears black. When children appear mixed or ambiguous, others make varied assessments about their racial identity and/or directly ask: what are you? The question is important because it clarifies how others will respond to the mixed-race child. These reactions have an effect on how mixed-race children come to understand their racial identity. In some cases, a child's physical appearance and social environment make it relatively easier to blend their blackness and whiteness. In other cases, children's physical appearance and/or their environment make any blending a challenge.

It is our contention that it is most healthy for mixed-race children to resolve the truth of multiracial parentage and develop a firm sense of racial self-understanding that acknowledges and blends all the aspects of their ancestry. This blending may result in racial identification that is anywhere along the COBI model. Because physical appearance and social context interact in identity development, there are really two questions at hand: 1) What can children do in situations where their physical appearance does not reflect their mixed-race status and others respond to them in ways that assume they are either exclusively black or white? and 2) What can children do in situations where their physical appearance is ambiguous, and yet the context disallows "biracial" identity? For parents and other concerned adults, it is critical to foster the development of skills that mixed-race children can use to assist them in asserting their identities in situations where they may be miscategorized or where their racial identity may be directly challenged. To do this, it is useful to first prepare children for the possibility that they may be misidentified by others by providing them several possible ways to respond when such situations arise. We offer the following examples to illustrate how such preparation may occur.

Kim is a mixed-race teenager who has very light brown skin and blond, curly hair. [8] One day at school, she was talking with Sally, another student who is white. At some point in the conversation, Sally said to Kim: "I hate the way those black girls are so loud. Like it's just something about black people, they are always so loud. I just want to tell them to shut up, but they would probably just get louder." Clearly, Sally assumed Kim was white by the way she spoke about the black girls. Had she recognized that Kim had black ancestry, she most likely would not have made this statement, or else she might have qualified it to be sure Kim knew she considered her to be an "exception." Kim recognized Sally's implicit assumption and responded by saying, "From what you just said, I guess you think I'm white, so I just want to set the record straight, I'm only half white. My dad is black and my mom is white." Kim's response was direct and to the point, which is one way to respond in such situations.

In some cases, it may be advisable to respond less directly because the child may be either uncomfortable with direct confrontation, or because there is reason to suspect that a more direct response will create undesirable conflict or tension. If we return to the example of Kim and Sally, Kim could have been indirect by saying, "I don't think it's true that all black people are loud, I know some quiet black people and some loud white people. Like my dad, he's black and he's a very quiet person. My mom is white and she is the loud one in our family." This response is less direct, although no doubt challenging. Kim also could have responded by saying something with a more vulnerable tone such as, "I'm a little uncomfortable with what you just said because I am guessing that you only said that because you think I am white."

In addition to learning how to handle misidentification, there is the reality that *no matter how mixed-race children identify, they will experience some degree of rejection from others.* Whether it is black people who think they are acting uppity for asserting a biracial identity, or white people who challenge a black identity because the person doesn't "look black" to them, at some point, they will invariably have to respond to challenges about their identification. For example, consider the case of a teenager who appears black but identifies as biracial, as in the case of Dana.[9] According to Dana:

> When I meet someone who is black, a couple times they will assume that I am black, and when I tell them I am biracial, a lot of times they not only get an attitude about it, but sometimes someone will even say to me that I am not really biracial, I guess 'cause I look black. When that happens, it can be hard because I want the person to understand I'm not saying I'm biracial because I have any problem with black, it's just that I am also white. I am both, and I want to be honest about that.

As another example, consider Anthony, a light-skinned, green-eyed adolescent.[10] He reported that:

> Black people can always tell that I am mixed but most white people never realize it. Most white people assume I am white and they are surprised when I tell them. The thing is, I relate to being black and that's what I tell people I am. I mean, I know that I am really mixed, but what I identify with mostly is black. Once, this girl at school came up to me who was mixed and she said, "Oh you think you're black, but you're biracial. Why don't you admit it?" That made me mad. Who is she to tell me who I am? What does she know about me anyway?

In each of these cases, not only was the mixed-race adolescent's identity being challenged, but the person doing the challenging was also expressing a concern that had some relevance to their own identity. In both these cases, the challenger felt that the mixed-race person's asserted identity indirectly devalued their own racial identity. In cases like this, individuals should acknowledge the underlying reality that they have one black and one white parent, while also addressing the challenger's implied concern in a reassuring way. For example, Dana could say, "My mother is black and my father is white, so that's why I consider myself biracial. I am not trying to distance myself from my being black. I am proud of my black part. But I just want to be honest about the fact I am both black and white."

In Anthony's case, he might say, "My mother is white and my father is black, so of course I am biracial. But I identify more strongly with my black part. I was raised by my father and most of the people I was around are black and that is very strong inside of me, but that doesn't mean I don't understand and recognize that I have both." By responding in these ways, both Dana and Anthony would be accomplishing three things: 1) they would be acknowledging the underlying reality of their mixed-race background, 2) they would be addressing the implied concern of the challenger, and 3) they would be asserting their preferred way of defining themselves.

While the ways of responding to an identity challenge or rejection are numerous, the point is that adults need to work directly with their children to help them develop several different types of reactions that are appropriate for their age, their particular situation, and their personal comfort level. It is most important for adults to understand that challenge and rejection will inevitably happen to their children. Second, it is better to prepare their children for this possibility before it happens than to pick up the pieces after an incident occurs. While mixed-race children may be misidentified by others and may experience social environments in which their self-identification is not accepted, they will gain from exploring and practicing several different responsive strategies.

SUMMARY

When trying to understand mixed-race children's racial identity development, physical appearance is an important consideration. The relationship between appearance and racial identity is complicated by social context because different communities vary in the extent to which "biracial" identity is an acceptable and legitimate racial identification. It is clear that appearances do not absolutely determine racial identity among mixed-race children. How they are perceived by others is influenced by historical, cultural, and environmental factors. Considering these contextual factors also helps us to better appreciate:

1) why people with the same parental background (one black and one white parent) develop different racial identities, and 2) why their physical appearance does not always directly predict that outcome.

For parents of mixed-race children and social service providers, it is critically important to realize that while blended identities are beginning to emerge, there still exist many social contexts where the one-drop rule remains alive and well. The challenge is to teach children and adolescents how to negotiate situations where their identity is rejected, as well as strategies to resist invalidation. Caregivers' strategies must take into account the historical construction of blackness and the position of those whose beliefs negate the existence of biracial as a legitimate category of self-understanding.

The reality of racial identity development among mixed-race children is that they make increasingly varied choices, and that those choices may change over their lifetime. For those working with multiracial children and adolescents, it is imperative to understand that racial identification is both contextually and experientially bound, and much more than skin deep. In the following chapter, we add the final component to our identity development model: gender.

NOTES

1. John was a student of Rockquemore's and participated in the Survey of Biracial Experiences. See Kerry Ann Rockquemore and David L. Brunsma, *Beyond Black: Biracial Identity in America* (Thousand Oaks, Calif.: Sage Publications, 2002).

2. Rockquemore and Brunsma, *Beyond Black.*

3. F. James Davis, *Who Is Black?: One Nation's Definition.*(University Park: Pennsylvania State University Press, 1991).

4. See Theresa Williams, "Race as Process: Reassessing the 'What Are You?' Encounters of Biracial Individuals," *Racially Mixed People in America*, ed. Maria Root (Newbury Park, Calif.: Sage Publications, 1996).

5. This case is drawn from Kerry Ann Rockquemore and David Brunsma, "Beyond Black?: The Reflexivity of Appearances in Biracial Identification among Black/White Biracials," *Skin Deep: How Race and Complexion Matter in the "Color-Blind" Era*, ed. Verna Keith, Cedric Herring, and Hayward Horton (Urbana: University of Illinois Press, 2004).

6. Eduardo Bonilla-Silva, *Racism without Racists: Color-Blind Racism and the Persistence of Racial Inequality in the United States* (Lanham, Md.: Rowman & Littlefield, 2003).

7. Steve is an acquaintance of Rockquemore.

8. Kim was a student of Laszloffy.

9. Dana was Laszloffy's client.

10. Anthony was Laszloffy's student.

7

Just between Sisters: The Intersection of Race and Gender in the Lives of Mixed-Race Girls

Thus far, we have considered how mixed-race children are embedded in social environments that exert various influences on their racial identity development including their families, schools, neighborhoods, peers, and friends. We also examined how physical appearance mediates between how mixed-race children see themselves and how others respond to them. In this chapter, we focus on particular issues facing mixed-race girls. While all mixed-race children and adolescents encounter challenges in racial identity development, mixed-race girls face the intersecting dynamics of racial and gender oppression. This creates a unique set of issues for mixed-race girls that warrant closer attention.

In the research on the multiracial experience, gender has been conceptually underdeveloped.[1] When gender is considered, analyses tend to be rudimentary, focusing on whether men and women make different choices about their racial identities, or examining exclusively female clinical samples for patterns in attitudes, behaviors, and background experiences. Most researchers have found no gender effects using the first approach, paralleling studies of African Americans' racial identity.[2] Using the second method, both Jewelle Taylor Gibbs and Roger Herring report that gender does appear to impact racial identity among mixed-race women because women in therapy report similar experiences of rejection around identification and appearance issues.[3] Like Gibbs and Herring, we believe that racial identity development among mixed-race people is gendered. While it is not the case that boys and girls develop different racial identities, it is the case that the entire *process* of identity

131

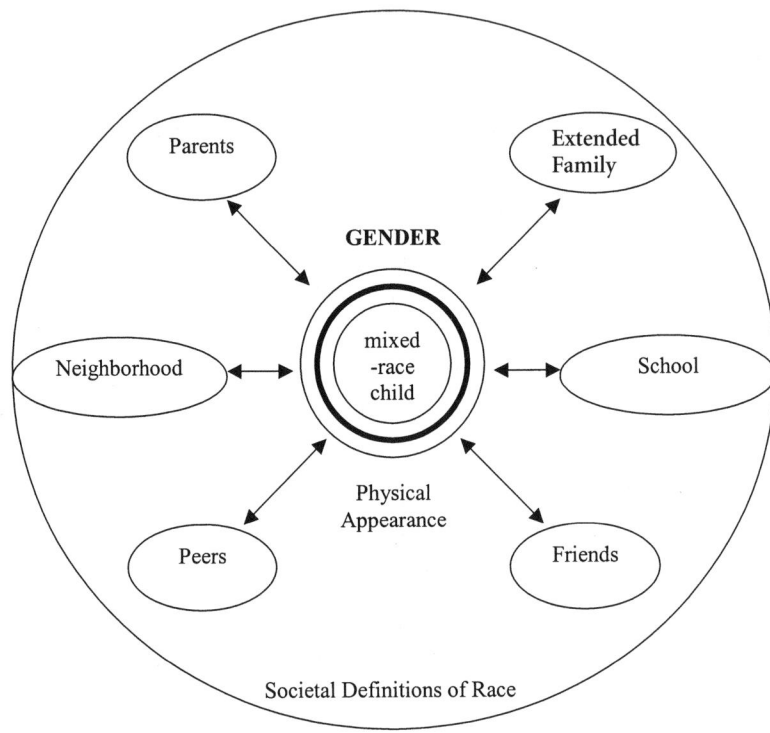

MODEL 7.1
Gender and Racial Identity Development

construction is shaped by gender, so that girls, unlike boys, tend to experience gender-specific stressors that shape racial identity development.

This chapter explores how race and gender interact to influence the racial identity development of mixed-race girls. It should not be a surprise that this influence occurs most often around physical appearance. The race and gender-specific meanings attached to physical characteristics have historical roots and result in differential treatment that can be painful for mixed-race girls. Because adolescent girls are especially vulnerable to identity issues around appearances, and because this vulnerability impacts their racial identity development, we put them at the center of our analysis. Our discussion is intended to articulate the unique pressures that girls face because the intersection of race and gender oppression creates tensions between light-skinned and dark-skinned girls.

THE HISTORICAL ROOTS OF THE COLOR COMPLEX

To understand how gender and race interact to shape racial identity development for mixed-race girls, it is necessary to consider the roots of skin color stratification, the differential meanings attached to various skin colors, and, finally, how this phenomenon is distinctly gendered.

Skin-color stratification is firmly grounded in the institution of slavery that produced both rampant miscegenation and the systematic privileging of lighter-skinned blacks. The nature of slavery with its skin-color stratification system was such that it pitted light-skinned and dark-skinned people against each other, forming the basis for the "color complex."[4]

This privileging of light skin continued long after the demise of slavery, so that even today, those with "good" (white) features are more likely to have higher personal income, educational attainment, and occupational prestige than those with "bad" (black) features.[5] Within the black community, where complexion and physical traits vary widely, the color complex remains a basis for deep tension. Light-skinned people who are more likely to receive privileges often feel that those with darker skin question their blackness and accuse them of identifying with whiteness and "thinking they are better." Darker-skinned people recognize, and often resent, that those with lighter skin receive unfair advantages. They are more likely to question the blackness of those with lighter skin and question whether or not those who are lighter think they are "better." The color complex organizes relations among blacks, but also between black and mixed-race people.

While the color complex affects all black people, it is important to recognize that skin-color stratification came into being as a distinctly gendered social phenomenon (via the rape of black female slaves). It continues today as one that disproportionately affects women because of the importance that physical appearance plays in the overall construction of female identity.[6] This is the case because patriarchal ideology dictates that men are inherently more valuable than women and, among women, worth is defined in terms of physical beauty and sexuality. Robin Lakoff and Raquel Scherr argue that for women, "beauty is power" because women's beauty is equivalent to men's intelligence, political influence, and/or physical strength in determining their value.[7] As a result, beauty standards are more rigorously applied to women than to men across all races and cause a sex-specific emphasis on body image.[8] Moreover, the definition of what is beautiful and sexually appealing is such that white skin and white European physical features are considered the ideal. Black women, held to a European standard of beauty, are socially and psychologically affected by skin-color stratification. Light-skinned women's desirability stems from their close physical approximation of the white beauty standard. They not only have higher educational attainment, personal incomes, and perception of success, but they are also considered more desirable as mates and more likely to marry a man with high income and prestige than dark-skinned women.[9] Despite the seeming success of the Black Power movement, the group-level gains from the Civil Rights movement, and the infusion of feminist ideas throughout society, the disturbing fact remains that light-skinned black women continue to be evaluated as more attractive than those with darker skin.

Because of the importance that appearance plays in the overall construction of female identity, and because physical appearance plays such a critical role in racial identity development for multiracial people, mixed-race girls encounter struggles related to their identity on the basis of both race and gender. Held to a white standard of beauty, mixed-race girls, like all girls, are raised in a society where light skin and "white" physical features are more cherished and more consistently rewarded. The challenge that mixed-race girls face is that so much of their sense of self-esteem is tied to their appearance. Our society has a narrow definition of what is considered beautiful, and this definition defines the ideal in terms of white skin and related physical traits (e.g., small, narrow nose, thin lips, blue eyes, straight, light hair). As a result, mixed-race girls who do not approximate whiteness are disadvantaged. Like most black girls, they are placed at odds with a society that devalues them racially, thereby setting them up for corresponding gender-based devaluation as well. However, by virtue of their mixed-race parentage, some mixed-race girls look white because they closely approximate white features. Within the patriarchal paradigm that evaluates femaleness in terms of physical beauty based on whiteness/lightness, this affords an advantage to this subgroup of mixed-race girls and creates the tension that often exists between black and mixed-race girls.

TENSION BETWEEN MIXED-RACE AND BLACK GIRLS

Most mixed-race people, *as people of color,* experience discrimination from whites at some point in their lives. However, it is sometimes surprising to white mothers of mixed-race children, as well as those having little contact with black communities, to find out that mixed-race people may not receive automatic acceptance from blacks. Research shows that it is not uncommon for mixed-race people to report having negative interactions with blacks. Women, however, report a higher frequency of negative encounters and go on to qualify that their problems are largely confined to interactions with black females.[10] This tension is articulated by Ann, a mixed-race woman who identifies as biracial. She said the following in response to an interviewer's question about whether or not she would consider attending a historically black college:

ANN: I don't have anything against historically black colleges, I just don't think that it would work out for me because of the complex that I have with black females, not that I, it's not like *my* complex toward them—it's just their hostility toward me. Um, I have nothing against them, I just chose to stay around [her hometown].

INTERVIEWER: Can you tell me a story about how you've experienced that hostility?

ANN: I am just constantly getting horrible looks, and a lot of stuff has been said about me. Most of it has to do with black males because they think like I'm tryin' to take their man or something. I mean, I don't really deliberately go out of my way to piss them off or anything, but, I mean it's there. I know it's there because if one of my friends is friends with a black female, they tell me what they say and I just see it, so I'm not even really assuming. I just look and *I know*, you know what I mean?

In this quoted exchange, Ann articulated the hostility that many mixed-race girls perceive from black girls. Of course, tension certainly exists between mixed-race and white girls as well. Such tension usually arises in situations where a mixed-race girl who physically appears white and identifies this way is found to have a black parent. In this instance, rejection from white girls arises around, "Oh, so you're not really white," which translates into, "You're no longer acceptable or as good as us." In other cases, a mixed-race girl may encounter rejection from white girls who simply see her as black and accordingly devalue her and her physical traits. While these tensions can and do arise, in their accounts of girl-to-girl conflict, mixed-race girls more frequently refer to tension with black girls, and they report a high degree of pain associated with these conflicts. A young woman named Sue was asked if she ever experienced discriminatory treatment from whites, and she said, "Sometimes, but not as much as from black people. . . . I mean, it's completely different sides of the spectrum. . . . Blacks don't accept me. . . . They don't really like me."[11]

Ann articulates a common sentiment expressed by mixed-race girls, who frequently tell us stories of strained relationships with black girls. The doubt and rejection they encounter is almost always painful, but it is especially so when girls feel a kinship with blackness and desire acceptance from blacks.

In summary, the extent to which rejection from black girls hurts varies on the basis of how one identifies racially. We have argued that it is important for children to feel validated in their preferred view of self. Irrespective of how an individual racially self-identifies, the degree to which others validate (or reject) this definition plays a salient role in how much they continue to assert this definition of self as well as their overall level of emotional and psychological well-being. For girls who identify with blackness and desire acceptance from black people, rejection of their blackness is especially painful. In the following section, we identify and explore several factors that are related to the tension that often develops between black and mixed-race girls.

THE PROBLEM OF IDENTITY "CHOICE"

A primary factor organizing the tension between black and mixed-race girls is "identity choice." Regardless of whether black girls are light-skinned or dark-skinned, they will develop a black racial identity. They may have various feelings about their racial group membership and they may be at different stages of consciousness in terms of black identity development models. However, irrespective of how they feel about their blackness, they are not in a position to choose an alternative racial identification. Even if they are multiracial by ancestry (and surely most black people are!), unless they have parents of different races, they are unlikely to ever consider themselves as anything other than black.

In contrast, mixed-race girls may develop a black, biracial, or white identity depending on their physical appearance and social context. This distinction is critically important because both light-skinned black and light-skinned mixed-race girls are privileged via their light skin. In the same way, dark skin continues to stigmatize dark-skinned black and dark-skinned mixed-race girls. However, for black girls, a black identity is a given. For them, the color complex is not a fundamental push or pull factor in terms of racial identity development or sense of group membership because there is no possibility of being anything other than black. On the other hand, mixed-race girls can choose how to identify themselves racially, and negative interactions around physical appearance can push them away from a black identity.

Lydia is a light-skinned black college student. While her complexion affords her certain privileges, she does not have the option to identify in any way other than black.[12] Unlike mixed-race women who can choose to identify as biracial, Lydia does not have to contend with the resentment that having the "option" to identify that way often generates. Ironically, not having this option feeds her sense of resentment for those who do have this option. As Lydia stated, "Sometimes I am angry with biracial sisters because they can either choose to say they are black or biracial. I'm not saying I'm not proud to be black, but when you have the option to choose, you can't understand what it's like when you don't have that option."

In contrast to Lydia, consider the case of Tina, a mixed-race woman with light brown skin, curly hair, and green eyes.[13]

> I consider myself biracial, but here's the thing, I really do not feel comfortable with black people, mainly black girls. I have had so many experiences of being snubbed because I'm biracial. They think that 'cause I say I'm biracial, that I'm against black people, which isn't the case. It's just that I happen to be biracial. I know I could say I was black and that would probably help, but frankly I'd rather just associate mostly with whites. They don't hassle me, and they accept me as biracial, so that works for me.

With the ability to choose one's racial identity comes the possibility of rejection, real or perceived. There is an interactive cycle that occurs such that the more black girls sense mixed-race girls pulling away from blackness, the more likely they are to reject them. In turn, the more rejection mixed-race girls perceive, the more likely they are to pull away from blackness—and the cycle persists. At the heart of this pattern is perceived rejection from both sides and a great deal of pain for both parties.

The Interaction between Identification and Appearance

The tension between mixed-race and black girls reflects a complicated interaction between issues of identification and physical appearance. Those who are mixed-race have the option to choose how to racially identify themselves, serving as a basis for tension. In addition, the particular choices that individuals make can contribute to further tension. While it may not be surprising that choosing to identify as biracial feeds suspicion and mistrust between those who are black and mixed-race, some may be shocked to realize that even when mixed-race people identify as black, this does not automatically translate into harmonious relations. For a light-skinned girl, adopting a black identity may not be enough to eliminate doubts and questions about her "authentic blackness." Hence, there is a complicated relationship between how one chooses to identify racially and one's physical appearance. Stated another way, at the heart of the tension between girls is the issue of physical appearance.

While physical appearance plays a salient role in racial identity development for all mixed-race people, its influence in the lives of girls tends to be much greater than for boys. In our society, the complex interaction between white supremacy and patriarchy spawns a litany of powerful messages that are sent to girls suggesting that their value as human beings is directly tied to their physical beauty. Because girls are socialized to evaluate themselves based on physical appearance, they are more likely to disparage one another on the basis of physical characteristics, and mixed-race girls are especially vulnerable to being "dissed" for their looks. As reported by psychologist Maria Root, "[Mixed race] girls sustained more ridicule and rejection around phenotype than boys for hairstyles, body size, eye color, eye shape, hair color, and bust size."[14] Because of the prominent role that appearance plays in female valuation, such disparagement tends to cut especially deep.

Maya and Kelly are both mixed-race girls who identify as black.[15] However, Maya is dark-skinned and "looks black," while Kelly is light-skinned and has an ambiguous appearance. Irrespective of their similar racial identification as black, their different appearances evoke fundamentally different responses from black people, especially black girls.

Maya reports that she has relatively stress-free relations with black girls. She said, "Since I look black and I identify as black, I really don't have any problems with black folks. When they find out my father is white, sometimes that makes them step back for a moment, but only for a moment." Conversely, Kelly, in spite of asserting a strong black identity, reports frequent negative encounters with black girls in particular. She stated,

> Even though I consider myself black, the fact that I don't really look black causes
> a lot of misunderstanding. Black girls are especially hostile to me at first because

I am so light. I've been accused of thinking I'm "Miss Thang" or thinking I'm "all that." It's not true, and anyone who takes the time to get to know me realizes it soon enough. The fact is that I am blacker than some black people, and once we move past the surface, most black people see that and are accepting of me. But some black girls, no matter what, just can't get over how I look. They just ride me no matter what.

A key issue underpinning the tension between black and mixed-race girls is the specific meanings that are attached to skin color and other physical traits. These meanings range from "this type of hair or skin color is good or bad" to "you think you're better" to "you are less." As a result, disparaging remarks hurled between black and mixed-race girls almost always refer to appearance-related issues. For example, note how issues of hair reside at the center of Laura's comments about the tension she experiences with black girls.[16] "Black girls just don't seem to like me. They act jealous of the fact that I have good hair. It's not my fault that I have pretty hair, but they make such a fuss about it and treat me bad like somehow it's my fault."

As Laura's comments reveal, the issue of hair is at the center of the tension she experiences with black girls. And of particular salience is her reference to having "good hair." While she wonders why black girls "make such a fuss" about her hair, it is clear that she believes her hair is good, and by implication, theirs must be bad. She, like the girls in question, links specific attributions to physical characteristics, in this case hair. No doubt, her belief that her hair is good, at least indirectly, fuels the tension between herself and the black girls in question because, both sides are operating on the same notion that certain physical characteristics are good while others are bad.

Competing for Male Attention—The Adolescent Explosion

The tension between black and mixed-race girls intensifies over the competition for boys attention.[17] The privileging of light skin becomes most painfully obvious for girls when they begin to develop interests in boys and dating. They are fully aware that black males prefer light-skinned females.[18] This preference results in a rank ordering of girls according to their attractiveness, where the more beautiful (i.e., white-appearing) a girl is, the greater her ability to secure male attention. In the heterosexual world of dating, all girls are objectified by male "observers," but black girls are at a particular disadvantage, given that their market "value" is determined by a racist beauty standard. This creates a situation in which dark-skinned girls are devalued, pressured to approximate the standards of beauty determined by the dominant (white) group, and, justifiably, resent the colorism practiced within the black community.[19] Light-skinned girls, aware of unearned privileges, feel that resentment, distrust, and rejection by others, and may even feel their sense of group belonging threatened.[20]

The tension between mixed-race and black girls increases exponentially when mixed-race girls display an interest in dating black boys. Because of the color complex, it is not uncommon for black boys to generally display a preference for lighter-skinned girls. This intensifies competition and resentment between light- and dark-skinned girls.[21] Here, dark-skinned black girls feel, in a very painful way, their devalued status, and it is here that they are most likely to lash out at lighter-skinned girls.

Moreover, while adolescent boys tend to choose white, black, Asian, Latino, and mixed-race partners, for black girls the dating pool is largely restricted to black boys. This in turn increases antagonism between black and mixed-race girls who may be competing for black male attention. The role that competition for male attention plays in the tension between mixed-race and black girls is reflected in the comments made by two mixed-race women, Sheila and Shannon, as they describe their adolescent experiences:

> SHEILA: The problems that I had, truthfully, were with the black girls. That's the problems I had. They didn't like me 'cause they said they thought I was "all that" 'cause I'm light-skinned and I've got pretty long hair and the boys like me. . . . 'Cause I never had any problems with the black guys. You know, they're the ones that watched over me and I guess black girls didn't like that too much.

> SHANNON: It was just different. . . . It was mainly [black] girls. It was never [black] guys. Guys didn't have a problem with me [being mixed-race], which I think made it worse with black girls. Yeah, the problems were always with the girls. And it was just like, some of them didn't want to be my friend because of the way that I looked. And they would just be mean. Like, "I don't like you yellow girl."

In these two accounts, several interesting patterns emerge. First and foremost, both Sheila and Shannon talk about black girls as a monolithic group, ignoring variations within that group. In other words, they paint black girls with a broad brush, generalizing the negative interactions they have had with a few to the group as a whole. This is particularly important because patterns of negative interactions that are generalized can lead to an expectation that such interactions will occur with other black girls, potentially encouraging the anticipated behavior. Second, both Sheila and Shannon are light-skinned, and what they do not mention here (but what is deeply embedded in their accounts) is that the negative interactions they encounter occur, without exception, with girls whose skin is darker than theirs. Differences in complexion are inextricably tied to underlying competition for boys' attention, which so often underscores the conflict between black and mixed-race girls.

THE CORE ISSUE: INTERNALIZED OPPRESSION

At the core of how girls understand themselves and each other, and come to develop a racialized and gendered self-concept, is the degree to which they have resolved issues of internalized oppression that occur at the nexus of white supremacy and patriarchy. Within these conditions, a common dynamic of oppression has developed, namely that the oppressed internalize the beliefs and behaviors of their oppressors. For hundreds of years, the forces of white supremacy and patriarchy have gnawed on the psyches of women and black people and, as a result, many have internalized negative messages about themselves and developed ways of relating with each other that reflect the attitudes and behaviors of whites and men as a collective. This is particularly salient for women of color who are bombarded by mediated messages that are doubly negative because they are both women (existing in a patriarchy) and racial minorities (in a predominantly white society).

What Is Internalized Oppression?

Individual and institutional racism continues to exist in the United States and is experienced by people of color daily. The term "internalized oppression" simply refers to the internalization of external oppression in the form of racism and sexism or, more simply stated, bringing the oppressor within.[22] In our society, we are constantly bombarded by white supremacist and patriarchal ideology. Internalized oppression occurs when individuals come to believe these messages, evaluate themselves and others in these terms, and adopt the belief system, values, and worldview that devalues their very existence. Paulo Freire refers to this process as "identification with the oppressor" to the degree that members of oppressed groups "internalize the image of the op-pressor and adopt his guidelines" for action and interaction in the world.

Children of color are embedded in a social context in which negative mes-sages are constantly swirling about them. If they are not supported by signif-icant others who consciously resist the messages of devaluation, it is difficult for them to develop a positive conception of their racial identity. Without ex-plicit support, children of color unconsciously internalize racist messages and incorporate these negative messages into their sense of self. The danger is that children will accept society's assessment of them as "less than" and incorpo-rate that negativity into their own identification and their attitudes toward other people of color.

If the pain, rejection, and exploitation of racism and sexism are not healed, a distress pattern is created that can lead individuals to reenact the distress with someone else in the victim role. Because of the pervasiveness of racism and sexism, women of color face systemic oppression by both individuals and institutions. Distress patterns created by racism are reenacted in the only places that are deemed "safe" in America: among members of the group, and within themselves through denial, self-invalidation, isolation, and fear.

Internalized oppression results in feelings of shame and the disowning of blackness. It manifests in various ways, but most relevant to our discussion are: relational difficulties, isolation, and the acceptance of negative stereotypes. In-dividuals project their unconscious feelings of rage, fear, and powerlessness onto other members of the group. It is not uncommon for internalized op-pression to drive some black people to avoid other blacks as much as possible. They may develop defensive patterns of interacting with other blacks and/or express shame and fear of other black people. In severe cases, individuals may feel safer among whites and make lifestyle choices that put them in social en-vironments in which they are totally isolated from contact with other black people. Internalized oppression may also result in the acceptance of negative stereotypes and evaluation of the self that incorporates ideas of "good hair/bad hair" and "light skin/dark skin" in determining overall value.

One can hardly speak of internalized oppression among black women without thinking of rap star Lil' Kim, who is well known for wearing blond wigs, blue contacts, ever-lightening skin, and plastic surgery. She is also, how-ever, well known for the frankness with which she discusses her own self-esteem problems and self-hatred. Reflecting on her own upbringing, Lil' Kim describes being bombarded with images of blonde-haired, blue-eyed girls as the ideal beauty. As a grown woman, she has often personified this Barbie image by transforming her physical presentation of self to conform to this ideal. She once described herself by saying, "I have low self-esteem and I always have. Guys always cheated on me with women who were European-looking. You know, the long-hair type. . . . Being a regular black girl wasn't good enough."[23]

This one brief quote illustrates several important ways that internalized oppression can manifest in black women. First and foremost, after internalizing messages that "blond + blue eyed = beautiful," and that her worth as a human being is dependent on her beauty and attractiveness to men, she experienced low self-esteem because of her inability to approximate these standards. Second, she articulates that she has repeatedly experienced men's preference for "European-looking" black women. Finally, in her adulthood, she has done everything possible to become that beauty ideal. As bell hooks describes her: "Donning blond wigs and getting a boob job so that she can resemble a cheap version of the white womanhood she adores wins her monetary success in the world of white supremacist, patriarchal capitalism and helps her cover up the fact that she has no self-worth."[24] hooks is correct that in a society where black girls are evaluated against a white beauty standard, we should not be surprised to find internalized oppression manifested as low self-worth, and that behaviors designed to approximate white standards are rewarded in the market.

Suzanne Lipsky, a black psychologist, describes her awareness of her own internalized racism in a way that summarizes and illustrates the various manifestations of internalized oppression:

> I can be sure that any time I feel intolerant of, irritated by, impatient with, embarrassed by, ashamed of, "not as black as," "blacker than," better than, not as good as, fearful of, not safe with, isolated from, mistrustful of, not cared about by, unable to support, or not supported by another black person, some pattern of internalized racism is at work. Any time I take action or do not take action on the basis of any of these feelings, I am giving in to a pattern of internalized oppression, racism, and powerlessness.[25]

We turn now to how these conflicts vary among dark- and light-skinned girls with the hope of providing caregivers with a window to both the surface issues that their children may face and the deeper issues that underlie them. Internalized oppression looks differently when it is enacted by dark-skinned and light-skinned girls so we discuss each of these separately and use examples to illustrate the variation.

Dark-Skinned Girls and Internalized Oppression

Internalized oppression for dark-skinned girls occurs when they are bombarded by negative messages that tell them their dark skin marks them as "ugly" and is a liability in attracting boys attention. Such messages come from the media but, more painfully, from members of their immediate and extended family and community members who reinforce the light skin/dark skin value system by differential treatment of children in the same family or by name-calling. If negative messages are internalized, dark-skinned girls can feel devalued and, in turn, express their rage toward lighter-skinned girls. At times, the easiest targets are light-skinned, mixed-race girls who are vulnerable due to their in-between status.

Light-skinned, mixed-race girls consistently report being told by dark-skinned (black) girls that they "thought they were better," or thought their light skin/white physical traits put them in a superior position. Listen closely to the interlocking nature of appearance and blackness in the way that three mixed-race women describe their childhood experiences with dark-skinned black girls and family members:

> SHEILA: They say I'm "stuck up," "a bitch," you know, "I think I'm better than everybody else because I'm light." Or "the only reason people like you is 'cause you're light and got curly hair." Or "you think you're better than everybody else because you're not really black." Yeah, they can be really cruel.

> MACEY: [My grandmother said] well, I don't know if that's my granddaughter. She's so light. My other grandchildren are dark skinned," and "she thinks she's better than everybody," and "look at her hair," and little things like that.

> KAYLA: In middle school, they would say "you have pretty hair" and "why do you have pretty hair?" And, of course, "her momma's white—she probably thinks she's better than everybody."[26]

When dark-skinned black girls feel devalued, this fuels negative interactions with mixed-race girls. However, the negative interactions have great potential for misinterpretation. For example, a mixed-race girl may interpret a negative comment about her appearance, not as a competitive joust (as intended), but as a rejection of her blackness. In fact, such a comment indicates precisely the opposite because the person making the comment is affirming her blackness, and thus her existence as a competitor for boys' attention. For mixed-race girls, such experiences can have devastating effects on their racial identity development. Dark-skinned black girls' competitive comments ("She thinks she's cuter than everybody else") are misinterpreted as group rejection ("They don't think I'm really black"). An ill-timed flip of "good" hair can end in fisticuffs that sow the very seeds of antiblack sentiment underlying an unhealthy biracial identification (i.e., "I'm *not* black, I'm biracial").

When darker-skinned girls behave in a rejecting way toward lighter-skinned girls, this usually is motivated by their own history of feeling rejected and negatively treated because of their skin color. Unlike rejection from whites that conveys superiority, rejection from dark-skinned females is rooted in the pain of inferiority. Driven by their own experiences of devaluation, they are more likely to perceive lighter-skinned girls as looking down on them, so their rejection responses are often formed around a defensive impulse. In other words, when white girls reject mixed-race girls, they do so from a place of privilege that communicates: "You are not white and therefore you aren't as good as I am." When black girls reject mixed-race girls, they do so from a place of pain that screams, "You are one of those people who have hurt me and so not only are you not a part of me, but I want you to feel some of the pain I feel." The pain that underpins this rejection is particularly harsh because it bleeds at the same time that it draws blood. The recipients find themselves in a conundrum because they are being rejected by those with whom they should be in solidarity. When white people are rejecting, this might hurt, but it is not unexpected. When black people are rejecting, it hurts more because it also alienates. It threatens to leave mixed-race girls with no place to go, and no place to turn for support or community.

Light-Skinned Girls and Internalized Oppression

Thus far, we have described how internalized oppression manifests in dark-skinned girl's rejection of light-skinned mixed-race girls. However, it is also important to discuss the flip side: light-skinned mixed-race girl's rejection of blackness and/or of black girls. As often as we hear about light-skinned girls experiencing hostility from dark-skinned girls, we hear about black girls who accuse mixed-race girls of thinking "they are better" because of their light skin.

While the literature is replete with discussions of how black women may be accusatory toward mixed-race women, it also happens that some mixed-race women honestly do think, feel, and act as if they are "better" than their darker-skinned sisters. The root cause of this sense of superiority is their internalized oppression. Because societal messages relentlessly communicate that light skin is more attractive than dark skin, we should not be surprised to find that some light-skinned girls have internalized this racist message and buy into the notion that they *are* "better" because of their skin color. This belief can fuel a deeply implanted sense of superiority that plays a catalytic role in the hostility they receive from darker-skinned girls.

When light-skinned girls internalize the white supremacist valuation of light skin, it can be devastating to their relationships with dark-skinned girls. If you recall, Ann (the light-skinned mixed-race woman who identifies as biracial) said she experienced difficulties with black women throughout her life. In reality, she had problems with a few darker-skinned girls whose behavior she then generalized to *all* black women. Ann currently has no black female friends, nor has she ever in her lifetime. This was not unusual considering that her childhood was spent in a predominately white suburban community where she had few opportunities to develop close ties with any black people. Ann described her problems with black women as "the complex I have with black women," and then paused to reframe the problem. In doing so, she attributed the blame to black women, and not herself. Later in her interview, she revealed the assumptions she brings to interactions with black women:

INTERVIEWER: Do you think you act differently around black people than you do around white people?

ANN: Um, yes, definitely. I'm a little bit more conscious of what I say. I don't think I'm gonna say something offensive. I'm just more conscious of [what I say] around black females

INTERVIEWER: Oh really?

ANN: If anything, I might seem a little more uptight around black um, around black people, but mostly black females, but it's kinda strange. My ex-boyfriend was black . . . and he thought that I had issues [with black people]. He always used to bring it up and say, "It's 'cause you're more comfortable around white people." And it pissed me off, but it was true somewhat. You're more comfortable with what you grow up with you know what I mean? So, yeah I guess I do act a little bit differently.

Ann's comments honestly illustrate that she 1) feels most comfortable with white people, 2) is uncomfortable around black people, 3) is *most* uncomfortable around black women, and 4) she behaves differently around black women. Ann has determined in her mind that black women cause problems in her life and that they will not accept her because, per her earlier quote, they think that she is trying to "take their man." Because she grew up in a white environment, she didn't have enough access to black people to realize that variation exists among black women and that all may not respond to her in the same manner. She also enjoys the attention she receives from black men and has internalized the idea that she *is* more beautiful than dark-skinned black women and that they resent her for her beauty. Ann brings all of these assumptions to her interactions with black women and admits adjusting her behavior.

It's not difficult to imagine how nervous and tense Ann is around black women, assuming that they are jealous of her and just waiting for a confrontation, which will only confirm her expectations of their behavior. Those interacting with her surely sense "the vibe"—that is, her tension, discomfort, and sense of superiority. Even black women who don't generally have problems with mixed-race women may find themselves in an agitated or defensive posture with Ann. At some level, Ann's interactions could be transformed if she could critically engage her deeply rooted sense of superiority and the way in which she projects it to others.

When answering a question after a lecture at Michigan State University, bell hooks illustrated the internalized-oppression-as-projected-superiority perfectly when she said, "Biracial women need to be aware of their hostile gestures." As she made this statement, she flicked an imaginary mane of waist-length hair over her shoulder, eliciting howling laughter from the black women in attendance. This was a gesture so recognizable that it did not require further explanation to the members of the audience. More directly, it was the one gesture that seemed to personify the historically rooted sense of superiority of those who approximate a white beauty standard. In the flicking of that hypothetical "good" hair, she signified how the flaunting of internalized superiority simultaneously projects hostility and a devaluation of blackness.

In the following section, we present strategies that parents and professionals can use to challenge internalized oppression and help girls acknowledge, articulate, and actively resist societal pressure to define their value according to existing beauty standards.

STRATEGIES FOR DEVELOPING CRITICAL CONSCIOUSNESS

Parents and professionals must assume an active role in deconstructing the ways in which racism and sexism converge and impinge on the lives of children of color. To do this, parents and other adults must foster the development of what hooks refers to as "critical consciousness," which is the ability to critique and analyze the overt and the subtle manifestations of oppressive ways of thinking, being, and doing. Those who possess critical consciousness look beneath the surface to identify and question the underlying ideologies that are reflected in any and all aspects of our socially constructed realities. For example, those who possess critical consciousness might probe to identify the messages about race and gender that are being conveyed in product advertising, popular films, music videos, the platforms espoused by candidates for political office, the types of institutional policies that are adopted, customs that dictate how holidays are celebrated, and implicit social "rules" that dictate everything from where people sit on public transportation, to how greetings are expressed, to who marries who, to how people express emotions. None of these things exist in a vacuum; instead, all of these ways of being and doing reflect specific values that are rooted in broader ideologies. Those with critical consciousness consistently question the underlying values and ideologies that are reflected and reinforced by social activity and cultural productions.

Teaching children to exercise critical consciousness is a way of preparing them to recognize and resist the numerous ways that racism and sexism are present in their social world. Parents and other adults can support the development of critical consciousness in children through a combination of both direct and indirect means. Direct methods consist of talking with children in a straightforward way about racism and sexism and providing them with examples from daily life. Direct methods also consist of sending overt messages that challenge racist and sexist values. For example, adults can do this by saying things such as: "Girls and boys are both smart and neither gender is better than the other," or, "In our society there is a tendency to act as if lighter skin is better, but that's not true. All skin colors are equally beautiful, just in different ways." Messages such as these directly counteract the racist and sexist conditioning that espouses men are better than women and light is better than dark. Children benefit from hearing adults disrupt these ideas and advocate countercultural messages that undermine racism and sexism.

Adults can indirectly foster the development of critical consciousness by asking children provocative questions to hone children's ability to deconstruct the racist and sexist messages that are woven into common cultural practices. For example, when watching a T.V. show, movie, or music video, parents might ask their children, "What messages do you think this ad (or T.V. show or movie) is conveying about women? What is it saying about women of color? About black people? The purpose of such questions is to invite children to start looking beneath the surface by examining the underlying messages in the media. These types of questions also orient them to consider race and gender issues. Most importantly, by asking questions, parents create space for dialogue, which is an essential dimension in the formation of critical consciousness.

While we have focused here on how the forces of sexism and racism impact mixed-race and black girls, it is necessary to teach *both* boys and girls to recognize and challenge these forces. Eventually, the boys of today will grow into the men of tomorrow, who, if not socialized to think critically about race and gender, will unwittingly reproduce sexist oppression. Teaching boys to respect women generally and value women of color specifically is a way of making a down payment on a future generation who will have the capacity to acting in nonoppressive ways.

Challenging Racial and Gender Biases from the Inside Out

One of the challenges parents and professionals may face as they strive to teach children to resist racism and sexism is the extent that they carry these values within themselves. Most, if not all, of us have been raised in a culture that supports white supremacist and patriarchal values. To some extent, we each carry these values in our own attitudes and behavior. If we are to support children in resisting sexism and racism, we must be willing to examine our own beliefs and biases.

In mixed-race families, a common way parents unwittingly reinforce racist and sexist ideology is through preferential behavior based on skin color and/or physical appearance. Most parents love all of their children, yet it is not uncommon for parents to prefer some of their children to others. Moreover, parental preferences sometimes reflect underlying race and gender preferences. For example, a father who has both a daughter and a son may display preferential treatment toward his son because he values boys more than girls. A mother who has three children whose complexions vary may prefer the lightest-skinned child because she unconsciously values lighter skin over darker skin.

Within families where there are parental preferences, most children are painfully aware of them and understand why they exist. For parents, recognizing their preferences, especially when they are linked to race and gender, can be difficult because of their desire to treat all children equally. Because most parents do, in fact, love all of their children, it can be extremely hard to see how they may extend preferential treatment to one child over others, or how they might invest higher hopes in, and have greater expectations of, one child than another. It is even more difficult to see how such preferences may be linked to underlying race and gender biases. Yet, the ability to look within is essential for any parent committed to treating all children fairly and to creating a family environment that resists (rather than replicates) race and gender biases. Seeing all aspects of our adult selves is the first step in confronting these problematic behavior patterns.

Resisting Societal Definitions of Female Worth and Beauty

For parents raising mixed-race children, it is important to send clear and consistent messages that teach children to value *all* skin colors and physical features. This is especially critical in the case of girls because, as we have argued, physical appearance is more important for girls than boys. While most children of color experience some devaluation on the basis of physical characteristics, this devaluation is intensified for girls because of the emphasis that society places on female beauty. Because girls receive countless messages that their worth is defined by their approximation of a white beauty standard, parents must actively convey that all of their daughters are beautiful and their worth is not determined by their physical characteristics.

There are many different ways adults can present countercultural messages about how girls' worth and beauty are defined. The reading materials suggested in appendix C should be helpful, but parents should also directly affirm each girl's physical beauty, even when it does not conform to conventional societal standards. This can also be accomplished indirectly by referring to specific physical characteristics that are not valued by the broader society, and making a point to affirm the beauty of these qualities. For example, an adult might make a point to comment on the beauty of a particular woman's dark skin to provide children with alternative ways of defining what is beautiful. Actions such as these resist narrow definitions of beauty advanced by the broader culture and provide children with a more inclusive and healthy way of conceptualizing beauty.

While it is useful to broaden the definition of what is considered beautiful, it is even more helpful to support girls in seeing themselves as more than just their physical bodies. In other words, it is imperative to support girls in developing their intellectual, athletic, and spiritual capacities, which fosters the notion that they are multidimensional beings and not merely defined in terms of their bodies and beauty.

Promoting Sisterhood

It is especially important to actively socialize girls to think in terms of a "sisterhood" that goes beyond their siblings. Girls must be proactively taught to recognize their shared connection and interrelatedness. By promoting sisterhood among girls of color, adults socialize them to use their energies to lift each other up instead of pulling each other down. Not only is sisterhood a way of disrupting racist and sexist socialization, but it also provides girls of color with a buffer against the racism and sexism that is pervasive in the wider world around them.

Cultivating sisterhood within families can be challenging because sibling rivalry is inevitable and children experience conflicts as a normative part of development. However, when conflicts between sisters have racialized and gendered tensions, parents must be vigilant in disrupting them from the outset. For example, it is not uncommon for children to become embroiled in arguments and to hurl insults at each other. But when these insults contain racist and sexist messages, parents must assume a proactive role in curtailing them. Failing to do so is tacit approval. For example, Cecile, an African American woman, had four mixed-race daughters of varying complexions.[27] One afternoon, Cecile overheard two of the older girls arguing. The lighter of the two called the other "a nappy-headed bitch." Cecile did not hesitate to intervene by sitting both girls down and telling them:

> I don't know what you two were arguing about, but I know that whatever it was, I will not tolerate having you tear each other apart as young women of color. It's okay to have disagreements and to get mad at each other, but it is never okay to start dissing each other as young women, or on the basis of how you look. There are enough people out there who will do that, you two don't need to do it to each other. In fact, no matter how mad you get with each other, the bottom line is that you are sisters and you need to focus on lifting each other up, not pulling each other down. You are both beautiful in different ways and you need to affirm each other's beauty, even when you don't agree about something. Trust me, if you don't stand together in sisterhood, neither one of you will stand alone for very long.

Promoting a Sense of Wholeness When One Has Been Devalued

As we have discussed, it is all too common for tension to exist between light-skinned and dark-skinned girls. The stories of a light-skinned girl coming home in tears because a darker-skinned girl accused her of being "stuck up" and "thinking she's better because she's light," or of a darker-skinned girl coming home in tears because lighter-skinned girls rejected her and made her feel ugly, are all too common. The question is: What specific steps can parents and other adults take to help girls understand and work through situations when they have been insulted, devalued, or rejected because of their physical appearance? We propose the following guidelines.

1) Validate the Pain the Child Has Experienced

It is crucial to begin by validating the pain the child in question is experiencing. Adults should devote considerable energy toward understanding the emotions a child is feeling at the moment by acknowledging how hard the experience must be for her. Hearing and validating have a comforting effect and help ease the angst the child is feeling.

2) Encourage Role-Taking

After a child has been sufficiently validated, it becomes possible to ease into a specific discussion about what happened. After the facts have been recalled, then shift to ask the child to assume the position of those who assaulted her and try to imagine what reasons there may have been for their actions/ inactions. For example, a parent might ask: "So those two girls were mean to you because they believe you think you're better because you're lighter-skinned. Why do you think that's something they are even thinking about and worried about?" If this is a child who has been encouraged to think critically about issues of race and gender, she will probably be able to explain some of the dynamics underpinning this phenomenon. If not, this becomes a teachable moment where an adult might say: "Well, we live in a society where people with darker skin are often treated worse than people with lighter skin. Of course, this isn't fair or right, but it happens. How they treated you was not right, but I want you to understand why they may have done that and to try to understand how they might feel."

In another example, a dark-skinned child might have been mistreated by lighter-skinned children. In this situation, an adult might start by asking the child: "Why do you think those girls made mean comments about your complexion?" Again, this creates an opportunity for the child to identify how racist conditioning distorts how many people perceive skin color. If the child does not seem aware of these dynamics, or even if she is, it would be appropriate for the adult to offer the following: "We live in a society where some people think lighter skin is better than darker skin. Now, those people are wrong, and when you meet people like that you have to remember that whatever they say or do, this idea is wrong. Your dark skin is beautiful and don't let anyone try to convince you otherwise. In fact, it's sad that these girls don't understand this."

3) Discuss Empowering Responses

Finally, parents should conclude by asking the child to consider what they would like to do now so they can feel okay. This allows the child to feel a sense of mastery and control because, while she cannot control how others treat her, she has a choice about how she will respond, and this is the essence of empowerment. For example, an adult might say, "How those girls treated you is not nice, I agree, and I can see why it hurt your feelings. But you can't control them; you can only control yourself. So how would you like to handle this situation now? What do you think you should do now so you can feel okay about this?"

As we have argued, the interaction of race and gender oppression creates unique challenges for mixed-race girls. However, there are various strategies parents and professionals can employ to help them negotiate the dilemmas and difficulties that they may encounter in their racial identity development. Each conscious effort taken on the part of caregivers can help mixed-race girls move closer to the goal of finding ways to live in balance with themselves and with those around them.

NOTES

1. The notable exceptions are Helena Herschel, "The Influence of Gender and Race Status on Self-Esteem during Childhood and Adolescence," in *Race/Sex: Their Sameness, Difference, and Interplay*, ed. Naomi Zack (New York: Routledge, 1997); and Maria Root, "Resolving 'Other' Status: Identity Development of Biracial Individuals," *Women & Therapy* 9.1–2 (1990): 185–205.

2. See Michael Hughes and Bradley Hertel, "The Significance of Color Remains: A Study of Life Chances, Mate Selection, and Ethnic Consciousness among Black Americans," *Social Forces* 68.4 (1990): 1105–20.

3. Jewelle Taylor Gibbs, "Biracial Adolescents," in *Children of Color: Psychological Interventions with Culturally Diverse Youth*, eds. Jewelle Taylor Gibbs and Larke Nahme Huang (San Francisco, Calif.: Jossey-Bass, 1998): 305–32; Roger Herring, "Biracial Children: An Increasing Concern for Elementary and Middle School Counselors," *Elementary School Guidance & Counseling* 27.2 (1992): 123–30; Kerry Ann Rockquemore, "Negotiating the Color Line: The Gendered Process of Racial Identity Construction among Black/White Biracial Women," *Gender & Society* 16.4 (2002): 485–503.

4. Kathy Russell, Midge Wilson, and Ronald Hall, *The Color Complex: The Politics of Skin Color among African Americans* (New York: Harcourt Brace Jovanovich, 1992).

5. Ronald E. Hall, "Bias among African Americans Regarding Skin Color: Implications for Social Work Practice," *Research on Social Work Practice* 2.4 (1992): 479–86; Angela Neal and Midge Wilson, "The Role of Skin Color and Features in the Black Community: Implications for Black Women and Therapy," *Clinical Psychology Review* 9.3 (1989): 323–33; Russell, Wilson, and Hall, *The Color Complex: The Politics*

of Skin Color among African Americans. See also Hughes and Hertel, "The Significance of Color Remains" and Verna Keith and Cedric Herring, "Skin Tone and Stratification in the Black Community," *American Journal of Sociology* 97.3 (1991): 760–78.

6. St. Clair Drake and Horace R. Cayton, *Black Metropolis: A Study of Negro Life in a Northern City* (New York: Harcourt Brace, 1945); William H. Grier and Price M. Cobbs, *Black Rage* (New York: Basic Books, 1968).

7. Robin Lakoff and Raquel Scherr, *Face Value: The Politics of Beauty* (Boston, Mass.: Routledge & Kegan Paul, 1984).

8. See Nancy Baker, *The Beauty Trap: Exploring Woman's Greatest Obsession* (New York: Franklin Watts, 1984), and Thomas F. Cash and Thomas Pruzinsky, *Body Images: Development, Deviance, and Change* (New York: Guilford Press, 1990).

9. Drake and Cayton, *Black Metropolis*; Grier and Cobbs, *Black Rage*; Margaret L. Hunter, "Colorstruck: Skin Color Stratification in the Lives of African American Women," *Sociological Inquiry* 68.4 (1998): 517–35; Charles Spurgeon Johnson, *Growing up in the Black Belt: Negro Youth in the Rural South* (Washington, D.C.: American Council on Education, 1941).

10. Rockquemore, "Negotiating the Color Line."

11. Sue was an undergraduate student in Laszloffy's course called Families and Society.

12. Lydia was a member of a focus group that explored race relations among students of color at a midsize Northeastern university.

13. Tina was a member of the focus group that explored race relations among students of color at a midsize Northeastern university.

14. Maria Root, "Experiences and Processes Affecting Racial Identity Development: Preliminary Results from the Biracial Sibling Project," *Cultural Diversity & Mental Health* 4.3 (1998): 237–47, 243.

15. Maya and Kelly were both undergraduates who were members of the students of color focus group.

16. Laura was Laszloffy's client in therapy.

17. The literature on skin-color stratification in dating and marriage has a heterosexist bias. Because we are drawing our discussion form existing empirical

studies, and because researchers have yet to begin systematically studying the same processes among homosexuals and/or determining whether differences occur on the basis of sexual orientation, we do not address this issue in the text. We do, however, recommend readers interested in same-sex interracial households to recent and notable exploratory work in Bea Wehrly, Kelley Kenney, and Mark Kenney, *Counseling Multiracial Families* (Thousand Oaks, Calif.: Sage Publications, 1999).

18. Selena Bond and Thomas Cash, "Black Beauty: Skin Color and Body Images among African American College Women," *Journal of Applied Social Psychology* 22.11 (1992): 874–88.

19. Neal and Wilson, "The Role of Skin Color and Features in the Black Community."

20. Margo Okazawa-Rey, Tracy Robinson, and Janie Ward, "Black Women and the Politics of Skin Color and Hair," *Women & Therapy* 6.1–2 (1987).

21. Both black and mixed-race boys receive the same messages as girls about skin color and physical features. However, for boys, the color complex typically manifests as a preference for light-skinned (or white) girls as dating and/or sexual partners. While boys may also experience the general valuing of light skin over dark, they are not in an analogous position to girls in terms of dating, or the dependency of their self-worth on physical appearance. Often, mixed-race boys experience the benefit of their scarcity, interpreting black girl's attention as validation of their blackness. Mixed-race boys don't compete with black boys for a small pool of mates the way that teenage girls do; they are advantaged in a seller's market and, therefore, do not experience the same level of hostility and rejection from darker-skinned boys.

22. Fanon Frantz, *Black Skin, White Masks* (New York: Grove Press, 1967).

23. Chisolm, Jamilya, "Imitation of Life." *The Source* (2002): 114–17.

24. bell hooks, *Rock My Soul: Black People and Self-Esteem* (New York: Atria Books, 2003).

25. Suzanne Lipsky, *Internalized Racism*, (Seattle, Wash.: Rational Island Publishers, 1987).

26. These cases are drawn from Kerry Ann Rockquemore and Patricia Arend, "Opting for White: Choice, Fluidity, and Black Identity Construction in Post-Civil Rights America." *Race & Society* 5.1 (2003): 51–66 (forthcoming).

27. Cecile was a client of Laszloffy's colleague.

8

Multiracialism in America: Reflections and New Directions

At the heart of the COBI model is the fact that mixed-race people develop various racial identities. However, what is important is that their choices reflect an underlying acceptance, rather than a denial, of mixed-race ancestry. The fundamental truth in all mixed-race people's lives is that they are the children of interracial families. No matter how hard, uncomfortable, or even unacceptable this reality may be for some, this is their truth, and their life task is to resolve their in-between status in a society that negates and devalues their existence.

We believe that psychological health requires an acceptance of truth and, in this case, it requires acceptance of the truth that one has both black and white parents. On this foundational acceptance, it is possible to develop a singular identity that emphasizes one race more than another, a blended identity that balances both, or a transcendent identity where a person acknowledges their full ancestry but elects to subjugate the meaning of race to a broader understanding of self. For those who do not accept their mixed-race ancestry, this denial may also manifest in a singular identity (where one acknowledges only one part) or a blended identity (where one does not authentically accept both parts of self but is "forced" by external conditions to present one's self in a blended way as biracial) or as a transcendent who refuses to acknowledge either part and claims a "raceless" identity.

For caregivers of mixed-race children, it is important to understand the role socialization experiences play in shaping the identity children eventually establish. The racial ideologies, life experiences, and ways that parents and other adults define themselves racially greatly affect children's identity development. When parents and other adults are able to acknowledge children's blackness *and* whiteness, they convey a message to children that supports the acceptance and blending of their ancestry. More importantly, when parents and other adults are able to truly value both blackness and whiteness, this is communicated to children and establishes a foundation for acceptance. Conversely, when adults implicitly or explicitly deny, reject, or devalue either blackness or whiteness, this undermines children's capacity to accept both parts of self. Hence, the role that adults play in shaping children's identity is crucial and it is imperative that they understand the power of the messages they send to children.

One of the strands we have tried to weave throughout this book is our strong belief that the process of racial identity development occurs within a broader social context. In the United States this context is greatly informed by the ideology of white supremacy, the legacy of slavery, the one-drop rule, and contemporary manifestations of racism at all levels of society. This context inevitably influences how mixed-race people learn to think and feel about themselves. We live in a society that overvalues whiteness and devalues blackness, which makes the matter of accepting both black and white parts of one's self complicated. Our historical and contemporary racial contexts work against the very process that we are arguing is essential to health—namely, that mixed-race people accept their full self. Moreover, the social context makes it difficult for parents and other adults to develop a balanced view of blackness and whiteness such that they can support children in developing a healthy relationship with both aspects of their ancestry.

While it is true that society is slanted in ways that make it challenging for mixed-race people to accept and value their mixed-ancestry, this does not preclude the role of individual agency in the process of identity development. Adults who are involved in the lives of mixed-race children and children themselves can act in ways that resist conventional norms that limit how mixed-race people can and should self-identify. We live in a racially polarized society that views black and white in extreme oppositional and unrelated terms. This separation is designed to reinforce the assumption that white represents all goodness and black all badness. For mixed-race people to develop a healthy sense of themselves, regardless of whether they adopt a singular, blended, or transcendent identity, they must resist these polarizations and the unequal values attached to both white and black. This requires personal agency and a conscious, willful choice to resist racist conclusions and the categories that stem from these conclusions.

We have presented a range of strategies for parents and practitioners that assume that individuals can make purposeful choices that push back against the grain of the prevailing social order. While society most certainly influences our views on race and racial identity, each person can elect to think critically about these issues and act in ways that disrupt conventional logic. It is possible and, as we argue throughout, healthy for mixed-race people to think explicitly about matters of race, and to make conscious, informed choices about how and why they self-identify that hopefully will reflect an underlying acceptance of both whiteness and blackness and a balanced view of the "good" and "bad" reflected in each. Toward this end, we also include three appendices at the end of this book that we offer as resources to aid and support parents and other adults in helping mixed-race children develop ways of being, thinking, and behaving that involve empowerment and acceptance.

As the frequency of interracial relationships increases, the pressure to reconsider existing racial classifications is also increasing. We already have seen this in the 2000 Census, where the long-standing norm of mutual exclusivity between categorizations has melted away to include a "check all that apply" directive. However, even as the assumption that one can only belong to one racial group is being challenged, the sense that race (as we know it) is an illusion, is not. And so, while we may consider the acknowledgment of mixed-race identities a progressive movement in race-relations, the eight-hundred-pound gorilla is still sitting in the middle of the living room. In other words, while the acknowledgment of multiracial identity is a sign of progress, it still assumes that there is some biological basis for grouping human into five racial categories. As we have argued throughout, this view is flawed. However, until the social reality catches up to the biological evidence, or until we start understanding in our social lives what we already know scientifically, progress will remain slow.

Multiracial children growing up today exist at a transitional moment in history—when race is both real and unreal, trapped somewhere between the enduring legacy of slavery and the promise of the Multiracial movement. As caregivers, it is our responsibility to understand the current moment for what it is politically, culturally, and sociologically and to support children in developing healthy racial identities. This means that we have to help them to understand the racial realities of the broader society we live in, and to understand how race influences their relationships with family members, teachers, friends, and peers. It is our deepest hope that mixed-race children will learn to better understand the social realities of race while using their personal power to push against narrow social conventions and oppressive social constructions. Certainly, we look forward to the day when the very concept of "mixed-race" will be obsolete because race as a social system for categorizing and defining people will have given way to the truth of our common humanness. Until that day comes, or rather, as a step in that direction, we hope that this book serves as a useful resource for raising mixed-race children who, grounded in a foundation of acceptance, will develop and proudly assert varied and diverse ways of racial self-definition.

Appendix A

Multiracial Organizations

NATIONAL ORGANIZATIONS

AMEA (Association of Multiethnic Americans)
>   The mission of AMEA is "to educate and advocate on behalf of multiethnic in-
>   dividuals and families by collaborating with others to eradicate all forms of dis-
>   crimination."
>   Association of MultiEthnic Americans, Inc.
>   P.O. Box 341304
>   Los Angeles, CA 90034-1304
>   www.ameasite.org

A Place for Us
>   "A Place for Us National . . . is the largest multiracial establishment designed to
>   promote racial harmony. In doing so, we support multiracial families and their
>   extended families (and confront the issues of the day head on)."
>   A Place for Us National Headquarters
>   Luneda Quincy Ali
>   P.O. Box 357
>   Gardena, CA 90248
>   Email: rita@aplaceforusnational.com
>   www.aplaceforusnational.com/home.html

The Center for the Study of Biracial Children
"Produces and disseminates materials for and about interracial families and biracial children. The Center provides advocacy, training and consulting. Its primary mission is to advocate for the rights of interracial families, biracial children, and multiracial people."
Dr. Francis Wardle
2300 S. Kramaria Street
Denver, CO 80222
Email: francis@csbc.cncfamily.com
www.csbc.cncfamily.com

MAVIN Foundation
"MAVIN Foundation is the nation's leading nonprofit organization that is redefining diversity by celebrating multiracial and transracially adopted youth. Through our programs, we are helping to create a cohesive, multicultural society."
MAVIN Foundation
600 First Avenue, Suite 600
Seattle, WA 98104
Phone: (888) 77-MAVIN or (206-622-7101)
Email: info@mavinfoundation.org
www.mavinfoundation.org

National Advocacy for the Multi-Ethnic (NAME)
NAME "provides support and advocacy for individuals from diverse backgrounds through education, fellowship and unity."
rmail: info@namecentral.org
www.namecentral.org

Project RACE
"Project RACE advocates for multiracial children and adults through education, community awareness and legislation. Our main goal is for a multiracial classification on all school, employment, state, federal, local, census and medical forms requiring racial data."
Susan Graham
Project RACE
2910 Kerry Forest Parkway, D4-129
Tallahassee, FL 32309

Email: projrace@aol.com

www.projectrace.com

Swirl

"Swirl aims to unite the mixed community by providing support to mixed families, individuals, adoptees, and interracial couples."

Jen Chau

16 West 32nd Street, Suite 10A

New York, NY 10001

ListServ: http://groups.yahoo.com/group/SWIRLinc

www.swirlinc.org

STATE ORGANIZATIONS

Arizona

MOSAIC (Multiethnics of Southern Arizona in Celebration)

Levonne Gaddy

P.O. Box 8335

Tucson, AZ 85738

Phone: (520) 825-6754

Email: levonne@theriver.com

Arkansas

A Place for Us, Arkansas

DeWaldon & Rita Frazier

P.O. Box 724

North Little Rock, AR 72114

Phone: (501) 744-8859

Email: rita@aplaceforusnational.com

www.angelfire.com/nv/aplaceforus/arkansas.html

Interracial Lifestyle Connection

Gary Bowden

4406 North 54th Street

Fort Smith, AR 72904

Phone: (501) 785-4304

Swirl, Arkansas

Charlie Johnson

Email: zebraboy_72@yahoo.com

California

A Place for Us, Northern CA
 Judy McGee,
 1668 Seville Street
 Salinas, CA 93906
 Phone: (408) 442-8651 or (408) 770-2190

Hapa Issues Forum
 Hapa Issues Forum, Inc.
 1840 Sutter Street
 San Francisco, CA 94115-3220
 Phone: (415) 409-HAPA
 Email: hif@hapaissuesforum.org
 http://hapasissuesforum.org

 Southern California Chapter
 231 East Third Street, Suite G-104
 Los Angeles, CA 90013-1493
 Phone: (213) 694-0286
 Email: socal@hapaissuesforum.org

I-Pride, Interracial/Intercultural Pride
 I-Pride
 P.O. Box 11811
 Berkeley, CA 94712-2811
 Phone: (510) 633-0975
 Email: (510) 633-0975
 hwww.i-pride.org

Multiracial Americans of Southern California (MASC)
 12228 Venice Blvd., Suite 542
 Los Angeles, CA 90066
 Phone: 310-836-1535
 Email: MASCorg@yahoo.com
 http://AMEAsite.org/masc.asp

National Multi-Ethnic Families Association (NaMEFA)
 2073 N. Oxnard Blvd., Suite 172
 Oxnard, CA 93030
 Email: yaz@earthlink.net

Our Colors Inc.
    3919 Lusk Street
    Oakland, CA 94608
    Email: info@ourcolors.net
    Phone: (510) 655-8264 ext. 2
    www.ourcolors.net

Race Unity Matters! of Northern California
    4309 Linda Vista Avenue
    Napa, CA 94558

Swirl, Silicone Valley
    Phone: (408) 236-3460
    Email: SVSwirl@yahoo.com

Swirl, Bay Area
    Email: swirl_rsvp@yahoo.com

Swirl, Los Angeles
    Email: adiahoag@hotmail.com

Colorado
Center for the Study of Biracial Children
    Francis Wardle
    2300 South Krameria Street
    Denver, CO 80222
    Phone: (303) 692-9008
    Email: francis@csbc.cncfamily.com
    www.csbc.cncfamily.com

Families of Color Communiqué
    C. Lessman
    P.O. Box 478
    Fort Collins, CO 80522
    Phone: (303) 223-9658

Connecticut
The Metis Nation in New England
    P.O. Box 1013
    Washington, NH 03280-1013

Email: METISNwEng@aol.com
http://members.aol.com/METISNwEng/vision.html

District of Columbia
Interracial Family Circle of Washington, D.C.
P.O. Box 53291
Washington, D.C. 20009
Phone: (202) 393-7866
Email: info@interracialfamilycircle.org
www.interracialfamilycircle.org

Florida
Biracial & Natural Children (BRANCH)
P.O. Box 50051
Lighthouse Point, FL 33074
Phone: (305) 781-6798

Lifeline for Children
P.O. Box 17184
Plantation, FL 33318
Email: a032725t@bc.seflin.org

Tallahassee Multiracial Connection
2001 Holmes Street
Tallahassee, FL 32310
Phone: (904) 576-6734

Unity—A Multiracial Social Group
B. J. Winchester
P.O. Box 2902
Orange Park, FL 32073-2902
Phone: (904) 276-6668
Email: BJWinchester@alliedprint.com

Swirl, South Florida
Rachael Lee
Email: anaxita@bellsouth.net

Georgia
Interracial Family Alliance
  P.O. Box 450473
  Atlanta, GA 31145
  (770) 924-8453
  Email: atlantaifa@hotmail.com

Illinois
Adoptive Parents Together
  Linda Russo
  427 N. Wheaton Avenue
  Wheaton, IL 60187

Biracial Family Network (AMEA Affiliate)
  P.O. Box 2387
  Chicago, IL 60690-2387
  Phone: (773) 288-3644
  Email: info@bfnchicago.org

Champaign County Crayola Club
  Ellyn Bullock
  1311 W. University
  Champaign, IL 61821
  Phone: (217) 359-7416
  Email: ejbullock@nhb-law.com

Child International
  4121 Crestwood
  Northbrook, IL 60062
  Phone: (847) 272-2511

Families for Interracial Awareness
  Linda Thomas
  Phone: (708) 869-7117

Interracial Family Network
  Dickelle Fonda
  P.O. Box 5380
  Evanston, IL 60204-5380

Phone: (847) 491-9748
Email: mfonda@aol.com

Multiracial Families of Oak Park
Linda Bailey
P.O. Box 1158
Oak Park, IL 60304
Phone: (708) 524-4577

North Shore Race Unity Task Force
536 Sheridan Rd.
Wilmette, IL 60091

Tapestry
Sherry Blass
40 Francis Avenue
Crystal Lake, IL 60014

Louisiana
Creole Heritage Center
Janet Ravare Colson
NSU Box 5675
Natchitoches, LA 71497
Phone: (318) 357-6685
Email: colsonj@nsula.edu
www.nsula.edu/creole

Maryland
Amegroid Society of America
Deanna Lewis
P.O. Box 30149
Baltimore, MD 21270
Email: hobustel@aol.com
www.ameribiz.com/asa/forum.htm

Massachusetts
Multiracial Family Group Network
Jane Chiong
P.O. Box 554 (Newton Branch)
Boston, MA 02258
Phone: (617) 332-6241

New England Alliance of Multiracial Families
    39 Dodge Street, No. 338
    Beverly, MA 01915
    Phone: (617) 962-3886
    Email: neamforg@aol.com
    www.neamf.org

Students of Mixed Heritage
    SU 3187, Williams College
    Williamstown, MA 01267
    Phone: (413) 597-3354

Swirl, Boston
    Email: lambesusan@yahoo.com
    www.synthscribe.com/swirl/events.htm

Michigan
Multiracial Family and Youth Network
    P.O. Box 7521
    Bloomfield Hills, MI 48302
    Phone: (313) 335-7629

Multiracial Group at University of Michigan
    Karen E. Downing
    122 Undergraduate Library
    Ann Arbor, MI 48109-1185
    Phone: (313) 763-5084
    Email: kdown@umich.edu

Society for Interracial Families
    Pam D'Souza
    P.O. Box 4942
    Troy, MI 48099
    Phone: (313) 643-6652

Minnesota
Multi-Cultural Development Center
    US Bank Building
    9633 Lyndale Avenue South
    Bloomington, MN 55420

Phone: (952) 881-6090
Email: info@mcdc.org
www.mcdc.org

TIRAH Society
Chris McCoy
P.O. Box 241016
Apple Valley, MN 55124
Phone: (612) 891-3415
Email: natirah@aol.com

Swirl, Minneapolis
Brian Kelley
Email: kelley01@visi.com

Missouri
Interracial Family Unity Network
Diana Page
1015 Dulle Street
Jefferson City, MO 65109-2576
Phone: (314) 635-6375 or (314) 635-9899

Multiracial Family Circle of Kansas City, MO
Kevin L. Barber
P.O. Box 32414
Kansas City, MO 64171
Email: MFCircle@aol.com
www.matracore.com/mfc/intro.htm

Nevada
A Place for Us Nevada
Email: aplaceforus@counsellor.com

New Jersey
4C (Cross Cultural Couples & Children) of Plainsboro New Jersey
Lisa Edwards
P.O. Box 8
Plainsboro, NJ 08536-4104

Phone: (609) 448-8823 or (609)-275-9352 (eve)
Email: tango-sierra@geocities.com
www.geocities.com/Heartland/Meadows/7936/7936.html

Getting Interracial/cultural Families Together (G.I.F.T.)
Pete & Lois Donegan
P.O. Box 1281
Montclair, NJ 07042
Phone: (973) 783-0083
Email: info@njgift.org
http://groups.yahoo.com/group/NJGIFT

InterRacial Life
Dave Seibel
2 George Street
East Brunswick, NJ 08816
Phone: (732) 390-7316
Email: david_seibel@ml.com

Multiracial Family Support Group
Bobbi Joels
265 Hempstead Drive
Somerset, NJ 08873
Phone: (732) 296-0734
Email: BobbiJoels@aol.com

New York
A Place for Us/Multiethnic Women for Media Fairness/Interracial Women's Political Consortium
Valerie Wilkins-Godbee
P.O. Box 859
Peekskill, NY 10566
Phone: (914) 788-1482
Email: vwilkins@hotmail.com

INTERace
P.O. Box 582
Forest Hills, NY 11375-9998

Interracial Club of Buffalo
Mary Murchison-Edwords
Box 400 (Amherst Branch)
Buffalo, NY 14226
Phone: (716) 875-6958
Email: MEdwo32688@aol.com

Jewish Multiracial Network
307 Seventh Avenue, Suite 900
New York, NY 10001
Phone: (212) 242-5598
Email: info@jmnetwork.org
www.jmnetwork.org

Swirl, Long Island
Darin Vest
Email: adlvest@aol.com

North Carolina
GIFT
Carri Uram
103 Green Lake Drive
Greenville, NC 29607
Phone: (864) 233-4872
Email: speclink@greenville.infi.net

Triangle Interracial and Multicultural Experience (TIME)
Marsha Alston
15A Woodbridge Drive
Chapel Hill, NC 27516

Ohio
Cleveland Area Interracial Families (CAIFA)
Michael & Joylyn Schweglar
808 East 203 Place
Euclid, OH 44119

Cincinnati Multiracial Alliance
P.O. Box 17163
Street Bernard, OH 45217
(513) 791-6023

Heights Multicultural Group
Sylvia Billups
South Euclid, OH 44121
Phone: (216) 382-7912
Email: ladyshep@aol.com

Interracial Family Association
Reginald A. Saxton
P.O. Box 34323
Parma, OH 44134
Phone: (216) 348-3500

Interracial Families in Friendship
P.O. Box 82628
Columbus, OH 43202
Email: Columbus/Central area: janet@simplyliving.org
Delaware/Northern area: wolftale@wolftale.net
Newark/Eastern area: alexnan@alltel.net
www.simplyliving.org/ifif

Rainbow Families of Toledo
Nancy Shanks
1920 S. Shore Blvd.
Oregon, OH 43618
Phone: (419) 693-9259

Oregon
Honor Our New Ethnic Youth (HONEY)
Sarah Ross
P.O. Box 23241
Eugene, OR 97402
Phone: (541) 343-4023
Email: EugeneHoney@aol.com

Interracial Family Network
  P.O. Box 12505
  Portland, OR 97212

Oregon Council on Multicultural Affairs (AMEA Affiliate)
  7218 N.E. Sandy Blvd., Suite 3
  Portland, OR 97213
  Phone: 503-249-3926
  Email: cirector@ocma-multiracial.org
  http://ocma-multiracial.org/

People of Every Stripe
  Ed Cooper
  P.O. Box 12505
  Portland, OR 97212
  Phone: (503) 282-0612

Pennsylvania
Interracial Families, Inc.
  5450 Friendship Avenue
  Pittsburgh, PA 15232
  Phone: (412) 661-7414

Rainbow Circle
  Broadfield Association
  P.O. Box 242
  Chester, PA 19016

SOME Families
  1798 Unionville-Lenape Rd.
  West Chester, PA 19382
  Phone: (215) 793-1533

Swirl, Philadelphia
  Email: swirlphillyevents@yahoo.com

South Carolina
One Love
  104 Brookwood Drive
  Seneca, SC 29678

Tennessee

A Place for Us
    Marie Beck
    P.O. Box 11303
    Memphis, TN 38111
    Phone: (901) 272-9067

Texas

A Place for Us
    Brad & Amy Russell
    Dallas, TX
    Phone: (214) 517-1498

The Interracial Family Alliance of Houston
    Chris Townsend
    P.O. Box 6297
    Katy, TX 77491
    Phone: (281) 579-9005
    Email: ctownsendchris@yahoo.com

Virginia

Interracial Connection
    Pat Barner
    P.O. Box 7055
    Norfolk, VA 23509
    Phone: (757) 622-9260 or (757) 461-2510
    Email: mbarner@livenet.net
    www.multirace.org

Washington

Interracial Family Network of Seattle-King County
    16541 Redmond Way, Suite 105
    Redmond, Washington 98052-4482
    Email: ifns@isomedia.com
    www.isomedia.com/homes/duncan/interracial.html

Wisconsin

Multiracial Alliance of Wisconsin
    Barbara Golden
    P.O. Box 9122
    Madison, WI 53715
    Phone: (608) 836-0616

Appendix B

Online Resources

American Love Stories
www.pbs.org/weblab/lovestories
The PBS website is a companion to the documentary *An American Love Story*.

A Place for Us
www.aplaceforusnational.com/home.html
"A Place for Us National . . . is the largest multiracial establishment designed to promote racial harmony. In doing so, we support multiracial families and their extended families (and confront the issues of the day head on)."

Beautiful Biracial
beta.communities.msn.com/BeautifulBiRacial
"This community is for those of a biracial background with a positive outlook on life who would like to share and communicate with others."

Biracial Kids.org
www.biracialkids.org
"This site is geared primarily towards teens and to parents of mixed or transracially adopted children."

Center for the study of Biracial Children
www.csbc.cncfamily.com
"The center provides advocacy, training and consulting. Its primary mission is to advocate for the rights of interracial families, biracial children, and multiracial people."

All descriptions are quoted directly from the organizations' websites.

Colorful Couples

www.kudoku.com/colorful

"Colorful Couples is an organization of interracial couples who meet to discuss social influences on their relationship and family."

EbonyIvoryMe

www.ebonyivoryme.com

"A worldwide forum where people of interracial interests can meet, discuss and share their thoughts, feelings and experiences about love, life and embracing our differences."

Eurasian Nation

www.eurasiannation.com

"This website is the premier online resource for people of mixed European and Asian descent. It aims to provide quality content on Eurasian issues and to act as a discussion forum for Eurasians."

Interracial Voice

www.interracialvoice.com

"IV is an independent, information-oriented, networking news journal, serving the mixed-race/interracial community in cyberspace. This electronic publication advocates universal recognition of mixed-race individuals as constituting a separate 'racial' entity and wholeheartedly supported the initiative to establish a multiracial category on the 2000 Census."

Karen Downing's Homepage

www-personal.umich.edu/~kdown/karen.html

"This homepage is a combination of information the Peer Information Counseling students and I have put together, and interesting links to other homepages. It is continually under construction, so expect some changes periodically!"

The Half Korean Page

www.halfkorean.com

"This is a groundbreaking Web page for half-Koreans of all backgrounds."

Hapa Issues Forum

www.hapaissuesforum.org

"Founded in 1992, HIF is a California-based nonprofit with five chapters focused on Asian and Pacific Islanders of mixed heritage."

iCelebrateDiversity.com!

www.icelebratediversity.com/index3.htm

"iCelebrateDiversity.com celebrates differences, encourages understanding, and promotes peace & unity!"

The Interracial Connection

www.multirace.org

"The InterRacial Connection is dedicated to improving race relations and providing a window for viewing African American heritage, history and contributions."

Interracial/Intercultural Pride

www.i-pride.org

"I-Pride's mission is education, and this organization has many activities, which reflect this goal. I-Pride strives to educate our selves, our children, and our community about the facts of intercultural and interracial identity."

MAVIN Foundation

www.mavinfoundation.org

"MAVIN Foundation is the nation's leading nonprofit organization that is redefining diversity by celebrating multiracial and transracially adopted youth. Through our programs, we are helping to create a cohesive, multicultural society."

Mixed Folks.com

www.mixedfolks.com

"This website features multiracial celebrity biographies, message boards, and resources for multiracial people."

Mixed Race

www.mixedrace.com

"Mixedrace.com is an online community that brings together people from all races and ethnicities to celebrate the beauty of diversity."

Multi-Racial: Association of Multiethnic Americans

www.ameasite.org

"AMEA aims to educate and advocate on behalf of multiethnic individuals and families by collaborating with others to eradicate all forms of discrimination."

Multiracial Kids

www.multiculturalkids.com

"Our mission is to provide quality multicultural materials to preschool and elementary school-age children in the home and classroom. We are committed to providing fun, informative and diverse materials, which can be used to increase a child's knowledge of him/herself and others, thereby enhancing self-esteem while fostering tolerance and an appreciation of differences."

The Multiracial Activist

www.multiracial.com

"The Multiracial Activist believes that biracial/multiracial people, interracial couples/families, and transracially adopted individuals have unique needs that cannot or will not be met by traditional civil rights groups who tend to brush off our community or denigrate us. We need to handle our own affairs. Join The Multiracial Activist in taking charge of our community!"

My Shoes

www.myshoes.com

"My shoes is a support group in cyberspace hosted by clinical psychologist Dr. Juanita Brooks for biracial/multiracial children, adolescents, and adults who have a white appearance."

New People Magazine

www.newpeoplemagazine.com

"New People is an online magazine for the multiracial community."

Other Colors

www.kqed.org/w/baywindow/othercolors/about/index.html

"Bay Window takes a look at what it's like to be a multiracial person in the Bay Area with Other Colors: Being Multiracial in America."

Our Colors

www.ourcolors.net

"Our Colors is a Community of Lots of Races—the multiracial community. We are a grassroots nonprofit organization committed to fostering hope, courage, self-esteem, and confidence in our children in this race conscious society."

Polly Wanna Cracka?

www.pollywannacracka.com

"*Polly Wanna Cracka?* is devoted to presenting quality websites regarding interracial, multiracial, and multicultural families, relationships, organizations, and topics."

Project Race

www.projectrace.com

Project Race "advocates for multiracial children and adults through education, community awareness, and legislation. Our main goal is for a multiracial classification on all school, employment, state, federal, local, census and medical forms requiring racial data."

Swirl

www.swirlinc.org

"Swirl aims to unite the mixed community by providing support to mixed families, individuals, adoptees, and interracial couples."

Appendix C

Research and Reading for Interracial Families

CHILDREN'S BOOKS

Adoff, Arnold. *Black Is Brown Is Tan*. New York: HarperCollins, 1992.

Adoff, Arnold. *Hard to Be Six*. New York: HarperCollins, 1991.

Bartlett, Theresa. *When You Were Born in Vietnam*. St. Paul, Minn.: Yeong & Yeong Book Company, 2001.

Boyd, Brian E. *When You Were Born in Korea*. St. Paul, Minn.: Yeong & Yeong Book Company, 1993.

Czech, Jan M. *An American Face*. Minneapolis, Minn.: Sagebrush, 2000.

Czech, Jan M. *The Coffee Can Kid*. Washington, D.C.: Child and Family Press, 2002.

Davol, Marguerite W. *Black, White, Just Right!* Morton Grove, Ill.: Albert Whitman & Company, 1993.

Friedman, Ina R., and Allen Say. *How My Parents Learned to Eat*. Boston, Mass.: Houghton Mifflin, 1987.

Garland, Sarah. *Billy and Belle*. New York: Penguin, 1992.

Hamanaka, Sheila. *All the Colors of the Earth*. New York: HarperTrophy, 1999.

Hoffman, Mary. *An Angel Just Like Me*. New York: Dial Books for Young Readers, 1997.

Igus, Toyomi. *Two Mrs. Gibsons*. San Francisco, Calif.: Children's Books Press, 2001.

Jenness, Aylette. *Families: A Celebration of Diversity, Commitment, and Love*. Boston, Mass.: Houghton Mifflin, 1993.

Johnson, Angela, and David Soman. *The Aunt in Our House*. New York: Orchard Books, 1996.

Karvoskaia, Natacha. *Dounia*. New York: Kane/Miller Book Publishers, 1995.

Kates, Bobbi Jane. *We're Different, We're the Same*. New York: Random House, 1992.

Katz, Karen. *The Colors of Us.* New York: Henry Holt and Co., 1999.

Kissinger, Katie. *All the Colors We Are: The Story of How We Get Our Skin Color.* St. Paul, Minn.: Redleaf Press, 1994.

Koh, Frances M. *A China Adoption Story.* Morton Grove, Ill.: Albert Whitman & Company, 1997.

Lacapa, Kathleen, and Michael Lacapa. *Less Than Half, More Than Whole.* Flagstaff, Ariz.: Northland Publishing, 1994.

Lionni, Leo. *Little Blue and Little Yellow.* New York: HarperTrophy, 1995.

Lucado, Max. *You Are Special.* Wheaton, Ill.: Crossway Books, 1997.

Mandelbaum, Pili. *You Be Me, I'll Be You.* Brooklyn, N.Y.: Kane/Miller, 1990.

Monk, Isabell. *Family.* Minneapolis, Minn.: Carolrhoda Books, 2001.

Monk, Isabell. *Hope.* Minneapolis, Minn.: Carolrhoda Books, 1998.

Nikola-Lisa, W. *Bein' with You This Way.* New York: Lee & Low Books, 1994.

Otey-Little, Mimi. *Yoshiko and the Foreigner.* New York: Farrar, Straus & Giroux, 1996.

Pellegrini, Nina. *Families Are Different.* New York: Holiday House, 1991.

Rosenberg, Maxine, and George Ancona. *Living in Two Worlds.* New York: Lothrop, Lee & Shepard Books, 1986.

Rosove, Lori, and Heather Burrill. *Rosie's Family: An Adoption Story.* New York: Asia Press, 2001.

Schmidt, Jeremy, and Ted Wood. *Two Lands, One Heart.* New York: Walker & Company, 1995.

Senisi, Ellen B. *For My Family, Love Allie.* Morton Grove, Ill.: Albert Whitman & Company, 1998.

Simon, Norma. *Why Am I Different?* Morton Grove, Ill.: Albert Whitman & Company, 1993.

Viglucci, Pat Costa. *Sun Dance at Turtle Rock.* Rochester, Minn.: Stone Pine Books, 1996.

Wyeth, Sharon Dennis. *Ginger Brown: Too Many Houses.* New York: Random House, 1996.

YOUNG ADULT

Adoff, Arnold. *All the Colors of the Race.* New York: HarperCollins, 1982.

Bell, William. *Zack.* Madison, Wis.: Turtleback Books, 1999.

Carvell, Marlene. *Who Will Tell My Brother?* Concord, N.H.: Hyperion Press, 2002.

Crutcher, Chris. *Whale Talk.* New York: Greenwillow, 2001.

Dorris, Michael. *Window.* New York: Hyperion Books for Children, 1997.

Gay, Kathlyn. *"I Am Who I Am": Speaking out about Multiracial Identity.* New York: Scholastic, 1995.

Hamilton, Virginia. *Arilla Sun Down*. New York: Scholastic, 1995.

Hamilton, Virginia. *Plain City*. New York: Scholastic, 1996.

Hewett, Lorri. *Lives of Our Own*. New York: Dutton Books, 1998.

Katz, William L. *Black Indians: A Hidden Heritage*. New York: Atheneum, 1986.

Lipsyte, Robert. *The Brave*. New York: HaperCollins Children, 1991.

Nash, Renea D. *Coping as a Biracial/Biethnic Teen*. New York: Rosen Publishing Group, 1995.

Nash, Renea D. *Everything You Need to Know about Being a Biracial/Biethnic Teen*. New York: Rosen Publishing Group, 1995.

Nichols, Joan Kane. *All but the Right Folks*. Owings Mills, Md.: Stemmer House Publishing, 1985.

Okimoto, Jean Davis. *Molly by Any Other Name*. Minneapolis, Minn.: Scholastic, 2000.

Porte, Barbara Ann. *I Only Made Up the Roses*. New York: Greenwillow Books, 1987.

Porte, Barbara Ann. *Something Terrible Happened*. New York: Orchard Books, 1994.

Pullman, Philip. *The Broken Bridge*. New York: Laurel Leaf, 1994.

Screen, Robert Martin. *With My Face to the Rising Sun*. New York: Harcourt Brace Jovanovich, 1977.

Szumski, Bonnie. *Interracial America*. San Diego, Calif.: Greenhaven Press, 1996.

Woodson, Jacqueline. *If You Come Softly*. New York: Putnam, 2000.

Woodson, Jacqueline. *The House You Pass on the Way*. New York: Puffin, 2003.

Wyeth, Sharon Dennis. *The World of Daughter McGuire*. New York: Random House, 1994.

FICTION

Bowman, Elizabeth Atkins. *White Chocolate*. New York: Forge, 1998.

Brown, Rosellen. *Half a Heart*. New York: Farrar, Straus & Giroux, 2000.

Crouch, Stanley. *Don't the Moon Look Lonesome: A Novel*. New York: Pantheon Books, 2000.

Dickey, Eric J. *Milk in My Coffee*. New York: Signet, 1999.

Fulbeck, Kip. *Paper Bullets: A Fictional Autobiography*. Seattle, Wash.: University of Washington Press, 2001.

Gibbons, Reginald. *Sweetbitter*. Seattle, Wash.: Broken Moon Press, 1994.

Gibbs, Susan. *The Bend in the River*. Sterling Heights, Md.: Hawkshadow Publishing Co. Inc., 2002.

Grau, Shirley A. *The Keepers of the House*. Baton Rouge: Louisiana State University Press, 1995.

Guymon, Shannon. *Never Letting Go of Hope*. Cedar Fort Press, Utah: 2001.

House, Silas. *A Parchment of Leaves*. Chapel Hill, N.C.: Algonquin Books, 2002.

Himes, Chester B. *The End of a Primitive*. New York: W. W. Norton & Company, 1997.

Kitt, Sandra. *Significant Others*. New York: Onyx Books, 1996.

Larsen, Nella. *Passing*. New York: Penguin Books, 1997.

Larsen, Nella. *Quicksand*. New York: Penguin Books, 2002.

Lauber, Lynn. *21 Sugar Street*. New York: Norton, 1993.

Lent, Jeffrey. *In the Fall*. New York: Knopf Publishing Group, 2001.

Liu, Aimee, E. *Cloud Mountain*. New York: Warner Books, 1998.

Liu, Aimee, E. *Face*. New York: Warner Books, 1994.

Margolies-Mezvinsky, Marjorie. *They Came to Stay*. New York: Putnam Publishing Group, 1976.

McLarin, Kim. *Meeting of the Waters*. New York: William Morrow & Co., 2001.

McReynolds, Patricia Justiniani. *Almost Americans: A Quest for Dignity*. Santa Fe, N.M.: Red Crane Books, 1997.

Parks, Mary Anderson. *The Circle Leads Home*. Boulder: University Press of Colorado, 1998.

Powers, Richard. *The Time of Our Singing*. New York: Farrar, Straus & Giroux, 2003.

Webb, Frank, Harriet B. Stowe, and Robert Reid-Pharr. *The Garies and Their Friends*. Baltimore, Md.: Johns Hopkins University Press, 1997.

Rizzuto, Rahna R. *Why She Left Us*. New York: HarperCollins Publishers, Inc., 1999.

Roy, Lucinda. *Lady Moses: A Novel*. New York: HarperFlamingo, 1998.

Sanders, Dori. *Clover*. Chapel Hill, N.C.: Algonquin Books, 1990.

Senna, Danzy. *Caucasia*. New York: Riverhead Books, 1998.

Senna, Danzy. *Symptomatic*. New York: Riverhead Books, 2004.

Smith, Lillian. *Strange Fruit*. Fort Washington: Harvest Books, 1992.

AUTOBIOGRAPHIES, BIOGRAPHIES, AND MEMOIRS

Andrews, Lori. *Black Power, White Blood: The Life and Times of Johnny Spain*. New York: Pantheon Books, 1996.

Arboldea, Teja. *In the Shadow of Race: Growing up as a Multiethnic, Multicultural, and "Multiracial" American*. Manwah, N.J.: Erlbaum, 1998.

Camper, Carol. *Miscegenation Blues: Voices of Mixed Race Women*. Toronto, Canada: Sister Vision, 1994.

Delman, Carmit. *Burnt Bread and Chutney: Growing up between Cultures—A Memoir of an Indian Jewish Girl*. New York: Random House, 2002.

Doss, Helen G. *The Family Nobody Wanted*. Boston, Mass.: Northeastern University Press, 2001.

Douglas, David, and Barbara Douglas. *Marriage beyond Black and White: An Interracial Family Portrait*. Wilmette, Ill.: Baha'i Publishing Trust, 2002.

Funderberg, Lise. *Black, White, Other: Biracial Americans Talk about Race and Identity.* New York: William Morrow, 1994.

Gaskins, Pearl Fuyo. *What Are You? Voices of Mixed-Race Young People.* New York: Henry Holt, 1999.

Glancy, Diane, and C. Truesdale. *Two Worlds Walking: Short Stories, Essays, and Poetry by Writers with Mixed Heritages.* New York: New Rivers Press, 1994.

Haizlip, Shirlee Taylor. *The Sweeter the Juice: A Family Memoir in Black and White.* New York: Touchstone, 1995.

Hall, Wade. *Passing for Black: The Life and Careers of Mae Street Kidd.* Lexington: University Press of Kentucky, 1998.

John, Jaiya. *Black Baby White Hands: A View from the Crib.* Silver Spring, Md.: Soul Water, 2002.

Johnson, Kevin R. *How Did You Get to be Mexican? A White/Brown Man's Search for Identity.* Philadelphia, Pa.: Temple University Press, 1999.

Lazarre, Jane. *Beyond the Whiteness of Whiteness: Memoir of a White Mother of Black Sons.* Durham, N.C.: Duke University Press, 1996.

McBride, James. *The Color of Water: A Black Man's Tribute to His White Mother.* New York: Riverhead Books, 1996.

Minerbrook, Scott. *Divided to the Vein: A Journey into Race and Family.* New York: Harcourt, 1996.

Obama, Barak. *Dreams from My Father: A Story of Race and Inheritance.* New York: Random House, 1995.

O'Hearn, Claudine C. *Half and Half: Writers on Growing up Biracial and Bicultural.* New York: Pantheon Books, 1998.

Santiago, Esmeralda. *Almost a Woman.* New York: Random House, 1999.

Santiago, Esmeralda. *When I Was Puerto Rican.* New York: Vintage Books, 1994.

Scales-Trent, Judy. *Notes of a White Black Woman: Race, Color, Community.* University Park: Pennsylvania State University Press, 1995.

Walker, Rebecca. *Black, White, and Jewish: Autobiography of a Shifting Self.* New York: Riverhead Books, 2001.

Williams, Gregory. *Life on the Color Line: The Story of a White Boy Who Discovered He Was Black.* New York: Dutton, 1995.

PARENTING

Collison, Michele. *It's All Good Hair: The Guide to Styling and Grooming Black Children's Hair.* New York: Amistad, 2002

Ferrell, Pamela. *Kids Talk Hair: An Instruction Book for Grown-Ups and Kids.* Washington, D.C.: Cornrows and Company, 1999.

Hopson, Darlene Powell. *Different and Wonderful: Raising Black Children in a Race Conscious Society.* New York: Prentice Hall Press, 1991.

Lazarre, Jane. *Beyond the Whiteness of Whiteness: Memoir of a White Mother of Black Sons.* Durham, N.C.: Duke University Press, 1996.

McAdoo, Hariette Pipes, and John Lewis McAdoo. *Black Children: Social, Parental, and Educational Environments.* 5th ed. Thousand Oaks, Calif.: Sage Publications, 2001.

Nakazawa, Donna Jackson. *Does Anybody Else Look Like Me? A Parent's Guide to Raising Multiracial Children.* Oxford, U.K.: Perseus, 2003.

Reddy, Maureen. *Crossing the Color Line: Race, Parenting, and Culture.* New Brunswick, N.J.: Rutgers University Press, 1994.

Reddy, Maureen T., ed. *Everyday Acts against Racism: Raising Children in a Multiracial World.* Seattle, Wash.: Seal Press, 1996.

Root, Maria, and Matt Kelley. *Multiracial Child Resource Book: Living Complex Identities.* Seattle, Wash.: MAVIN Foundation, 2003.

Wardle, Francis. *Tomorrow's Children: Meeting the Needs of Multiracial and Multiethnic Children at Home, in Early Childhood Programs, and at School.* Denver, Colo.: Center for the Study of Biracial Children, 1999.

Wright, Marguerite A. *I'm Chocolate, You're Vanilla: Raising Healthy Black and Biracial Children in a Race-Conscious World.* San Francisco, Calif.: Jossey-Bass, 1998.

INTERRACIAL, INTERFAITH, AND INTERCULTURAL RELATIONSHIPS

Bode, Janet. *Different Worlds: Interracial and Cross-Cultural Dating.* New York: Scholastic, 1989.

Crohn, Joel. *Mixed Matches: How to Create Successful Interracial, Interethnic, and Interfaith Relationships.* New York: Fawcett, 1995.

Dalmage, Heather M. *Tripping on the Color Line: Black-White Multiracial Families in a Racially Divided World.* New Brunswick, N.J.: Rutgers University Press, 2000.

Ho, Man Keung. *Intermarried Couples in Therapy.* Springfield, Ill.: Charles C Thomas Publishing, Ltd., 1990.

Kaeser, Gigi. *Of Many Colors: Portraits of Multiracial Families.* Amherst: University of Massachusetts Press, 1997.

Kennedy, Randall. *Interracial Intimacies: Sex, Marriage, Identity, and Adoption.* New York: Vintage. 2003.

McNamara, Robert, Maria Tempenis, and Beth Walton. *Crossing the Line: Interracial Couples in the South.* Westport, Conn.: Greenwood Press, 1999.

Moran, Rachel. *Interracial Intimacy: The Regulation of Race and Romance.* Chicago, Ill.: University of Chicago Press, 2001.

Nash, Gary. *Forbidden Love: The Secret History of Mixed-Race America.* New York: Henry Holt and Co., 1999.

Root, Maria. *Love's Revolution: Interracial Marriage*. Philadelphia, Pa.: Temple University Press, 2001.

Rosenblatt, Paul, Terri Karris, and Richard Powell. *Multiracial Couples: Black and White Voices*. Thousand Oaks, Calif.: Sage Publications, 1995.

Sollors, Werner. *Interracialism: Black-White Intermarriage in American History, Literature, and Law*. New York: Oxford University Press, 2000.

Yancey, George A., and Sherelyn Wittum Yancey. *Just Don't Marry One: Interracial Dating, Marriage, and Parenting*. Valley Forge, Pa.: Judson Press, 2002.

TRANSRACIAL ADOPTION

Aldridge, Jane, and Ivor Gaber. *In the Best Interests of the Child: Culture, Identity and Transracial Adoption*. London: Free Associated Books, 1995.

Alperson, Myra. *Dim Sum, Bagels, and Grits: A Sourcebook for Multicultural Families*. New York: Farrar, Straus & Giroux, 2001.

Alperson, Myra. *The International Adoption Handbook: How to Make an Overseas Adoption Work for You*. New York: Henry Holt & Company, Inc., 1997.

Alstein, Howard, and Rita J. Simon. *Adoption across Borders*. London: Rowman & Littlefield, 2000.

Alstein, Howard, and Rita J. Simon. *Adoption, Race, and Identity: From Infancy through Adolescence*. New York: Praeger, 1992.

Alstein, Howard, Marygold S. Melli, and Rita J. Simon. *The Case for Transracial Adoption*. Washington, D.C.: The American University Press, 1994.

Anderson, David C. *Children of Special Value: Interracial Adoption in America*. New York: St. Martin's Press, 1971.

Bates, J. Douglas. *Gift Children: A Story of Race, Family, and Adoption in a Divided America*. New York: Ticknor & Fields, 1993.

Cox, Susan Soon-Keum. *Voices from Another Place: A Collection of Works from a Generation Born in Korea and Adopted to Other Countries*. St. Paul, Minn.: Yeong & Yeong Book Company, 1999.

Crumbley, Joseph. *Transracial Adoption and Foster Care: Practice Issues for Professionals*. Washington, D.C.: Child Welfare League of America, 1999.

Day, Dawn. *Adoption of Black Children: Counteracting Institutional Discrimination*. Lanham, Md.: Lexington Books, 1979.

Fogg-Davis, Hawley. *The Ethics of Transracial Adoption*. Ithaca, N.Y.: Cornell University Press, 2002.

Freundlich, Madelyn. *Adoption and Ethics: The Role of Race, Culture, and National Origin in Adoption*. Washington, D.C.: Child Welfare League of America, 2000.

Hall, Beth, and Gail Steinberg. *Inside Transracial Adoption*. Fort Wayne, Ind.: Perspectives Press, 2000.

John, Jaiya. *Black Baby, White Hands: A View from the Crib*. Silver Spring, Md.: Soul Water, 2002.

Nelson-Erichsen, Jean, and Heino R. Erichsen. *Butterflies in the Wind: Spanish/Indian Children with White Parents*. The Woodlands, Tex.: Los Niños International, 1992.

Patton, Sandra. *Birthmarks: Transracial Adoption in Contemporary America*. New York: New York University Press, 2000.

Pertman, Adam. *Adoption Nation: How the Adoption Revolution Is Transforming America*. New York: Perseus, 2000.

Rankin, Jo, and Tonya Bishoff. *Seeds from a Silent Tree: An Anthology By Korean Adoptees*. San Diego, Calif.: Pandal Press, 1997.

Register, Cheri. *"Are Those Kids Yours?" American Families with Children Adopted from Other Countries*. New York: Free Press, 1990.

Rush, Sharon. *Loving across the Color Line: A White Adoptive Mother Learns About Race*. New York: Rowman & Littlefield Publishers, 2000.

Simon, Rita, and Howard Altstein. *Transracial Adoptees and Their Families: A Study of Identity and Commitment*. New York: Praeger, 1987.

Simon, Rita, and Rhonda Roorda. *In Their Own Voices: Transracial Adoptees Tell Their Stories*. New York: Columbia University Press, 2000.

Smolowe, Jill. *An Empty Lap: One Couple's Journey to Parenthood*. New York: Atria, 1998.

Steinberg, Gail, and Beth Hall. *Inside Transracial Adoption*. Indianapolis, Ind.: Perspective Press, 2000.

Tessler, Richard, Gail Gamache, and Liming Liu. *West Meets East: Americans Adopt Chinese Children*. Westport, Conn.: Bergin & Garvey, 1999.

Wolff, Jana. *Secret Thoughts of an Adoptive Mother*. Kansas City, Mo.: Andrews and McMeel, 1997.

RACE RELATIONS AND RACIAL IDENTITY

Anzaldúa, Gloria. *Borderlands/La Frontera: The New Mestiza*. 1st ed. San Francisco, Calif.: Spinsters/Aunt Lute, 1987.

Azoulay, Katya Gibel. *Black, Jewish, and Interracial: It's Not the Color of Your Skin but the Race of Your Kin*. Durham, N.C.: Duke University Press, 1997.

Bethel, Elizabeth Rauh. *The Roots of African American Identity: Memory and History in Antebellum Free Communities*. New York: St. Martin's Press, 1997.

Bost, Suzanne. *Mulattas and Mestizas: Representing Mixed Identities in the Americas, 1850–2000*. Athens: University of Georgia Press, 2003.

Brown, Ursula. *The Interracial Experience: Growing Up Black/White Racially Mixed in the United States*. Westport, Conn.: Praeger, 2001.

Burroughs, W. Jeffrey, and Paul R. Spickard. *We Are a People: Narrative and Multiplicity in Constructing Ethnic Identity*. Philadelphia, Pa.: Temple University Press, 2000.

Chideya, Farai. *The Color of Our Future*. New York: William Morrow, 1999.

Chiong, Jane Ayers. *Racial Categorization of Multiracial Children in Schools*. Westport, Conn.: Bergin & Garvey, 1998.

Cross, William. *Shades of Black: Diversity in African American Identity*. Philadelphia, Pa.: Temple University Press, 1991.

Daniel, G. Reginald. *More Than Black? Multiracial Identity and the New Racial Order*. Philadelphia, Pa.: Temple University Press, 2001.

Davis, F. James. *Who Is Black? One Nation's Definition*. University Park: Pennsylvania State University Press, 1991.

Frazier, Sundee Tucker. *Check All That Apply: Finding Wholeness as a Multiracial Person*. Downers Grove, Ill.: Intervarsity Press, 2002.

Gibbs, Jewelle Taylor, and Larke-Nahme Huang. *Children of Color: Psychological Interventions with Culturally Diverse Youth*. San Francisco, Calif.: Jossey-Bass, 1989.

Gunthorpe, Wayne West. *Skin Color Recognition, Preference, and Identification in Interracial Children*. Lanham, Md.: University Press of America: 1998.

Helms, Janet E. *Black and White Racial Identity: Theory, Research, and Practice*. New York: Greenwood Press, 1990.

Ignatiev, Nowl, and John Garvey. *Race Traitor*. New York: Routledge, 1996.

Jones, Lisa. *Bulletproof Diva: Tales of Race, Sex, and Hair*. New York: Doubleday, 1994.

Katz, Ilan. *The Construction of Racial Identity in Children of Mixed Parentages: Mixed Metaphors*. Bristol, Pa.: J. Kingsley Publishers, 1996.

Kenney, Kelly R., Bea Wehrly, and Mark E. Kenney. *Counseling Multiracial Families*. Thousand Oaks, Calif.: Sage Publications, 1999.

Kilson, Marion. *Claiming Place: Biracial Young Adults of the Post–Civil Rights Era*. Westport, Conn.: Bergin & Garvey, 2001.

Korgen, Kathleen Odell. *From Black to Biracial: Transforming Racial Identity Among Americans*. Westport, Conn.: Praeger, 1998.

Lott, Juanita Tamayo. *Asian Americans: From Racial Category to Multiple Identities*. Walnut Creek, Calif.: AltaMira Press, 1998.

Malcomson, Scott L. *One Drop of Blood: The American Misadventure of Race*. New York: Farrar, Straus & Giroux, 2000.

Menchaca, Martha. *Recovering History, Constructing Race: The Indian, Black, and White Roots of Mexican Americans*. Austin: University of Texas Press, 2001.

Moraga, Cherrie. *The Last Generation: Prose and Poetry*. Cambridge, U.K.: South End Press, 1993.

Olumide, Jill. *Raiding the Gene Pool: The Social Construction of Mixed Race*. Sterling, Va.: Pluto Press, 2002.

O'Toole, James M. *Passing for White: Race, Religion, and the Healy Family.* Boston: University of Massachusetts Press, 2002.

Parker, David, and Miri Song. *Rethinking "Mixed Race."* London: Pluto Press, 2000.

Penn, William. *As We Are Now: Mixblood Essays on Race and Identity.* Berkeley: University of California Press, 1997.

Rockquemore, Kerry Ann, and David L. Brunsma. *Beyond Black: Biracial Identity in America.* Thousand Oaks, Calif.: Sage Publications, 2001.

Rodriguez, Richard. *Brown: The Last Discovery of America.* New York: Penguin Books, 2002.

Root, Maria P. P. *Racially Mixed People in America.* Thousand Oaks, Calif.: Sage Publications, 1992.

Root, Maria P. P. *The Multiracial Experience: Racial Borders as the New Frontier.* Thousand Oaks, Calif.: Sage Publications, 1996.

Sheets, Rosa Hernandez, and Etta R. Hollins. *Racial and Ethnic Identity in School Practices: Aspects of Human Development.* Mahwah, N.J.: L. Erlbaum Associates, 1999.

Shigematsu, Stephen Murphy. *Multicultural Encounters: Cases Narratives from a Counseling Practice.* New York: Teachers College Press, 2002.

Socha, T., and R. Diggs. *Communication, Race, and Family: Exploring Communication in Black, White, and Biracial Families.* Mahwah, N.J.: L. Erlbaum Associates, 1999.

Sollors, Werner. *Neither Black Nor White Yet Both: Thematic Explorations of Interracial Literature.* New York: Oxford University Press, 1997.

Spencer, Jon Michael. *The New Colored People: The Mixed-Race Movement in America.* New York: New York University Press, 1997.

Spencer, Rainier. *Spurious Issues: Race and Multiracial Identity Politics in the United States.* Boulder, Colo.: Westview Press, 1999.

Tizard, Barbara, and Ann Phoenix. *Black, White, or Mixed Race? Race and Racism in the Lives of Young People of Mixed Parentage.* London: Routledge, 1993.

Wallace, Kendra. *Relative/Outsider: The Art and Politics of Identity among Mixed-Heritage Students.* Westport, Conn.: Ablex, 2001.

Williams-Leon, Teresa. *The Sum of Our Parts: Mixed-Heritage Asian Americans.* Philadelphia, Pa.: Temple University Press, 2001.

Williamson, Joel. *New People: Miscegenation and Mulattoes in the United States.* New York: Free Press, 1980.

Winters, Loretta I., and Herman L. DeBose. *New Faces in Changing America: Multiracial Identity in the Twenty-first Century.* Thousand Oaks, Calif.: Sage Publications, 2003.

Zack, Naomi, *American Mixed Race: The Culture of Microdiversity.* Lanham, Md.: Rowman & Littlefield, 1995.

Zack, Naomi. *Race and Mixed Race.* Philadelphia, Pa.: Temple University Press, 1993.

Appendix D

Movies and Documentaries

An American Love Story
A PBS documentary condensed from a thousand hours of filming the biracial Wilson Sims family: Karen Wilson (a white woman), Bill Sims (a black man), and their two daughters.

Banana Split: 25 Stories
In this film, Kip Fulbeck focuses on biracial ethnicity exploration and Asian self-identity. He examines the relationship between his father who is Caucasian and his mother who is Asian and also explores ethnic patterns and media stereotypes of Asian American men.

Beyond Black and White
Although Americans have traditionally treated race relations as a matter of black and white, race in this country is much more complex. *Beyond Black and White* brings new perspectives to the oversimplification of racial categories and new insight into the complexity of social relationships in these two important regions. All those interested in race and public policy as well as social activism directed toward racial, ethnic, and gender issues will find in these thought-provoking analyses a doorway to deeper understanding.

Catfish in Black Bean Sauce
This comedy, directed by, produced by, and starring Chi Muoi Lo, centers on the marriage proposal and birth mother discovery of two adult Vietnamese Americans adopted by an African American couple after the fall of Saigon.

All descriptions are drawn directly from the movie or documentary publicity materials.

Children of Mixed Race = Who You Wanna Be
> This is a study of the various types of identities that interracial people have had to invent for themselves. It is based on interviews with racially mixed students at the University of California, Berkeley, who speak about their perceptions of their own personal identities.

Coffee-Colored Children
> The film is a semiautobiographical story set in England of racism, prejudice, and self-definition experienced by biracial children of a Caucasian/Nigerian marriage.

Come See the Paradise
> Set against the background of a controversial period in American history, the internment of Japanese Americans during World War II, *Come See the Paradise* is the love story of an Irish American man and a Japanese American woman.

Days of Waiting
> A documentary about artist Estelle Peck Ishigo's internment with her Japanese American husband during World War II and the difficulties of readjustment at war's end.

Do Two Halves Really Make a Whole?
> This video features the diverse viewpoints of people with multiracial Asian heritages and their personal experiences in growing up as multiracial Asian Americans.

Doubles: Japan and America's Intercultural Children
> This film by Regge Life is the first in-depth look at the lives of intercultural children of Japanese and Americans from inside America as well as inside Japan.

Domino: Interracial People and the Search for Identity
> Portrays the stories of six interracial people, exploring issues of identity, cultural isolation, and the search for community. Through these personal stories, each person recounts how their identity is affected by their parents' history, hierarchies of race, gender roles, and class. Ultimately, these six individuals demonstrate how living intimately with two cultures can be a source of strength and enrichment.

En Ryo Identity: A Reclamation

This experimental documentary addresses the complexities inherent in establishing and asserting a biracial identity. Berges also explores mainstream media constructions and stereotypical images of Asian American identity juxtaposed with Hollywood representations of Asians and interviews with his Japanese American grandmother on her internment camp experiences.

Family Name

As a white child attending school in Durham, North Carolina, Macky Alston thought it curious that many of his African American classmates shared his last name. For years, when Macky broached the subject with family members, he was met with uncomfortable silence. It was not until his father, a minister and civil rights leader, finally gave him a book about the history of the Alston family that Macky learned the disquieting facts about the Alston's slave-owning past. This first-person documentary tracks Macky's efforts to disinter long-buried secrets and establish familial connections between the white and African American branches that bear the Alston name. His journey takes him from New York to Alabama, to family reunions, picnics, housing projects, churches, graveyards, archives and to original Alston plantations. He begins to focus on a great-great-great-great-granduncle named Chatham Jack, a well-known slave owner, who may have fathered biracial children. Like an intriguing detective story, Macky's search for relatives across the color line moves in unexpected directions. At the film's poignant conclusion, black and white Alstons gather for the first time on the site of one of the Alston plantations. Yet, in a surprisingly ironic epilogue, viewers discover that Macky may have been investigating a family history not his own.

First Person Plural

Deann Borshay Liem was adopted from Korea by a White American family in 1966. Her memory of her birth family was almost forgotten until dreams inspired her to look at her past and try to unite her adoptive and biological families.

Guess Who's Coming to Dinner

A liberal white couple (Hepburn and Tracy, in Tracy's last appearance) put their platitudes to the test. They always taught their daughter (Houghton, Hepburn's niece) that all people are created equal, regardless of race or religion; that is until she unexpectedly brings home a black doctor (Poitier) and announces that they're engaged.

Hapa

Marathon runner Midori Sperandeo talks personally about her biracial heritage and reflects on the phenomenon of being biracial, with interviews from a number of ethnically mixed-raced people with additional viewpoints.

Jungle Fever

A black architect begins an affair with his working class Italian secretary. Their relationship causes them to be scrutinized by their friends, cast out from their families, and shunned by their neighbors in this view of inner-city life.

Just Black? Multiracial Identity

In this documentary, several young people whose parents are of mixed racial heritage talk about their struggle to establish, acquire and assert a racial identity

Juxta

This film observes the deep and complex psychological effects of racially mixed children of Japanese women and American servicemen in the 1950s and mid-1980s.

Losing Isaiah

Directed by Stephen Gyllenhaal and starring Jessica Lange and Halle Berry, this movie centers on a black mother's struggle to regain custody of her abandoned son from his white adoptive mother.

Mixed Blood

Mixed blood takes a personal view of interracial relationships between Asian Americans and non-Asian Americans. Valerie Soe, the director combines interviews with over thirty concerned individuals, text and clips from scientific films and classic miscegenation dramas. This video explores the complexities of crosscultural intimacy and whether such choices have public and political implications (1992).

Mixed Feelings

Through interviews with five University of California–Berkeley students, producer and director Mikko Jokela examines what it is like to grow up of mixed Asian heritage in American society in this experimental documentary.

Multi-Facial

Vin Diesel wrote, directed, starred in and financed this debut short film about a struggling multiracial actor (1994).

One Drop
This film explores the recurring and divisive issue in African American communities of skin color. The film inter-cuts intimate interviews with darker skinned African Americans, lighter skinned African Americans and interracial children of black and white parents. It investigates the sensitive topic of color consciousness within the African American community with great tact and a clear commitment to healing divisions.

Outside Looking In: Transracial Adoption in America
Phil Bertelsen provides a unique perspective as both an adoptee and filmmaker in his exploration of transracial adoption and identity through three families located in three different regions of the country.

Rocky Road
Picking up where *Guess Who's Coming to Dinner* left off, *Rocky Road* explores the problems and prejudices one interracial couple experiences from their families and society in a modern dramedy. Rather than shy away from the racial issues, *Rocky Road* serves a heaping scoop of contemporary cultural conflict as the story weaves through the life of Talia (Nicole Smith), the eldest daughter of prosperous Caribbean immigrants in Los Angeles.

Secrets and Lies
After her adoptive parents die, a young black woman seeks out her natural birth mother only to discover that her mother is white. Equally shocked to learn the daughter she gave up for adoption is black, Cynthia insists that it's a mistake. But she soon realizes that it's true and when she springs her newfound daughter on the rest of the family, the resulting chaos leads to a series of secrets and lies being revealed at last.

Suzanne Bonnar: The Blacksburg Connection
Suzanne Bonnar grew up as the only black child in a small seaside town on the west coast of Scotland. Her mother, a local Scottish woman, lived near an American military base and fell in love with an African American serviceman. Longing to meet the father whom she had not seen since she was two, twenty-five-year-old Bonnar contacted an organization specializing in uniting families of servicemen. This moving documentary chronicles Bonnar's emotional reunion with her long-lost father at a London train station and her subsequent voyage of discovery to the United States. Traveling to her father's hometown of Blacksburg, South Carolina, Bonnar is welcomed by a large ex-

tended family and learns for the first time that she has three half-brothers. Known in Scotland as a vibrant blues singer, Bonnar is surprised and pleased to find her musical roots among relatives in the American South. In a stirring scene, Bonnar performs at the church where her grandfather was once pastor, and coincidentally sings selections that were particularly close to his heart.

Tanto Tiempo

This is Cheryl Quintana Leader's award-winning story of Mia and her Mexican mother, who had adopted an Anglo lifestyle. Mia rediscovers her Aztec heritage and incorporates both it and her mother back into her life.

Unforgettable Face

George Oiye, one of the Japanese American soldiers who liberated people from Dachau in 1945, and Yanina Cywinska, then a sixteen-year-old prisoner in the death camp, reunite some forty years after World War II.

Unlocking the Heart of Adoption

This film chronicles the journey of birthmother and filmmaker, Sheila Ganz, and compelling first person stories of adoptees, birthparents, and adoptive parents in both same race and transcracial adoptions.

References

Anzaldúa, Gloria. *Borderlands/La Frontera: The New Mestiza.* San Francisco: Spinsters/Aunt Lute, 1987.

Baker, Nancy. *The Beauty Trap: Exploring Woman's Greatest Obsession.* New York: Franklin Watts, 1984.

Berger, Maurice. *White Lies: Race and the Myths of Whiteness.* 1st ed. New York: Farrar, Straus & Giroux, 1999.

Besharov, Douglas, and Timothy Sullivan. "One Flesh." *The Nation* 8.4 (1996): 19–21.

Billingsley, Andrew. *Black Families in White America.* Englewood Cliffs, N.J.: Prentice-Hall, 1968.

Bond, Selena, and Thomas Cash. "Black Beauty: Skin Color and Body Images among African American College Women." *Journal of Applied Social Psychology* 22.11 (1992): 874–88.

Bonilla-Silva, Eduardo. *Racism without Racists: Color-Blind Racism and the Persistence of Racial Inequality in the United States.* Lanham, Md.: Rowman & Littlefield, 2003.

———. "'We Are All Americans': The Latin Americanization of Race Relations in the United States." *Race & Society* (forthcoming).

Bowles, Dorcas D. "Bi-Racial Identity: Children Born to African American and White Couples." *Clinical Social Work Journal* 21.4 (1993): 417–28.

Boyd-Franklin, Nancy. *Black Families in Therapy: A Multisystems Approach*. New York: Guilford Press, 1989.

Boykin, A. Wade, and F. Toms. "Black Child Socialization: A Conceptual Framework." *Black Children: Social, Educational, and Parental Environments*. Eds. Hariette Pipes McAdoo and John Lewis McAdoo. Beverly Hills, Calif.: Sage Publications, 1985. 15–22.

Brown, Nancy G., and Ramona E. Douglass. "Making the Invisible Visible: The Growth of Community Network Organizations." *The Multiracial Experience: Racial Borders as the New Frontier*. Ed. Maria Root. Thousand Oaks, Calif.: Sage Publications, 1996. 323–40.

Brown, Philip M. "Biracial Identity and Social Marginality." *Child & Adolescent Social Work Journal* 7.4 (1990): 319–37.

Brunsma, David L., and Kerry Ann Rockquemore. "The New Color Complex: Appearances and Biracial Identity." *Identity* 1.3 (2001): 225–46.

Cash, Thomas F., and Thomas Pruzinsky. *Body Images: Development, Deviance, and Change*. New York: Guilford Press, 1990.

Chisolm, Jamilya. "Imitation of Life." *The Source* (2002): 114–17.

Clark, Kenneth B., and Mamie P. Clark. "Racial Identification and Preference in Negro Children." *Readings in Social Psychology*. Eds. T. M. Newcombe and E. L. Hartley. New York: Holt, Rinehart and Winston, 1947. 159–69.

Conley, Dalton. *Being Black, Living in the Red Race, Wealth, and Social Policy in America*. Berkeley: University of California Press, 1999.

Cross, William, Thomas A. Parham, and Janet E. Helms. "The Stages of Black Identity Development: Nigrescence Models." *Black Psychology*. 3rd ed. Ed. Reginald L. Jones. Berkeley, Calif.: Cobb & Henry Publishers, 1991. 319–38.

Daniel, G. Reginald. "Black and White Identity in the New Millennium: Unsevering the Ties That Bind." *The Multiracial Experience: Racial Borders as the New Frontier*. Ed. Maria Root. Thousand Oaks, Calif.: Sage Publications, 1996. 121–39.

———. *More Than Black?: Multiracial Identity and the New Racial Order*. Philadelphia, Pa.: Temple University Press, 2002.

Davis, Allison, Burleigh Gardner, Mary Gardner, and W. Lloyd Warner. *Deep South: A Social Anthropological Study of Caste and Class*. Chicago: University of Chicago Press, 1941.

Davis, F. James. *Who Is Black?: One Nation's Definition*. University Park: Pennsylvania State University Press, 1991.

Dollard, John. *Caste and Class in a Southern Town*. 3rd ed. Garden City, N.Y.: Doubleday, 1957.

Drake, St. Clair, and Horace R. Cayton. *Black Metropolis: A Study of Negro Life in a Northern City*. New York: Harcourt Brace, 1945.

Emerson, Michael, and Christian Smith. *Divided by Faith: Evangelical Religion and the Problem of Race in America*. New York: Oxford University Press, 2000.

Fanon, Frantz. *Black Skin, White Masks*. New York: Grove Press, 1967.

Farley, John E. "Housing Segregation in the School Age Population and the Link between Housing and School Segregation," *Journal of Urban Affairs* 6.4 (1984): 65–80.

Fernandez, Carlos A. "Government Classification of Multiracial/Multiethnic People." *The Multiracial Experience: Racial Borders as the New Frontier*. Ed. Maria Root. Thousand Oaks, Calif.: Sage Publications, 1996.

Field, Lynda D. "Piecing Together the Puzzle: Self-Concept and Group Identity in Biracial Black/White Youth." *The Multiracial Experience: Racial Borders as the New Frontier*. Ed. Maria Root. Thousand Oaks, Calif.: Sage Publications, 1996. 211–26.

Frankenberg, Ruth. *White Women, Race Matters: The Social Construction of Whiteness*. Minneapolis: University of Minnesota Press, 1993.

Franklin, John Hope. *From Slavery to Freedom: A History of Negro Americans*. 5th ed. New York: Knopf, 1980.

Frazier, Edward Franklin. *Black Bourgeoisie*. Glencoe, Ill.: Free Press, 1957.

Funderburg, Lise. *Black, White, Other: Biracial Americans Talk About Race and Identity*. 1st ed. New York: W. Morrow and Co., 1994.

Gamoran, Adam. "Is Ability Grouping Equitable?" *Educational Leadership* (October 1992): 11–17.

———. "The Variable Effects of High School Tracking," *American Sociological Review* 57 (1992): 812–29.

Garroutte, Eva Marie. *Real Indians: Identity and the Survival of Native America*. Berkeley: University of California Press, 2003.

Gaskins, Pearl Fuyo. *What Are You? Voices of Mixed-Race Young People*. New York: Henry Holt, 1999.

Gibbs, Jewelle Taylor. "Biracial Adolescents." *Children of Color: Psychological Interventions with Culturally Diverse Youth*. Eds. Jewelle Taylor Gibbs and Larke Nahme Huang. San Francisco: Jossey-Bass, 1998. 305–32.

Gordon, Milton Myron. *Assimilation in American Life: The Role of Race, Religion, and National Origins*. New York: Oxford University Press, 1964.

Graham, Susan. "The Real World." *The Multiracial Experience: Racial Borders as the New Frontier*. Ed. Maria Root. Thousand Oaks, Calif.: Sage Publications, 1996.

Grier, William H., and Price M. Cobbs. *Black Rage*. New York: Basic Books, 1968.

Gwaltney, John Langston. *Drylongso: A Self-Portrait of Black America*. 1st ed. New York: Random House, 1980.

Hacker, Andrew. *Two Nations: Black and White, Separate, Hostile, Unequal*. New York: Ballantine, 1992.

Hale-Benson, and Janice E. Black. *Children: Their Roots, Culture, and Learning Styles*. Rev. ed. Johns Hopkins Paperbacks. Baltimore, Md.: Johns Hopkins University Press, 1986.

Hall, Christine. "The Ethnic Identity of Racially Mixed People: A Study of Black-Japanese." Los Angeles: University of California, 1980.

Hall, Ronald E. "Bias among African Americans Regarding Skin Color: Implications for Social Work Practice." *Research on Social Work Practice* 2.4 (1992): 479–86.

Hardy, Kenneth V., and Tracey A. Laszloffy. "Deconstructing Race in Family Therapy." *Journal of Feminist Family Therapy* 5.3/4 (1994): 5–33.

———. "The Dynamics of a Pro-Racist Ideology: Implications for Family Therapists." *Re-Visioning Family Therapy: Race, Culture, and Gender in Clinical Practice*. Ed. Monica McGoldrick. New York: Guilford Press, 1998. 118–28.

Harris, David R., and Jeremiah Joseph Sim. "Who Is Multiracial? Assessing the Complexity of Lived Race." *American Sociological Review* 67.4 (2002): 614–27.

Harvey, Aminifu R. "The Issue of Skin Color in Psychotherapy with African Americans." *Families in Society* 76.1 (1995): 3–10.

Helms, Janet E. *Black and White Racial Identity: Theory, Research, and Practice*. Westport, Conn.: Greenwood Press, 1990.

Henriques, Fernando. *Children of Conflict: A Study of Interracial Sex and Marriage.* New York: Dutton, 1975.

Herman, Melissa. "Forced to Choose: Some Determinants of Racial Identification in Multi-Racial Adolescents." *Child Development* 75.3 (2004): 730–48.

Herring, Cedric, Verna Keith, and Hayward Derrick Horton. *Skin Deep: How Race and Complexion Matter in the "Color-Blind" Era.* Urbana: University of Illinois Press, 2004.

Herring, Roger D. "Biracial Children: An Increasing Concern for Elementary and Middle School Counselors." *Elementary School Guidance & Counseling* 27.2 (1992): 123–30.

――――. "Developing Biracial Ethnic Identity: A Review of the Increasing Dilemma." *Journal of Multicultural Counseling & Development* 23.1 (1995): 29–38.

Herschel, Helena. "The Influence of Gender and Race Status on Self-Esteem during Childhood and Adolescence." *Race/Sex: Their Sameness, Difference, and Interplay.* Ed. Naomi Zack. New York: Routledge, 1997.

Herskovits, Melville J. *The American Negro: A Study in Racial Crossing.* Bloomington: Indiana University Press, 1964.

Holtzman, Linda. *Media Messages: What Film, Television, and Popular Music Teach Us about Race, Class, Gender, and Sexual Orientation.* Armonk, N.Y.: M. E. Sharpe, 2000.

hooks, bell. *Rock My Soul: Black People and Self-Esteem.* New York: Atria Books, 2003.

――――. *Salvation: Black People and Love.* 1st ed. New York: William Morrow, 2001.

――――. *Where We Stand: Class Matters.* New York: Routledge, 2000.

――――. *Yearning: Race, Gender, and Cultural Politics.* 1st ed. Boston, Mass.: South End Press, 1990.

Hughes, Diane. "Correlates of African American and Latino Parents' Messages to Children about Ethnicity and Race: A Comparative Study of Racial Socialization." *American Journal of Community Psychology* 31.1–2 (2003): 15–33.

Hughes, Michael, and Bradley R. Hertel. "The Significance of Color Remains: A Study of Life Chances, Mate Selection, and Ethnic Consciousness among Black Americans." *Social Forces* 68.4 (1990): 1105–20.

Hunter, Margaret L. "Colorstruck: Skin Color Stratification in the Lives of African American Women." *Sociological Inquiry* 68.4 (1998): 517–35.

———. "Light, Bright, and Almost White: The Advantages and Disadvantages of Light Skin." *Skin Deep: How Race and Complexion Matter in the "Color-Blind" Era.* Eds. Cedric, Herring, Verna Keith, and Hayward Derrick Horton. Urbana: University of Illinois Press, 2004.

Jacobs, James H. "Identity Development in Biracial Children." *Racially Mixed People in America.* Ed. Maria Root. Thousand Oaks, Calif.: Sage Publications, 1992. 190–206.

Johnson, Charles Spurgeon. *Growing up in the Black Belt: Negro Youth in the Rural South.* Washington, D.C.: American Council on Education, 1941.

Johnson, Deborah J. "Developmental Pathways: Toward an Ecological Theoretical Formulation of Race Identity in Black-White Biracial Children." *Racially Mixed People in America.* Ed. Maria Root. Thousand Oaks, Calif.: Sage Publications, 1992. 37–49.

Jones, Lisa. *Bulletproof Diva: Tales of Race, Sex, and Hair.* 1st ed. New York: Doubleday, 1994.

Jones, Nicholas, and Amy Symens Smith. *The Two or More Races Population: 2000.* Washington, D.C.: U.S. Census Bureau, 2001.

Kato, S. "Coats of Many Colors: Serving the Multiracial Child and Adolescent." *Journal of Family and Consumer Sciences* 92 (2000): 37–40.

Keith, Verna M., and Cedric Herring. "Skin Tone and Stratification in the Black Community." *American Journal of Sociology* 97.3 (1991): 760–78.

Kerwin, Christine, Joseph Ponterotto, Barbara Jackson, and Abigail Harris, "Racial Identity in Biracial Children: A Qualitative Investigation." *Journal of Counseling Psychology* 40.2 (1993): 221–31.

Kich, George Kitahara. "The Developmental Process of Asserting a Biracial, Bicultural Identity." *Racially Mixed People in America.* Ed. Maria Root. Thousand Oaks, Calif.: Sage Publications, 1992. 304–17.

Kilson, Marion. *Claiming Place: Biracial Young Adults of the Post–Civil Rights Era.* Westport, Conn.: Bergin & Garvey, 2001.

Knowles, Louis, and Kenneth Prewitt. *Institutional Racism in America.* Englewood Cliffs, N.J.: Prentice Hall, 1967.

Kozol, Jonathan. *Savage Inequalities: Children in America's Schools.* New York: Crown Pub., 1991.

Ladner, Joyce A. *Mixed Families: Adopting across Racial Boundaries.* Garden City, N.Y.: Anchor Press/Doubleday, 1977.

LaFromboise, Teresa, Hardin L. K. Coleman, and Jennifer Gerton. "Psychological Impact of Biculturalism: Evidence and Theory." *The Culture and Psychology Reader.* Eds. Nancy Rule Goldberger and Jody Bennet Veroff. New York: New York University Press, 1995. 489–535.

Lakoff, Robin Tolmach, and Raquel L. Scherr. *Face Value: The Politics of Beauty.* Boston: Routledge & Kegan Paul, 1984.

Landry, Bart. *The New Black Middle Class.* Berkeley: University of California Press, 1987.

Laszloffy, Tracey. "An Exploratory Study of Family Therapists Working as Consultants to Address the Interaction between Race and Education in an Elementary School." Doctoral dissertation, Syracuse University, 1997.

Laszloffy, Tracey A., and Kenneth V. Hardy. "Uncommon Strategies for a Common Problem: Addressing Racism in Family Therapy." *Family Processes* 39.1 (2000): 35–50.

Levine, David P. *Rethinking Schools: An Agenda for Change.* New York: New Press, 1995.

Lewis, Amanda E. *Race in the Schoolyard: Negotiating the Color Line in Classrooms and Communities.* New Brunswick, N.J.: Rutgers University Press, 2003.

Lipsky, Suzanne. *Internalized Racism.* Seattle, Wash.: Rational Island Publishers, 1987.

Lomotey, Kofi. *Going to School: The African American Experience.* Albany: State University of New York Press, 1990.

Losen, Dan, and Gary Orfield. *Racial Inequality in Special Education.* Cambridge, Mass.: Harvard Educational Publishing Group, 2002.

McBride, James. *The Color of Water: A Black Man's Tribute to His White Mother.* New York: Riverhead Books, 1996.

McIntosh, Peggy. "White Privilege: Unpacking the Invisible Knapsack." *Re-Visioning Family Therapy: Race, Culture, and Gender in Clinical Practice.* Ed. Monica McGoldrick. New York: Guilford Press, 1998. 147–52.

McIntyre, Alice. *Making Meaning of Whiteness: Exploring Racial Identity with White Teachers.* Albany: State University of New York Press, 1997.

Mead, George Herbert. *Mind, Self, and Society.* Chicago, Ill.: University of Chicago Press, 1934.

Miller, Robin L. "The Human Ecology of Multiracial Identity." *Racially Mixed People in America.* Ed. Maria Root. Thousand Oaks, Calif.: Sage Publications, 1992. 24–36.

Miller, Robin L., and Barbara Miller. "Mothering the Biracial Child: Bridging the Gaps between African American and White Parenting Styles." *Women & Therapy* 10.1–2 (1990): 169–79.

Myrdal, Gunnar, Richard Mauritz Edvard Sterner, and Arnold Rose. *An American Dilemma: The Negro Problem and Modern Democracy.* New York: Harper, 1944.

Nakashima, Cynthia L. "An Invisible Monster: The Creation and Denial of Mixed-Race People in America." *Racially Mixed People in America.* Ed. Maria Root. Thousand Oaks, Calif.: Sage Publications, 1992. 162–78.

Nakazawa, Donna. *Does Anybody Else Look Like Me? A Parent's Guide to Raising Multiracial Children.* Cambridge, Mass.: Perseus, 2003.

Neal, Angela, and Midge Wilson. "The Role of Skin Color and Features in the Black Community: Implications for Black Women and Therapy." *Clinical Psychology Review* 9.3 (1989): 323–33.

Norment, Lynn. "Lenny Kravitz: Brother with a Different Beat." *Ebony* (1994).

Obama, Barak. *Dreams from My Father: A Story of Race and Inheritance.* New York: Random House, 1995.

Okazawa-Rey, Margo, Tracy Robinson, and Janie V. Ward. "Black Women and the Politics of Skin Color and Hair." *Women & Therapy* 6.1–2 (1987): 89–102.

Oliver, Melvin L., and Thomas M. Shapiro. *Black Wealth/White Wealth: A New Perspective on Racial Inequality.* New York: Routledge, 1995.

Omi, Michael, and Howard Winant. *Racial Formation in the United States: From the 1960s to the 1990s.* 2nd ed. New York: Routledge, 1994.

Orfield, Gary, and Chungmei Lee. *Brown at 50: King's Dream or Plessy's Nightmare?* Cambridge, Mass.: Civil Rights Project, 2004.

Park, Robert Ezra. *Race and Culture*. New York: Free Press, 1928.

Parker, Rob. "Jeter Doesn't Choose Sides." *Newsday* (1998).

Porter, J. R., and Robert E. Washington. "Minority Identity and Self-Esteem." *Annual Review of Sociology* 19 (1993): 139–61.

Poston, W. Carlos. "The Biracial Identity Development Model: A Needed Addition." *Journal of Counseling & Development* 69.2 (1990): 152–55.

Reddy, Maureen T. *Everyday Acts against Racism: Raising Children in a Multiracial World*. Seattle, Wash.: Seal Press, 1996.

Renn, Kristen. *Mixed Race Students in College: The Ecology of Race, Identity, and Community on Campus*. Albany: State University of New York Press, 2004.

Rist, Ray C. "Student Social Class and Teacher Expectations: The Self-Fulfilling Prophecy in Ghetto Education." *Harvard Educational Review* 40.3 (1970): 411–51.

Rockquemore, Kerry Ann. "Between Black and White: Exploring the 'Biracial' Experience." *Race & Society* 1.2 (1998): 197–212.

———. "Negotiating the Color Line: The Gendered Process of Racial Identity Construction among Black/White Biracial Women." *Gender & Society* 16.4 (2002): 485–503.

Rockquemore, Kerry Ann, and David L. Brunsma. *Beyond Black: Biracial Identity in America*. Thousand Oaks, Calif.: Sage Publications, 2002.

Rockquemore, Kerry Ann, and David L. Brunsma. "Socially Embedded Identities: Theories, Typologies, and Processes of Racial Identity among Biracials." *Sociological Quarterly* 43.3 (2002): 335–56.

Rockquemore, Kerry Ann, and Tracey A. Laszloffy. "Exploring Multiple Realities: Using Narrative Approaches in Therapy with Black/White Biracials." *Family Relations: Interdisciplinary Journal of Applied Family Studies* 52.2 (2003): 119–28.

Rockquemore, Kerry, and Patricia Arend. "Opting for White: Choice, Fluidity, and Black Identity Construction in Post-Civil Rights America." *Race & Society* 5.1 (2003): 51–66 (forthcoming).

Rockquemore, Kerry, and David Brunsma. "Beyond Black?: The Reflexivity of Appearances in Biracial Identification among Black/White Biracials." *Skin Deep: How Race and Complexion Matter in the "Color-Blind" Era*. Ed. Verna Keith, Cedric Herring, and Hayward Horton. Urbana: University of Illinois Press, 2004.

Root, Maria. "The Multiracial Experience: Racial Borders as Significant Frontier in Race Relations." *The Multiracial Experience: Racial Borders as the New Frontier.* Ed. Maria Root. Thousand Oaks, Calif.: Sage Publications, 1996.

———. "Experiences and Processes Affecting Racial Identity Development: Preliminary Results from the Biracial Sibling Project." *Cultural Diversity & Mental Health* 4.3 (1998): 237–47.

———. "Resolving 'Other' Status: Identity Development of Biracial Individuals." *Women & Therapy* 9.1–2 (1990): 185–205.

———. *Racially Mixed People in America.* Newbury Park, Calif.: Sage Publications, 1992.

———. *Love's Revolution: Interracial Marriage.* Philadelphia, Pa.: Temple University Press, 2001.

———. "Racial Identity Development and Persons of Mixed Race Heritage." *Multiracial Child Resource Book.* Eds. Maria Root and Matt Kelley. Seattle, Wash.: MAVIN Foundation, 2003. 34–41.

Rosenthal, Robert, and Lenore Jacobson. *Pygmalion in the Classroom: Teacher Expectation and Pupils' Intellectual Development.* New York: Holt, Rinehart and Winston, 1968.

Rothenberg, Paula S. "How It Happened: Race and Gender Issues in U.S. Law." *Race, Class, and Gender in the United States: An Integrated Study.* 3rd ed. Ed. Paula S. Rothenberg. New York: St. Martin's Press, 1995. 427–35.

Russell, Kathy, Midge Wilson, and Ronald E. Hall. *The Color Complex: The Politics of Skin Color among African Americans.* New York: Harcourt Brace Jovanovich, 1992.

Scales-Trent, Judy. *Notes of a White Black Woman: Race, Color, and Community.* University Park: Pennsylvania State University Press, 1995.

Smith, William. "The Black Self-Concept: Some Historical and Theoretical Reflections." *Reflections on Black Psychology.* Eds. D. William, K. H. Burlew Smith, M. H. Mosley, and W. M. Whitney. Lanham, Md.: University Press of America, 1979. 149–59.

Spencer, Rainier. *Spurious Issues: Race and Multiracial Identity Politics in the United States.* Boulder, Colo.: Westview Press, 1999.

Stephen, Cookie W., and Judith H. Langlois. "Mixed-Heritage Individuals: Ethnic Identity and Trait Characteristics." *Racially Mixed People in America.* Ed. Maria Root. Newbury Park, Calif.: Sage Publications, 1992.

Stone, Gregory. "Appearance and the Self." *Human Behavior and Social Processes.* Ed. Arnold Rose. Boston: Houghton Mifflin, 1962.

Storrs, Debbie. "Whiteness as Stigma: Essentialist Identity Work by Mixed-Race Women." *Symbolic Interaction* 22.3 (1999): 187–212.

Thornton, Michael, Linda Chatters, Robert Taylor, and Walter Allen. "Sociodemographic and Environmental Correlates of Racial Socialization by Black Parents." *Child Development* 61.2 (1990): 401–19.

Tizard, Barbara, and Ann Phoenix. "The Identity of Mixed Parentage Adolescents." *Journal of Child Psychology & Psychiatry & Allied Disciplines* 36.8 (1995): 1399–410.

Twine, France Winddance. "Brown Skinned White Girls: Class, Culture, and the Construction of White Identity in Suburban Communities." *Gender, Place, and Culture* 3.2 (1996): 205–24.

Udry, Richard J., Karl E. Bauman, and Charles Chase. "Skin Color and Mate Selection." *American Journal of Sociology* 76.4 (1971): 722–33.

U.S. Census. *Guidance on Aggregation and Allocation of Data on Race for Use in Civil Rights Monitoring and Enforcement.* Washington, D.C.: Office of Management and Budget Bulletin, no. 00–02, 2000.

Van Ausdale, Debra, and Joe R. Feagin. *The First R: How Children Learn Race and Racism.* Lanham, Md.: Rowman & Littlefield, 2001.

Wallace, Kendra. *Relative/Outsider: The Art and Politics of Identity Among Mixed-Heritage Students.* Westport, Conn.: Ablex, 2001.

———. "Contextual Factors Affecting Identity among Mixed Heritage College Students." *Multiracial Child Resource Book.* Eds. Maria Root and Matt Kelley. Seattle, Wash.: MAVIN Foundation, 2003. 87–92.

Wardle, Francis. *Biracial Identity: An Ecological and Developmental Model.* Denver, Colo.: Center for the Study of Biracial Children, 1992.

Waters, Mary C. *Ethnic Options: Choosing Identities in America.* Berkeley: University of California Press, 1990.

Wehrly, Bea, Kelley R. Kenney, and Mark E. Kenney. *Counseling Multiracial Families.* Multicultural Aspects of Counseling Series, vol. 12. Thousand Oaks, Calif.: Sage Publications, 1999.

West, Cornel. *Race Matters.* Boston, Mass.: Beacon Press, 1993.

Wijeyesinghe, Charmaine. "Towards an Understanding of the Racial Identity of Biracial People: The Experience of Racial Self-Identification of African American/Euro American Adults and the Factors Affecting their Choices of Racial Identity." Doctoral dissertation, University of Massachusetts, 1992.

————. "Relationships and Black/White Multiracial People." *Multiracial Child Resource Book.* Eds. Maria Root and Matt Kelley. Seattle, Wash.: MAVIN Foundation, 2003. 160–67.

Williams, Carmen Braun. "Claiming a Biracial Identity: Resisting Social Constructions of Race and Culture." *Journal of Counseling & Development* 77.1 (1999): 32–35.

Williams, Gregory Howard. *Life on the Color Line: The True Story of a White Boy Who Discovered He Was Black.* New York: Dutton, 1995.

Williams, Theresa. "Race as Process: Reassessing the 'What Are You?' Encounters of Biracial Individuals." *Racially Mixed People in America.* Ed. Maria Root. Newbury Park, Calif.: Sage Publications, 1996.

Zuberi, Tukufu. *Thicker Than Blood: How Racial Statistics Lie.* Minneapolis: University of Minnesota Press, 2001.

Index

About the Authors

Kerry Ann Rockquemore is associate professor of African American studies and sociology at the University of Illinois at Chicago. She is coauthor of *Beyond Black: Biracial Identity in America* (2002). Her research focuses on racial socialization in interracial families and racial identity development.

Tracey Laszloffy is a relationship therapist in private practice in Connecticut. Prior to this, she served on the faculty at Seton Hill University, where she directed the master's level marriage and family therapy program. Dr. Laszloffy has published extensively in the area of race, oppression, and family therapy.